JIHĀD

JIHĀD

The Origin of Holy War in Islam

Reuven Firestone

OXFORD
UNIVERSITY PRESS

OXFORD
UNIVERSITY PRESS

Oxford New York
Athens Auckland Bangkok Bogotá Buenos Aires Cape Town
Chennai Dar es Salaam Delhi Florence Hong Kong Istanbul Karachi
Kolkata Kuala Lumpur Madrid Melbourne Mexico City Mumbai Nairobi
Paris São Paulo Shanghai Singapore Taipei Tokyo Toronto Warsaw

and associated companies in
Berlin Ibadan

First published in 1999 by Oxford University Press, Inc.
198 Madison Avenue, New York, New York 10016

First issued as an Oxford University Press paperback, 2002

Library of Congress Cataloging-in-Publication Data
Firestone, Reuven, 1952–
Jihad : the origin of holy war in Islam / Reuven Firestone.
p. cm.
Includes bibliographical references and index.
ISBN 0-19-512580-0; 0-19-515494-0 (pbk.)
1. Jihad—History. 2. War—Religious aspects—Islam. I. Title.
BP182.F5 1999
297.7'2'09—dc21 98-36384

1 3 5 7 9 8 6 4 2

Printed in the United States of America
on acid-free paper

Preface

Time, as we understand it, is linear. It progresses along a chronological path, always moving forward, never reversing itself, backtracking, or becoming distracted by sliding sideways. Perhaps because of the strict linearity of our concept of time, humans have the tendency to view history in strictly linear terms as well. We observe trends or note consistencies according to certain patterns that we detect, and we tend to ignore contradictory evidence that distracts from those patterns of observation. We latch onto certain perceived trajectories of behavior, ideas, or forces that we believe move through time and history. Then, either to build our argument or perhaps simply to make sense of life, we tend to disregard or forget about parallel, colliding, or contradictory vectors that cloud the crispness of those trajectories we are attracted to. Scientific arguments are often articulated in linear form in order to make a case; in such arguments, distracting data or points of view must be treated as much as possible, although they are not always perceived.

The science of history, like most other modern scientific disciplines, tends to be articulated in linear terms because of the nature of scholarly argument, but it is not at all certain that the human individuals and groups the science of history studies move through the perceived linearity of time in similar longitudinal patterns. While time is perceived as linear, human history seems not to be. Human behavior fluctuates, sometimes radically, and is affected by innumerable forces. It might be helpful to imagine human behavior through history as being shaped by a multitude of vectors of influence. While each one may affect human behavior in a consistent and even linear manner, when the entirety of vectors are at work simultaneously as occurs in real life, the result is a complex mechanism of forces that affect human conduct in such a way that it is impossible to successfully anticipate the directionality of group or even individual behavior in a consistent manner. Although human behavior has never been successfully predicted in a consistent manner, observers of humanity have had the tendency to describe and anticipate human behavior in terms that seem to do just that. Such is the thrust of the famous dictum, for example, that those who do not learn from history are forced to repeat it. My point here is simply to caution that the perceived patterns of history are nothing more than human constructs imposed on an extraordinarily complex reality. While we tend to view history as a broad river of many currents that are all swept along through time in the same direction, a more accurate metaphor might be an ocean whose innumerable currents are completely multidirectional.

This book represents a reexamination of an old accepted idea of history: that the Islamic concept of "holy war" evolved in a consistent and linear manner in response to certain historical trends during the early to middle periods of Muḥammad's mission as prophet in seventh-century Arabia. This idea, which was developed by Muslims during the eighth or ninth centuries and accepted largely at face value by critical scholarship, assumes as part of its larger assumption of the linearity of human history that the Muslim community during the mission of Muḥammad was unified in its view on warring. The literary evidence, however, confirms neither the smooth linearity nor the unanimity suggested by this point of view. On the contrary, the sources describe many different, non-parallel trajectories of influence and behavior that suggest that the early Muslim community was far from unanimous in its views about warring. They point to a rather bumpy ride through history in which various factions within the Muslim community competed for influence over the direction early Islam went in its views of war. The Qur'ān and early tradition literature tell us that some early Muslims were quite militant, while others refused to go to war. Some wished to promote Islam with the sword, while others were willing to do so only through the word. Some were ready to initiate war in order to advance the cause of the faithful, while others were only willing to fight in defense of the community.

I attempt to work through the evidence presently available in order to posit a theory of how and why Islam came to its classical position on war in the earliest period of its history, before its development of principles of interpretation and legal theory. All effort is made to be sensitive to conflicting trajectories of behavior represented by the sources and to avoid becoming stuck by forcing the evidence to conform to preconceived conceptual patterns. On the other hand, the very act of constructing an argument demands that the evidence be organized into patterns that support the conclusion that has been reached. My hope is that this book has succeeded in doing so honestly.

This book is written for both scholars and general readers. Each section includes an introduction to the major issues and literatures treated within it and lays out the problems to be analyzed. Each chapter treats a specific area or issue and examines it through citations and analyses of primary texts, all of which are provided in translation. The details of general analysis will be of interest to scholars, but the educated lay reader will certainly profit from the exercise as well. The notes are intended to enhance the analysis and direct the reader to relevant primary and secondary sources.

Although the concept, contents, conclusions, and errors contained in this book are entirely my own, it would never have seen the light of day without the valued support and assistance of a dedicated community of friends and colleagues. The many scholars from whose published works I have learned and grown are cited in the notes and bibliography. Most of my colleagues at Hebrew Union College in Los Angeles, however, are not. I am particularly indebted to David Ellenson, William Cutter, and Dean Lewis Barth for the innumerable discussions on related and unrelated topics, all of which have helped me in my thinking about this book. I am indebted to former Dean Lee Bycel for his constant support of my research and to Associate Dean Sheldon Marder for his encouragement. Librarian Harvey Horowitz of the Frances-Henry Library enabled me to access the necessary sources through his constant support, and special mention must be made of Krista Roesinger for her indefatigable labors on my behalf with interlibrary loans. Perhaps most of all, the collegiality and support of the institution engendered a feeling that truly anything is possible, a truth that must never be forgotten. Another community of great support for the development and encouragement of my, as well as many others', research and thinking is the Islamic Section of the American Academy of Religion, which welcomed me as a graduate student more than a decade ago under the leadership of Marilyn Waldman, of blessed memory, and Gordon Newby. I am further indebted to Johanna Afshani for her summer assistance and to Mathis Chazanov and Mitchel Miller for their assistance with the manuscript. I cannot hope to properly acknowledge my debt to my own extended family for its constant support, nor to the extended Abu Sneineh family of Hebron/Al-Khalīl and Jerusalem for their invitation to the study of Arab culture and Islam nearly thirty years ago. But most of all, my gratitude is to my wife and partner, Ruth H. Sohn, whose constant love and encouragement have sustained me throughout our years together.

Los Angeles, California R. F.
July 1998

Contents

PART III • THE ORAL TRADITION

Transliterations

Transliterations of Arabic words and names follow the alphabetical substitution provided below.

ا – ʾ (omitted at the beginning of a word)

ب – b	ذ – dh	ط – ṭ	ل – l
ت – t	ر – r	ظ – ẓ	م – m
ث – th	ز – z	ع – ʿ	ن – n
ج – j	س – s	غ – gh	ه – h
ح – ḥ	ش – sh	ف – f	و – w
خ – kh	ص – ṣ	ق – q	ي – y
د – d	ض – ḍ	ك – k	

Dipthongs are written *ay* [بَيْتْ] *aw* [يَوْمْ].

The three short vowels are represented by *a* for the *fatḥah, i* for the *kasrah*, and *u* for the *ḍammah.*

The long vowels are represented by *ā* for the *alif, ū* for the *waw*, and *ī* for the *yāʾ*.

Final *hāʾ* is represented by *a* at the end of the word, and by *at* when in construct.

Full declension (*iʿrāb*) is not employed in the transliterations.

The following system of annotation has been employed:

a. Transliteration marked (*with italics*).
b. Parenthetical comment or addition or substitution in translation marked [with brackets].

JIHĀD

Introduction

Comprehensive scholarly study of the phenomenon of "holy war," or war that is understood by its adherents and warriors as divinely sanctioned,[1] is surprisingly uncommon, this despite the ongoing prominence of news reports and discussion about militant groups and even leaders of nation-states threatening or claiming to engage in "holy war." The only exception to this rule is the study of war in the Hebrew Bible, a subdiscipline begun by Julius Wellhausen in his *Prolegomena to the History of Ancient Israel* in 1885. Friedrich Schwally coined the now common term "holy war" (*heilige Krieg*) in his monograph by that name published in 1901,[2] and a substantial volume and variety of excellent scholarship as well as popular works have been published on the topic to this day.[3] Some scholarly studies have been written also on holy war in the context of the medieval Christian Crusades, particularly as a possible deviation from the Western concept of the "just war."[4]

Although a number of studies have been published on holy war as it appears in Islam as well, only a fraction may be considered scholarly. Much must be deemed journalistic and some polemical, despite their attempt at objective appearance or their publication in well-known journals and magazines. One such example is W. R. Gardner's "Jihād," published in 1912 by *The Moslem World*, in which the author concludes: "That *jihād* is thus enjoined in the Koran for the establishment or extension of Islamic rule is, we have said, not surprising. One is almost inclined to say that it could scarcely have been otherwise with a Semitic race. Among all Semites, the idea that war was, or could be, dissociated from religion, may be said to have been almost unthinkable."[5]

Such polemics, in conjunction with the overwhelming fact of modern Western political and military domination, inspired Islamic apologetics ranging from the writings of Maulawi Cheragh ʿAlī[6] in India and Rashīd Riḍā[7] in Egypt to Āyatullāh Aḥmad Jannatī's "Defence and Jihād in the Qur'ān"[8] and S. K. Malik's *The Quranic Concept of War.*[9] A second school of Islamic responses to Western accusations and dominance, however, such as those of Abū al-Aʿlā al-Mawdūdī in Pakistan and Sayyid Qutb in Egypt, have tended to take a revivalist and more radical stance with regard to divinely sanctioned war than that of the apologists, further reworking classic medieval war ideas.[10] Such Islamic responses, whether apologist or revivalist, have in turn engendered further polemics ranging from John Laffin's alarmist *Holy War: Islam Fights* to the Hindu revivalist, Suhas Majumdar's *Jihād: The Islamic Doctrine of Permanent War.*[11] All of these approaches, whether polemical, apologetic, or revivalist, have distorted their representations by singling out only one trend or view among a broad range of thinking about war in Islamic civilization and by using it to generalize about Islam as a whole. A similar problem is evident in some recent attempts by Muslims in the West to challenge militant Islamic positions of war. The recent work edited by Abdel Haleem and others, for example, *The Crescent and the Cross: Muslim and Christian Approaches to War and Peace*, although commendable for its reexamination of Islamic texts and traditions, tends to avoid important but difficult traditional positions in its attempt to teach a unidimensional Islam promoting peace and reconciliatioin.[12]

Notwithstanding the clear influence of politics and polemics on discussions of such a controversial topic as holy war in Islam, a few excellent studies have been published in the last fifty years, most of which are descriptive. These include Majid Khadduri's *War and Peace in the Law of Islam*, which places Islam's legal tradition regarding war in the context of Islamic and international law.[13] Alfred Morabia's 1974 doctoral dissertation, "La notion de ğihad dans la'Islâm medieval,"[14] is less analytical in its broad description of the phenomenon and its application in Islamic history, although it also organizes various aspects of holy war ideology and theory. Rudolph Peters translated sections treating war from the medieval philosopher and legalist Ibn Rushd (*Bidāyat al-mujtahid*) and the modernist Maḥmūd Shaltūt (*Al-Qur'ān wal-qitāl*) and also published a study of holy war doctrine in modern Islamic movements, the latter of which especially includes some careful discussion of holy war notions in Islamic tradition.[15] Mention should also be made of two Arabic studies, both of which have been influenced by the appearance of Western writings on Islamic holy war. These are Wahba al-Zuḥaylī's *Āthār al-ḥarb fīl-fiqh al-islāmī*[16] and Muḥammad Haykal's *Al-jihād wal-qitāl fīl-siyāsa al-sharʿiyya*,[17] both of which describe the place of war in Islamic tradition and jurisprudence. A dozen or so excellent articles also have been written on various aspects of Islamic holy war, ranging from portrayals of "classic" Islamic war ideas to specific "sectarian" formulations among Shiʿite and Aḥmadī expressions, to modernist reworkings of medieval doctrine.[18]

As noted above, however, the scholarly studies tend to be descriptive, attempting to characterize rather than explain the phenomenon of holy war in Islamic civilization.[19] Little has been done to study the formation and evolution of the notion of divinely sanctioned war in Islam or to critically examine the spectrum of Islamic views on the subject. Classical Islamic tradition has developed its own canonical view on the formation and evolution of holy war and, with some small variation among the legal schools, a more or less standard view on the meaning and application of divinely sanctioned war in general. Scholarly studies of holy war in Islamic civilization have tended to accept uncritically, or at least not challenge, these standard views. The purpose of the present volume is to critically examine the origin of the holy war phenomenon in Islam, to test whether the traditional Islamic position on its origin and development is sound, and to employ methodologies and assumptions current in the social sciences as well as philology in order to describe and explain the early importance of holy war ideas and their implementation in primitive Islam.

The term "holy war" suggests a great many things to different people. Perhaps it is best, then, in defining the scope of this study, to begin with what this book does not attempt to accomplish. This book is not about warfare in Islam. It does not treat tactics, rules of engagement, weaponry, or legal justification, nor does it examine why the early Muslims were so successful militarily during their great conquest beginning in the seventh century. Neither is it a study of the morality of war, religiously sanctified or otherwise. It does not engage in "just-war" theory as defined by Western tradition, and it does not attempt to find parallels in Islam and in no way attempts to justify or condemn the engagement in war by Muslims at any point in history, ancient or modern. It will treat neither legal issues, political expressions, nor developments of religiously sanctioned warring that evolved after the earliest period, such as those directed against apostatizing or dissenting Muslim groups.

It is, rather, simply a study of the origins of the concept and application of warring that we now define as "holy war" in the earliest period of Islamic history. Questions are posed, such as: When and under what circumstances did the concept first appear in Islam, and as a result of what historical, political, religious, and sociological stimuli did it mature into its classical expressions? What were its antecedents in pre-Islamic Arabian civilization? Might it have been influenced by parallel concepts in neighboring civilizations?

Underlying such questions is the indisputable fact that divinely justified war became an item of major importance in the earliest Islamic period,[20] and that the concept of holy war quickly became a powerful motivator that has had an extremely important impact on the extent of Islamic empires and spheres of influence, on personal religious behavior, political and religious policy, international economics and law, and the self-perception of individual Muslims and the universal Muslim community as a whole. The study of the holy war phenomenon in early Islam is all the more interesting when we take into account the overwhelming evidence that pre-Islamic Arabia knew of no notion of ideological war of any kind, let alone religiously sanctioned war. How and why, then, did "holy war" become such a major component of early Islam?

Equally important questions regarding the origin of Islamic holy war are, What are the contexts for discussion about war in the early literature, and what are the authoritative sources for positions taken in later legal literature? How was warring understood by the earliest Muslim warriors? Was the early Muslim community of one mind on the matter, or were there different positions on warring and its justification in early Islam?

The problem may be stated most clearly as follows: while there is no evidence of any pre-Islamic expression of religiously sanctioned war, it appears very early in Islam as a highly developed and applied concept. How and why did holy war become such an important item in Islam?

This very question raises more general questions about the appearance of religiously sanctioned war in human cultures. How universal is the phenomenon? For how long in the history of human civilization have "holy war" concepts functioned? Does holy war exist more readily in complex, stratified societies than in more "primitive," less-stratified cultures? Is there a corresponding relationship between the existence of holy war concepts in any given culture and the structure or ideas of its religious system? Its economic system? Its leadership structure? Its gender roles? Can we postulate a transitional period in human cultures during which religiously sanctioned war might have evolved out of materially driven war? Can the existence of holy war ideas be explained through an objective "social Darwinist" theory?[21]

Answers to such big questions can hardly be guessed at in this stage of our knowledge about holy war phenomena. Additional study of the topic in the fields of anthropology, social psychology, and the academic study of religion is a desideratum and might yet bring us closer to understanding one of the more perplexing phenomena that has endured from ancient times well into the modern and postmodern[22] age.

At this point, an introduction to the data is in order, which in a study of this sort means a few words on sources and methodological approaches. Sources for this study are taken largely from Islamic literature itself, and they may be divided into three sometimes overlapping categories: sources that provide information about pre-Islamic Arabian cultures and worldviews, the Qurʾān, and the Ḥadīth, the tradition literature. A discussion about each category and the methodologies applied to their examination is provided in each chapter in which the specific genre of sources is studied. It should be noted here, however, that wherever feasible, the sources are cited both in their original languages and in translation in order to provide access to the nonspecialist in Islamic studies.

The three categories of sources from which the data for this study are extracted parallel the threefold division of this book. Part I centers on Arabia, particularly in the pre-Islamic period, and sets the parameters for the study of the early Islamic period by examining pre-Islamic cultural paradigms that may have influenced ideas about war during the transition into Islam. Chapter 1 examines preconceived notions about the various topics and subtopics to be studied and establishes the approach employed here. Chapter 2 examines the sources and provides an outline of pre-Islamic thinking about issues related to warring in order to establish paradigms against which developing Islamic views are analyzed.

Part II centers on the Qurʾān as the earliest Islamic text and transition marker from pre-Islamic Arabian civilization to the religio-cultural civilization that became Islam. Chapter 3 critically analyzes the canonical Islamic reading of the Qurʾān on the origin of holy war based on early commentaries (*tafāsīr*) and early historical and analytical studies (*asbāb al-nuzūl* and *naskh* collections). Chapter 4 provides a new reading based on a different method of analysis.

Part III centers on the tradition literature of Islam in the prophetic *sunna* and the biographical literature of Muḥammad. Chapter 5 concentrates on the Ḥadīth par excellence, the *sunna* of the Prophet, extracting information that might shed light on early beliefs and attitudes about warring during the mission of Muḥammad. Chapter 6 examines biographical (*sīra*) writings about Muḥammad from which cultural and historical data are extracted for comparison with that retrieved from the Qurʾān and Ḥadīth and for examining the relationship between formation of the new Muslim community (Umma) out of the old social systems of pre-Islamic Arabia and the development of religiously sanctioned war. Chapter 7 summarizes the prior findings and places them in historical context by linking the conceptual development of the Islamic holy war idea with the changes in the social structure and worldview of the new Muslim community.

PART I

Imaging Arabia

The term "Middle East" still conjures up images of adventure and romance, violence and intrigue, dusty bazaars and smoke-filled cafes. To the Westerner, it has been a region of mystery, the cradle of Western religion or perhaps even Western civilization itself, depending on how we define the extent of its borders and legacy—yet it is different from "us." The Middle East is not the West, the Orient not the Occident. We romantically acknowledge our intellectual and spiritual roots in the region, yet we deny any claim that the Middle East makes on us. It is adjacent to Europe, affects Europe, and has, in a way, given birth to Europe. It is perhaps because of this intimacy amid variance that Europe has so consistently used the Middle East as a paradigmatic means of defining the Other. The West considers the Middle East romantic, violent, and mysterious. It represents the extreme for which our civilization epitomizes the mean. As Edward Said has pointed out in somewhat broader terms, "European culture gained in strength and identity by setting itself off against the Orient as a sort of surrogate and even underground self."[1]

Western views of the Middle East tend to fold up regions, periods, cultures, and religions into an accordion bellows of overlapping images. Hammurabi, Moses, perhaps even Zoroaster, and certainly Muḥammad conflate into images of the ancient holy man, prophet, and lawgiver of our primitive forebears. Jesus, who represents the European escape from these primal images, is often left out of the picture among Christian believers, but even he cannot escape this primeval soup of ancient history among most postreligious Western intellectuals.

What stands out among the images of the Middle East is often the blood and gore or the anxiety of its potential: the story of the Flood, Pharaoh and the children of Israel and the destruction of the Egyptian armies at the Red Sea, Joshua at Jericho, John the Baptist's head on a platter, the Crucifixion, the destruction of the Jerusalem Temple, the intrigue and sudden death in *The Arabian Nights*, the Arab hordes riding out to the Conquest—and now the hijacker and suicide bomber. The Middle East is conjured up as the cradle of civilization, but it is nowhere the mature representative. It represents the potential that has been realized only elsewhere.

Our images of the Middle East are formed from movies and novels, storybooks and legends, television programs, news broadcasts, and newspapers. They are formed through these media and influenced by cultural and personal filtering mechanisms until they establish themselves in our psyches and become building blocks of our worldview. These are folk images, stereotypes that, although often consistent, hardly provide an accurate portrayal. The Middle East lies in our consciousness as the cradle of holy war. If our knowledge of the region provides us mental images for extremely ancient history, we may imagine Mesopotamian armies marching off to battle past the ziggurats of Babylon. We can certainly recall the biblical war images from illustrated Bibles, from such classic films as *The Ten Commandments*, *Ben Hur*, and *The Greatest Story Ever Told* and perhaps from sermons and homilies at religious services. But among our most secure images are those of the Arabs: dark warriors grasping scimitars in one hand and Qurʾāns in the other, a close-up of a swarthy giant, robed and bearded, brandishing a curved blade while breaking into a cunning grin—or a guerrilla aiming his Kalachnikov at innocent bystanders, a lone figure wired with explosives boarding an airplane or a city bus.

Stereotypical images of war in the Middle East often conflate a huge geographical area and thousands of years into an ongoing stream of warring and violence. In fact, however, the Middle East has been no more war-torn and perhaps a lot less so than many other regions of the world. To provide some perspective, the great historian of war Quincy Wright assembled a tally of 278 wars fought throughout the world from 1484 to 1945 based on a consistent set of criteria. Of those, 187 were fought mainly in Europe and 91 were fought everywhere else.[2]

Similar to the way in which we almost cannot help but distort the Middle East through our stereotypical images, so we in the West regularly misapply the term "holy war" when we so readily employ it to describe bloodshed between non-Western peoples and states. The Iran of Khomeini or the Iraq of Saddam Hussein have been regularly criticized as manipulating their populations into fighting wars by being told that they are fighting a holy war. But we do not apply the same criteria when our own presidents rally American citizens to be ready to engage the "evil empire" of the Soviet Union or destroy the satanic Saddam Hussein.[3] All governments when making the decision to go to war must rally their citizens to the cause. Because war has carried such a universally negative image in the twentieth century, political leaders and diplomats invariably articulate their countries' willingness to engage in war by using rhetoric that borders on the religious, particularly when describing "sacred duties" or in demonizing the enemy.

In fact, the motivations for engaging in war are complex and many, from the economic to the psychological, political, juridical, and ideological. Holy war, as will be seen below, is a subcategory of ideological war in which aggression is carried out against threats to the sacred values of a worldview, but no single motivation sends off armies to engage in battle. The reasons for war are multifaceted, complex, and fluid. One of the many categories that has been applied to warring and its justification is that of holy war, and holy war has been closely associated with Islam as it has with the Hebrew Bible and medieval Christendom. What follows is an examination of the provenance of holy war in its Islamic environment.

ONE

Islam and Holy War

Generalizations about Islam

Islam is perhaps the most misunderstood religion to the West, and many stereotypes still hinder clarity about its tenets and practices. Western prejudice toward Islam is as old as Islam itself. Even before Muḥammad, the nearly inaccessible Arabian Peninsula became a haven for practitioners of heterodox forms of Christianity that sought refuge from persecution by the Orthodox church. The church, in response, considered Arabia a "breeding ground of heresies" (*haeresium ferax*) even before the great Islamic Conquest began in the seventh century C.E.[1] The incredible success of the Conquest and the great civilization that arose along with it represented Europe's greatest threat, both politically and intellectually, for a thousand years. From the conquest of Spain in the early eighth century to the siege of Vienna by the Ottoman Turks in 1683, Islam represented a threat to the very physical existence of Christendom. This and Islam's achievement in all scientific and intellectual fields during its heyday in the Middle Ages caused a reaction in the West that epitomized Islam as cruel, evil, and uncivilized. This negative characterization began when Islam was powerful and Christianity weak but has continued into our own day.

Islam, as all religious civilizations, represents a complex system of values and ritual, theology and folklore, law and faith. Like all religions, it contains within it both the deep and the simple, the sublime and the cruel, the exalted and the ignoble. Like Judaism and Christianity, Islam is multifaceted, offering a variety of responses to the questions and perplexities of the human condition. It cannot fairly be forced into a single wrapping. Just as Judaism and Christianity rarely have a single view on issues of religious import, whether they be in the areas of theology, ritual, or epistemology, as well as the more commonly known issues of law and interpretation, so, too, Islam offers a range of views. Not only are there differences between Shiʿites, Sunnis, and Sufis, of which some educated Westerners may be generally familiar, within each of these and other Muslim groups may be found an abundance of subgroups expressing differing views and trends. As Aziz al-Azmeh articulates it, there are many "Islams."[2]

It is possible, nevertheless, and is indeed a desideratum in the field of religious studies, to speak of Islam as a coherent system, just as it is in relation to Judaism or Christianity—but only as long as we are willing to note the conflicting voices that may be found within it. The "Islam" that is the subject of analysis for the purposes of this study is the Islam in formation of the earliest period, during and immediately after the mission of Muḥammad, before the splits that eventuated in the division between Sunnis, Shiʿis, Khārijis, and Sufis. It took generations for qur'ānic studies, theology, and law to evolve from the days of Muḥammad into the disciplines of the classic period of the ʿAbbasid Caliphate, and it was during these generations that the "classical" or "orthodox" views and foundational concepts of a mainstream religious tradition were formed.[3] Our mission shall be to examine a portion of the complex early history of nascent Islam in order to reconstruct the conceptual development of its views on war.

The Meaning of Holy War

The study of war is a vast field comprising historical, phenomenological, legal, tactical, and psychological approaches, along with those in the fields of economics, political science, international relations, ethics, religious studies, anthropology, history, and so on. In these various disciplines, definitions must be established in order to limit and quantify the topic of study, but because of the great variety of interest and approach between them, even the definition of war itself finds no universal acceptance.[4] In most general terms, however, war may be defined as an organized, purposeful activity directed by one established group against a rival group that involves actual or potential application of lethal force.[5] The importance of distinguishing between the in-group and the "other" cannot be overstressed as the particular vehemence and tragedy of "civil war" suggests, for organized and sanctioned mass violence and killing can be conducted only against those who are identified, even if only temporarily, as outside the group—against "the enemy."[6]

War does not always mean combat. It may be a state of condition between human groups even when warfare is not actually being conducted. The cold war, for example, represented a state of affairs in which actual and direct combat between the principal parties never took place, and the doctrine of *jihād* in Islamic legal literature likewise defines a state of relationship between the Islamic world and the non-Islamic world.[7]

The term "holy war" is a European invention and derives from the study of war in its European context. It does not define types of warfare, such as "primitive" or "modern," nor does it define whether a specific engagement is defensive, preemptive, or initiatory. Rather, in its most broad definition, the term defines a form of justification for engaging in war by providing religious legitimization.[8] The question of justification is one that occupies many areas of scholarship on war, from anthropology to ethics, and it is the key issue in theories of "just war" that treat the *jus ad bellum*, a statement on the right or justification for making war.[9] Modern just-war theory relies on natural-law causes as justification for war, but medieval European just-war theory relied on religious justification as well, and such religious justification was ideological, based on religious doctrine. Today there is an attempt among international organs and, to a certain extent, in the West in general, to distinguish between legal and ideological justifications for warring, with the legal receiving greater legitimacy. Nonetheless, the distinction between holy war and just war is not always clear. Such distinction did not exist before the seventeenth century in Europe and has often been blurred since.

Western just-war ideas developed out of an amalgamation of Greco-Roman thought with Christian dogma and ethics and Teutonic cultural traditions.[10] The development of thinking that resulted in Western just-war doctrine includes holy war ideas and justifications as well, but the European expressions of holy war arose within historical and religio-cultural circumstances that were unique and certainly different from the equally unique Arabian context out of which arose the Islamic expressions of holy war. The two nevertheless share the ideological nature of justification for resorting to war. Both expressions therefore represent a subset of ideological war, which James Turner Johnson defines as "armed struggle against threats to the highest values accepted in the culture and against the values represented by the enemy."[11]

Although holy war is defined most broadly as any religious justification for engaging in war, it does not necessarily presume a connection of military activity to religious purposes, though this is often the case. Some expression of holy war exists in virtually all religious traditions and is certainly the most common and persistent expression of ideological war. Its representation across religious and cultural strata has taken many different forms and produced many different results. All, however, can be said to represent divinely justified engagement in war. Such justification contrasts most starkly with material justification for warring, which among ecological materialists has been said to lie at the bottom of many if not most decisions to engage in war.[12] Despite the continuing discussion between the various disciplines over the primary motivators for warring, it has become far more accepted in recent years to acknowledge that a multiplicity of motivations factor into any decision to go to war. Whatever the complexity of the motivational circumstances, however, justification—if not sanction—for embarking on a program in which many of one's own group are likely to be killed is a necessity.[13] As societies become more complex and hierarchical, justification based on material enhancement seems to decline, while ideological justification seems to rise. In the fully developed Islamic system, as will be demonstrated below, religious justification is provided along with the assurance that material enhancement or, in the event of death, heavenly reward will also accrue to the religious warrior. All expressions of holy war provide religious justification for engaging in war, whether or not a multiplicity of other factors affect the decision or likelihood of warring.

As might be expected given the variety of human religious experience, there are many different expressions of holy war. The divinity may gird its human warriors with extraordinary strength, determine the outcome before the beginning of the battle, or even fight on behalf of the people. Or the people might fight on behalf of the deity (or what it symbolizes), the ideals of religion, or against the false ideas of opposing religions or peoples. Divine authority for warring is established directly by the divine word communicated through speech or writ or indirectly through a prophet, priest, or religious functionary who determines the divine sanction through oracular means. Such a broad spectrum of holy war paradigms reflects the varied cultural and religious settings in which they may be found. Parallels may be found between the various expressions because of historical influence or simply because of phenomenological similarities. Yet the particular religious and cultural configurations of every individual tradition produce a unique expression of holy war that accurately reflects its history, theology, and anthropology. The particular expressions of holy war found in the Islamic world tend to be referred to in the West as *jihād*.

The Meaning of Jihād

The semantic meaning of the Arabic term *jihād* has no relation to holy war or even war in general. It derives, rather from the root *j.h.d.*, the meaning of which is to strive, exert oneself, or take extraordinary pains. *Jihād* is a verbal noun of the third Arabic form of the root *jahada*, which is defined classically as "exerting one's utmost power, efforts, endeavors, or ability in contending with an object of disapprobation."[14] Such an object is often categorized in the literature as deriving from one of three sources: a visible enemy, the devil, and aspects of one's own self. There are, therefore, many kinds of *jihād*, and most have nothing to do with warfare. "*Jihād* of the heart," for example, denotes struggle against one's own sinful inclinations, while "*jihād* of the tongue" requires speaking on behalf of the good and forbidding evil.[15] Various activities subsumed under *jihād* are said by Muḥammad to distinguish true believers who are loyal to God's Prophet:

> Every prophet sent by God to a nation (*umma*) before me has had disciples and followers who followed his ways (*sunna*) and obeyed his commands. But after them came successors who preached what they did not practice and practiced what they were not commanded. Whoever strives (*jāhada*) against them with one's hand is a believer, whoever strives against them with one's tongue is a believer, whoever strives against them with one's heart is a believer. There is nothing greater than [the size of] a mustard seed beyond that in the way of faith.[16]

Muḥammad is also credited with saying: "The best *jihād* is [speaking] a word of justice to a tyrannical ruler."[17]

The qualifying phrase "in the path of God" (*fī sabīl Allah*) specifically distinguishes the activity of *jihād* as furthering or promoting God's kingdom on earth. It can be done, for example, by simply striving to behave ethically and by speaking without causing harm to others or by actively defending Islam and propagating the faith. *Jihād* as religiously grounded warfare, sometimes referred to as "*jihād* of the sword" (*jihād al-sayf*), is subsumed under the last two categories of defending Islam and propagating the faith, though these need not be accomplished only through war. When the term is used without qualifiers such as "of the heart" or "of the tongue," however, it is universally understood as war on behalf of Islam (equivalent to "*jihād* of the sword"), and the merits of engaging in such *jihād* are described plentifully in the most-respected religious works.[18] Nevertheless, Muslim thinkers, and particularly ascetics and mystics, often differentiate between the "greater *jihād*" (*al-jihād al-akbar*) and the "lesser *jihād*" (*al-jihād al-aṣghar*), with the former representing the struggle against the self and only the "lesser *jihād*" referring to warring in the path of God.[19]

Even within its range of meaning as war on behalf of Islam, the term is often used in relation to conflicts between Muslims. Such examples of *jihād* include wars fought against groups of apostates rebelling against proper Islamic authority (*murtaddūn*), dissenting groups denouncing legitimate Muslim leadership (*baghī*), highway robbers and other violent people, and deviant or un-Islamic leadership.[20] The determination of when Muslim leaders may call for *jihād* and the requisite demands that such a call makes on the Muslim populace is developed in the legal literature. Because such religiously authorized war is determined in part by legal criteria that parallel Western Christendom's concerns identified with just-war thinking, John Kelsay has led other students of religious ethics in exploring Islamic legal thought associated with *jihād* in terms of just-war theory.[21]

Jihād thus cannot be equated semantically with holy war, for its meaning is much broader, includes many activities unrelated to warfare, and is determined in part by legal criteria that parallel modern just-war thinking in the West. It would not be inaccurate, however, to suggest a definition of the subcategory of "*jihād* of the sword" as any act of warring authorized by legitimate Muslim authorities on behalf of the religious community and determined to contribute to the greater good of Islam or the community of Muslims, either in part or as a whole. Because such a definition is framed by both ideological and legal criteria, even "*jihād* of the sword" is not quite equivalent to the common Western understanding of holy war.

The present volume centers on the origins of holy war in Islam, while not intending to provide a full understanding of the meaning of the term in classical Islam. It does not treat all of its meanings in the Qur'ān, for example, nor does it treat the newer interpretations of *jihād* that have developed in the twentieth century.[22] My purpose, rather, is to trace the genesis and development of religiously sanctified war in the earliest Islamic period, whether that is categorized in Islamic parlance as *jihād* or referred to through other terminology.

The issue of terminology finds some importance in a study of this sort, for just as it is impossible to equate *jihād* directly with holy war, Islam does not limit religiously authorized war to the term *jihād*. The terms *qitāl* (fighting) and *ḥarb* (war) found in the Qur'ān and in post-qur'ānic religious literature also treat warring. *Ḥarb* is a generic term for war and refers usually to wars that are not legitimized by religious authority, while *qitāl* and particularly *qitāl* in the path of God (*fī sabīl Allah*) is virtually synonymous with *jihād* when it is understood as warring in the path of God.[23]

TWO

The Pre-Islamic World

Holy war has been a well-known phenomenon in human civilization from long before the genesis of Islam. The Hebrew Bible contains many examples of warring on behalf of God or religion, and even the deity itself is depicted on occasion as engaging in the fray.[1] The Bible, in turn, reflects or parallels ideas of other peoples and religions in the ancient Near East, and the view that the tribal or national deity is actively involved in battle was common.[2] The prominent expression of holy war in the Bible subsequently influenced Christianity and Rabbinic Judaism as well, so that ideas of fighting on behalf of God's religion or God's people had been well established in the popular monotheistic religious traditions contemporary to the formative period of earliest Islam.[3] So, too, was divine association with warring and its outcome a part of Hindu religions and Zoroastrianism, with the latter certainly having an influence on the indigenous populations of Arabia before and during the early Islamic period.[4]

These great religious civilizations all had an impact on the new religious civilization of Islam, and scholarship on the question of their influence on early Islam continues to this day.[5] There is no doubt that foreign religious ideas and practices, particularly from Judaism and Christianity, had a profound effect on the development of Islam,[6] but in the case of holy war, the parallels that exist are phenomenological and not due to influence by the biblical traditions.[7] Notwithstanding the popularity of Western comparative studies between Islam and the biblical traditions, indigenous pre-Islamic cultural and religious concepts and ritual had an impact that was at least as powerful. Perhaps the most obvious example is that of pilgrimage to the *bayt* or Kaʿba in Mecca, which is a nearly wholesale adoption of pre-Islamic religious practice. The profound importance of pre-Islamic Arabian civilization for the development of warring in Islam requires its own independent examination.

Pre-Islamic Arabia

The history of pre-Islamic Arabia is garnered from reports from neighboring peoples, from occasional inscriptions found among ancient ruins, and from Muslim histories and related literature that were written centuries after the end of that era. The related literature referred to here includes oral Arabian poetry attributed to the pre-Islamic period but not committed to writing until a century or more into the Islamic period.[8] Although all historical documents have their own *tendenzen*, the typical view of Islamic literature, whether historical or otherwise, toward the pre-Islamic period merits a slight digression. The term for the pre-Islamic period in Islamic texts is *jāhiliyya*, which has come to hold the meaning of a state of ignorance. This period of ignorance is juxtaposed with the period of Islam, which is the era of moral and scientific enlightenment during which knowledge of God replaced the vanity of idolatry.[9] The term is revealing, for its very use illuminates the powerful Muslim historiographic bias regarding pre-Islamic Arabia. The ancient period is typified as being a time of ignorant idolatry, moral decadence, and near social anarchy. It was a period of hopeless human decay and darkness until the coming of light and hope with the advent of Islam.[10] This view presupposes, among other things, a radical break in values and worldview between the old pre-Islamic period and that even of early Islam, an assumption that is not supported by the results of this study. The bias against pre-Islamic times in Arabia expressed by the Islamic sources is quite clear and must certainly be taken into account, but its acknowledgment among Western scholars has too severely limited the amount of material that critical scholarship has been willing to accept for examination for the period.

A second and more difficult problem lies in the nature of early Islamic historical writing in general. Not only are those literary works that treat early Islam and the pre-Islamic era not contemporaneous with the age they treat, the earliest sources were compiled into their present form only 150 or 200 years after the end of the period in question. Although the available sources purport to contain material contemporaneous with the earliest period of Islam, Western scholarship has questioned their reliability since the middle of the nineteenth century.[11] Some recent studies of the pre-Islamic period try to bridge the data gap by extrapolating information from anthropological investigations of traditional groups that appear to have similar social, ethno-linguistic, economic, cultural, and climatic backgrounds but that live in the modern world.[12] The danger, however, of relying heavily on analogues that are separated from the subject in question by a millennium and a half of history is clear, for we cannot control for the innumerable natural evolutionary changes in culture and ideas that can skew the analogy.[13]

This study relies largely on Islamic texts for primary source material, notwithstanding the acknowledged difficulties of working with such information. Modern ethnographic studies of desert nomadic groups have also been consulted but not relied on for the extrapolation of data except in exceptional cases, which are acknowledged. This book, though neither a traditional study of historical events nor an ethnography, seeks to learn from historical and ethnographic data. As an examination of the concept of holy war in Islamic religious civilization, it attempts to understand cultural history. It therefore requires a critical examination of sources but not the same kind of examination as for a study of political history. It need not, for example, analyze why a primary source posits a particular motivation for, or outcome of, a particular event, because whether or not the events themselves even took place is often irrelevant. What is of importance for this study are the conceptual approaches and attitudes that the sources communicate. Do they distinguish between different qualities of fighting, different types of war, or the nature of justification for engaging in combat? How do they define the authority for the decision to engage in combat or for the obligation for doing so? What were the motivations for risking one's life on the battlefield? This information may sometimes be safely garnered even from texts that are unreliable for the purposes of recording political history, because such texts do not intend to manipulate the specific information being sought for this study. Sometimes materials that are suspect with regard to their historical accuracy may nevertheless provide accurate conceptual information even about the period they are suspected of misrepresenting. At the very least, they tend unselfconsciously to express beliefs and aspects of a worldview that represent their own period.[14]

Southern and Northern Arabia

The geographic term for peninsula in Arabic is *shibh jazīra*, which means, literally, "resembling an island." This is an appropriate term for the Arabian Peninsula because it is surrounded by water on three sides and thus largely isolated from other lands and peoples. Its northern border, however, extends into the settled areas of the eastern Mediterranean region and Mesopotamia, and, as a consequence, cultural, economic, and social interaction always moved between the arid Arabian steppe and the Fertile Crescent. This movement, however, was restricted by the northern desert, which tended to keep large population movements, including invading armies, from moving southward. The Arabian Peninsula remained, therefore, largely free from the direct control of the great powers of early antiquity—Egypt and Mesopotamia, and, later, Greece, Persia, Rome, and Byzantium. Communication across the boundary remained largely in the hands of Arab transporters who drove camel caravans back and forth between the southern tip of the peninsula and the southern Mediterranean in the west or the lower Tigris-Euphrates river valley in the east. Although the surrounding great powers were unable to conquer Arabia directly, they often succeeded through influence and proxies in preventing the formation of major rival commercial or political entities in Arabia. With the decline of these outside forces by the third quarter of the sixth century, however, the way was open for the growth of an indigenous Arabian power.[15]

Because the armies of the empires never succeeded in controlling Arabia, oppressed peoples wishing to flee state-imposed restrictions in the Fertile Crescent sometimes slipped south of the frontier. Such peoples included unorthodox expressions of Judaism and Christianity, which were pressured, oppressed, or outlawed by the external imperial authorities or their own internal religious hierarchies. There were, therefore, well-known Jewish and Christian communities in Arabia, which fled the state-controlled orthodoxy of Byzantine Christianity and Persian Zoroastrianism. These groups, which entered the stark and bleak landscape of Arabia in order to practice their religious traditions, assimilated greatly to Arabian culture, adopted Arabic names, and spoke the local languages.[16] As noted previously, these groups seem to have had a profound influence on the development of early Islam, but because we do not know the details of their particular, most likely heterodox, religious expressions, it is difficult to know the quality of their influence.[17]

The Arabian Peninsula hosted two general categories of indigenous populations: nomadic Arabs or Bedouin, and settled Arab agriculturists, with the former predominant in most habitable areas outside the southernmost region. The southern end of the peninsula, corresponding roughly to today's Yemen and known by the Romans as *Arabia Felix*, or "happy Arabia," was the most watered area and the only location, outside the occasional oasis, where agriculture could be practiced on an ongoing and year-round basis. The success of agriculture in South Arabia freed some of its population to pursue specialty skills necessary to build large and complex social structures necessary for the growth of large civilizations. Its major export crop was frankincense, which, because of the great demand for this commodity in the ancient Mediterranean world, provided the means to import goods and knowledge that helped establish a highly organized and developed society. South Arabia during this high period, beginning at least five centuries before the Common Era, was organized under the four major kingdoms of Sabā', Minaea, Ḥaḍramawt, and Qatabān, as well as some other minor states, but the social, religious, political, and cultural systems of South Arabia were so similar that they may be considered basically uniform.[18] The populations of South Arabia were largely settled in villages and towns practicing irrigation agriculture, but nomadic groups lived in areas not fit for productive farming. Notwithstanding the unique climatic and socioeconomic situation of South Arabia, there was common traffic and communication between it and the remainder of the peninsula, partly as a result of the caravan trade but, also, simply because of their proximity and the great success of South Arabian civilization. Rulers of South Arabia occasionally marched against other areas, as is preserved in the famous qur'ānic *sūra*, Al-Fīl (105, "The Elephant"), which refers to the attempt of an invader from the south to capture Mecca by attacking it with elephants.[19] Southern kingdoms established colonies in North Arabia, and ancient inscriptions describe the campaigns of southern kingdoms against nomadic tribes on the frontiers as well.[20] South Arabian peoples occasionally migrated northward, and although the two areas were linguistically separate (and remain so to an extent even to this day), they easily communicated and most certainly influenced one another.

Although South Arabia preserved no pre-Islamic literary tradition aside from the material sifted through the lenses of later Muslim writers, a number of ancient inscriptions in south Arabian languages have been discovered. These include a series of votive inscriptions dating up to the mid-fourth century C.E., which were dedications to statuettes in thanks for military and other successes. Most were found in a single area and dedicated to one national deity, Ilmuqah (*'lmqh*), in its cultic center of Awā near the famous ancient Marib and known today as Maḥram Bilqīs. These votive offerings were mounted on stone plinths containing a record of the dedication, and they provide information about the modes of warfare current in the Sabaean kingdom.[21] Similar votive offerings were made at the pre-Islamic shrine known as the Kaʿba in Mecca, although no inscriptions remain.[22] Despite the fact that these records of ancient campaigns were dedicated to tribal deities in thanks for success on the field of battle, the wars referred to in relation to the votive offerings do not fall into the category of "holy war." Motivations for warring derived from the inscriptions were almost exclusively the acquisition of plunder and the attainment of military glory. Warriors occasionally also received official awards at the conclusion of a campaign. In one case, rescue of a ruler's sister married to another ruler was cited as the reason for battle. There seems to be little obvious interest in territorial expansion and possession, but control of trade routes was important.[23] The casualties listed are almost always restricted to the number of combatants killed or taken prisoner, along with an accounting of the booty taken (usually in heads of camels, donkeys, and sheep and goats). Only one of thirty-eight such inscriptions noted the loss of noncombatants.[24] In one text, enemy casualties are listed as 2,000 men, but most of the battles were fought with only scores of troops on each side, extending upward to a few hundred. Reprisal operations were not uncommon, according to these records, but the victors are rarely cited as massacring captive troops. Battles were often waged by these settled South Arabian groups against nomads living on the peripheries of the settled areas.

Because of its unique climatic, economic, and sociopolitical conditions, South Arabia is usually considered to be a separate and distinct civilization significantly removed from the dominant nomadic Arabs to its north, but this was often not exactly the case. Among the southern regions, some were more and others were less centralized and organized around farming and commercialization. Some remained seminomadic, and all of them experienced periods of transition between village agrarianism and nomadism or vice versa, depending on the climatic, political, and economic conditions of the period.[25] During a crisis, nomadization increased, to such an extent at times that large populations migrated out of the south and into areas that are known to have been almost exclusively nomadic,[26] particularly when the important Mediterranean market for frankincense declined in late antiquity. The concomitant decrease in income resulted in the south's inability to keep up its irrigation system of dams and canals, which in turn accelerated its decline. Later and lesser southern kingdoms such as the Ḥimyar and the Kinda also declined by the sixth century, and with their decline came increased nomadization and northward migration of South Arabian peoples.[27] The decline did not spell an end to urban centers, however, even in the depressed period just before the rise of Islam, for towns were needed for trading and continued to grow up around cultic centers and oases.[28] But certainly by the century before the beginning of Muḥammad's mission, even predominantly agrarian South Arabia had taken on a considerably more nomadic character.

The Christian kingdom of Ethiopia (Abyssinia), opposite South Arabia and across the narrow Bāb al-Mandab straits separating the Red Sea from the Gulf of Aden, must also be mentioned. The mutual influence and interaction between South Arabia and Ethiopia are exemplified by the claim of each area as the ancient home of the Queen of Sheba, who according to the biblical report (1 Kings 10:1–10 and 2 Chronicles 9:1–9), went to Jerusalem with a great caravan of camels bearing spices, gold, and precious stones to test King Solomon's famous wisdom with difficult questions. Abyssinian rulers occasionally invaded South Arabia, and Abraha (a variant of Abraham), the leader of the aforementioned South Arabian expedition against Mecca recorded in the Qur'ān, was an officer originally sent by the Ethiopian negus to assist South Arabian Christians against the aggression of the last (and Jewish) king of the Ḥimyar dynasty, Dhū Nuwās.[29]

In North Arabia, and particularly in areas encroaching onto the Fertile Crescent, were organized Arab polities that reached very sophisticated levels of organization and culture. The prime example is the Nabataean kingdom (ca. 200 B.C.E.–200 C.E.) in today's southern Jordan, Israel, and northern Saudi Arabia.

The great civilization of Nabataea, centered in its rose-colored capital city hewn out of solid rock among the cliffs of Petra in today's Jordan, had so greatly assimilated to its Aramaic and Greco-Roman surroundings that it hardly qualifies as an indigenous Arabian kingdom. Its language of discourse was Aramaic, and its aesthetic, Greco-Roman. Only the personal names preserved reveal its Arabian origin.[30] The Nabataeans, however, offer a prime example of the course of migration and acculturation of Arabian peoples who moved northward from the arid Arabian steppe and into the more settled areas of the Fertile Crescent, a process continuing from the earliest times.[31]

Two other Arabian kingdoms in the north served as buffer states between the Byzantine and Persian Empires and the sporadic incursions of Bedouin migrants and raiders. These are the Ghassanids in the west and the Lakhmids in the east, both of which retained their Arabic language and culture although they took on forms of Christianity as their religion. They existed into the beginning of the seventh century but were weakened considerably by the time Muḥammad began preaching in Mecca in the early 600s.[32]

Both northern and southern Arabia were experiencing a period of decline during the time leading up to the birth of Muḥammad. The eastern Mediterranean region in general was in decline during this period, and the constant wars between Byzantium and Persia weakened the entire region. On the other hand, the central Arabian town of Mecca appears to have remained influential, primarily because of its position as the major cultic center of the west central Arabian region known as the Ḥijāz. Contrary to earlier assumptions among European scholars, Mecca may not have controlled a vast and influential network of trading contacts but, rather, a more modest trade in mostly local commodities.[33] The growth of sea trade, in which Arabia did not compete, drained resources away from the traditional Arab caravaning and trade of earlier centuries, and the collapse of powerful indigenous polities in southern and northern Arabia encouraged free reign among Bedouin tribes. This collapse, in turn, led to greater internecine feuding and wars, which resulted in a heightened insecurity throughout the peninsula. Nomadic tribes became increasingly dominant over sedentary communities, and Bedouin cultural influence rose. This trend away from organized polities and toward increased nomadism or at least nomadic influence has been termed the "bedouinization of Arabia."[34]

This term is somewhat misleading because the majority population of the peninsula did not make the transition from agrarianism or settled village or urban life to nomadism. On the contrary, the archaeological and literary evidence suggests that the majority population was in fact never nomadic, including the period leading up to the genesis of Islam. What did seem to change in this period, however, was a shift in power and influence away from sedentary communities and toward dominant nomadic tribes.

In the midst of the political dislocation and general decline of settled populations, the centrally located town of Mecca is depicted in the sources as maintaining itself as a powerful center exhibiting such urban traits as significant socioeconomic distinctions between clans and "classes." It is still unclear what specific factors may have contributed to a strong and influential Mecca at this time—beyond its importance as a religious cult center and the commerce that this importance would naturally attract—but the Arabic sources are quite consistent in their depictions. Such are the common features of Arabia toward the end of the sixth century. They make up the backdrop to the emergence of Islam.[35]

Central Arabia

Notwithstanding the importance of and influence exerted by the history, cultures, and religions of southern and northern Arabia on early Islam, the new Islamic order emerged out of the uniquely west central Arabian milieu of the Ḥijāz, and it is this environment that most strongly influenced the new order. It must be stressed, however, that the Ḥijāz does not equal Bedouin nomad. The majority population was probably settled among the agricultural oases scattered throughout the area, while the fewer but more ubiquitous nomads were spread throughout the steppe and deserts adjoining the occasional oases. The definitions of nomad and settled agriculturist were not static however, because there was movement between the two populations and even a sizable population of "seminomads" who practiced settled agriculture at certain times of the year and a localized form of nomadism at other times.[36] Indeed, most settled populations traced their origin from Bedouin nomadism, and, despite the difficult life of the desert pastoralist, the Bedouin image—and therefore its cultural importance and influence—remained the highest in status. The status of Bedouin culture and custom was enhanced by the fact that, for the most part, they held the reins of power in the region, and it is the dominant tribes of Bedouin who exercised the greatest influence. The strong tribes dominated not only weaker nomadic formations but also the less-mobile seminomads and the sedentary populations because of their fighting skills and mobility, which allowed them to attack and then retreat into the desert where they could not be pursued.[37]

Muḥammad was born and raised in the west central Arabian town of Mecca, and it was the environment of Mecca that had the greatest influence on the worldview of early Islam. Mecca was founded as a religious shrine, most likely because of its sacred spring, the *zamzam*, which gurgled up in an unlikely and inhospitable place.[38] Mecca and its sacred spring became a cultic center, which, by the sixth century, attracted pilgrims from throughout Arabia. Commercialism grew up alongside pilgrimage, and trading fairs were established in conjunction with the major periods of population influx. Mecca thus became a center for the visits of people with diverse cultural and religious backgrounds, thereby serving as a central focus for the intermingling of cultures, traditions, and ideas. It became "the most complex and heterogeneous place in Arabia," in which a variety of social, economic, and religious systems came together, causing ferment, tension, and opportunity.[39]

Muḥammad was of the Hāshim clan, a part of the large and dominant tribe of the region known as Quraysh. According to tradition, the Quraysh tribe left off from its previously nomadic lifestyle and took over the rule of Mecca some five generations before Muhammad.[40] Qurayshite cultural roots were therefore those of the Bedouin, and although as a settled urban tribe some Bedouin social and cultural values surely evolved and changed, these traditional Bedouin cultural realia must be examined in order that we can gain an appreciation of the dominant cultural norms of seventh-century Arabia and the part that they played in the development of an early Islamic worldview.

Bedouin Nomadism

It is appropriate as well as logical that the name "Bedouin" is derived from the Arabic word for desert, *al-bādiya*, for the Bedouin nomads of Arabia have been successful in living in extremely adverse desert conditions for millennia. The key to their success in such a hostile environment was the domestication of the camel, which may have been achieved in south central Asia as early as the last quarter of the third millennium B.C.E. Ancient rock drawings suggest that camel domestication entered Arabia after the sixteenth century B.C.E. The Bible (Judges 6–8) records the migration of what appear to be camel-herding bedouin in its reference to Midianites, Amalekites, and "children of the east" (*b^{e}ney qedem*) crossing the Jordan River from the north Arabian desert in the early eleventh century B.C.E. "They would come up with their livestock and their tents, swarming as thick as locusts; they and their camels were innumerable. Thus they would invade the land and ravage it. Israel was reduced to utter misery by the Midianites, and the Israelites cried out to the Lord."[41]

The domestication of the camel along with cultivation of the date palm provided the transportation and nourishment for deep penetration into arid regions. Under certain conditions, a camel can travel for weeks without drinking,[42] and the date, which supplies high caloric energy for sustenance, is easily preserved and does not spoil in the desert heat. The date pits and stems may also be fed to camels, and in an emergency the camels themselves may be slaughtered and their stored water drunk. The extreme mobility available to camel nomads made them formidable raiders of settled areas, for they could attack settled peoples unawares and then retreat into the desert where they could not be followed. Camels, however, were only one of a variety of animals tended by Bedouin: these included also donkeys for local transportation, sheep and goats for food, and, occasionally, horses for raiding.

As with any population spread over a large area and separated by the natural boundaries of water, mountains, and desert, it is impossible to speak of a single "Arabian culture" or even of a single Bedouin culture. There were and are, rather, a virtually infinite number of permutations of cultural norms. It is nevertheless possible to speak of the "ideal-typical" traits of a society, and it is this theoretical norm, which of course must vary considerably over time and place, that must be established here as a baseline against which changes brought about by Islam may be examined. Because of the political importance of Bedouin tribes in the Ḥijāzi highlands of the sixth century—the assumption among the settled populations themselves that they derived from Bedouin ancestors and what appears to have been in many respects their strong cultural influence if not dominance in some areas even of settled life—it is to Bedouin cultural values and concepts that we shall now turn.

Bedouin society was and remains a patriarchal system, and the sources providing data about camel-nomadism in ancient times stress male roles and the cultural traits that relate to those roles.[43] It is clear that female roles and cultural traits associated with those roles play a critical role in Bedouin life as they do in all human cultures, but the data on these topics in ancient Bedouin cultures is difficult to extract. The following discussion therefore centers on traits of great importance to the male role as leader and warrior in ancient nomadic Arabian cultures.

Fate

Pre-Islamic Arabian poetry contains a great amount of material treating the vicissitudes of fate. The vocabulary of the poetry is varied and sophisticated, with a number of different terms treating various nuances of what English renders generally as fate or destiny. *Manīya* or other forms of the root *m.n.w.* (*manā*, *munā*, the plural *manāyā*, etc.) convey this sense. As Helmer Ringgren notes in his monumental *Studies in Arabian Fatalism*, "[The root *m.n.w.*] is generally used to denote the allotting or apportioning carried out by Destiny, but as a rule we feel that the thing allotted is something dark and gloomy."[44] Other terms associated with fate include the verb *ḥamma* as in *uḥimmat* or *ḥummat manīya*, meaning "fate or death (*manīya*) is determined,"[45] *qadar* and *qaḍā'*, both of which are associated with the sense of decree and which later become the primary terms in Islam for divine decree;[46] and *dahr* (*miqdār*) and *zamān*, which are associated with the meaning of time as destiny and which often appear personified: "Time overcame ʿĀd by force, and Ḥimyar, troops after troops. . . ." "Time has killed him. . . ." "Time destroyed them (*ʾafnāhum al-dahr*). . . ." "Time is a thief who snatches away friends and relatives. . . ."[47]

To the pre-Islamic Arabian poet, fate cannot be avoided or escaped. It will find you wherever you may be, whether you fortify yourself in castles or even take refuge in the sun:

The young man runs, but his fated death (*ḥimām al-mawt*) reaches him.
Every day brings the fixed term nearer to him.
I know that my day will once reach me
And I shall not care for my world any more.

or

Time (*dahr*) is change, Time's fool is man,
Wealth or want, great store or small,
All is one since Death's (*manūn*) are all.[48]

What is inevitably fated in pre-Islamic Arabic poetry is the necessity of death, which is preordained. Destiny is, in fact, death, and a death that does not seem to include the possibility of an afterlife.[49] One will meet one's demise in a particular way at a particular place, so it is no use trying to avoid it by attempting to change the course of one's own history. Other events are not specifically mentioned as being destined to occur, however, so that decision making in general seems not to have been obstructed by the whims of fate. On the other hand, the overwhelming sense of fated death must have affected one's general view of history, both personal and general. Patient endurance (*ṣabr*) is the best attitude to be taken in the face of destiny. Destiny is capricious and impersonal, so that events occur without a sense of meaningful grounding. Whether one will die in an upcoming raid, in defense of one's honor while fighting, or through a mortal accident, one should be patient and courageous in facing the inevitable.

O my friends, a respected death
Is better than an illusory refuge;
Anxiety does not ward off the decree (*qadar*)
But endurance is a cause of victory.
Death (*manīya*) is better than vileness,
And having death before oneself is better than having it behind.
Thus, courage! There is no escape from death.[50]

It is still not clear how much pre-Islamic Arabian poetry reflects the actual worldview of daily life with regard to such beliefs as fate. Some of the great

European scholars of this poetry were hesitant, given the strictly formulaic use of common motifs and clichés in this oral medium, to consider it an accurate reflection of a common worldview.[51] At question is to what extent the poetic view of fate weakened or superseded traditional Arabian religious beliefs.[52] Ignaz Goldziher holds that the importance of the idea of fate lessened the influence of the old religious traditions, as do Watt and Ringgren.[53] The fact that religious motifs are rarely found in the poetic compilations, however, does not necessarily mean that they were not an important part of pre-Islamic Arabian culture. What seems clear is that several trajectories of belief were pulling pre-Islamic Arabian culture in different directions. Fatalism, the belief in the gods as controllers of human destiny; the Jewish and Christian religious belief systems held by newcomers and their resident Arabian converts; the indigenous pre-Islamic monotheistic expressions grouped together under the term *ḥanīfiyya*;[54] and what Watt terms "tribal humanism" associated with the important pre-Islamic traits of honor, generosity, and tribal solidarity all pulled at the minds and hearts of the populations of the region. These contrasting and competing systems added to the sense of dislocation that was affecting Arabia in the period immediately before the rise of Islam.

Honor

The harsh conditions and paucity of resources in the Arabian desert engendered a sociocultural system among Bedouin that promoted certain survival traits. These include hospitality and generosity, strength and bravery, good judgment, and an intense loyalty to one's kin and clan. Such characteristics tend to be subsumed under the Arabic term *murū'a* (or *muruwwa*), which is often defined today by the general term "manliness" but which is given a number of variant definitions in medieval Arabic lexicons. It seems to have had a broad range of meanings in ancient days but tended to define the qualities of a man's wealth and management of property, which therefore included such traits as generosity, judgment, and the abilities needed to acquire wealth in that society. The honor of a tribesman could be realized through hospitality, which often meant protection of a weaker individual (perhaps a refugee cut off from his own kinship group for some major offense) or an entire kinship group requesting aid. Weaker groups, for example, such as the Jewish clans of Yathrib/Medina,[55] attached themselves to the larger and more powerful Arab tribes (or clans) of the town. So, too, in the nomadic situation, strong tribes or tribal leaders would gather a number of dependents (*jār*, plural *jīrān*) whom they protected and who were in turn obligated to their superiors, and the most powerful tribes had a number of weaker tribal groups attached to them in various levels of clientship.[56] The most noble tribes (*sharīf*, plural *shurafā'*) were those that were strong enough to be independent of other tribes and could offer protection to many weaker groups. The following poem by the chief of the powerful Tamīm tribe exhibits the hierarchy of status and influence:

> We are the noble ones, and no other clan is our equal;
> From our number kings [are raised], and among us temples erected.
> How many clans we have overpowered during [our] raiding!
> It is [only] a surfeit of might [such as ours] that finds imitators. . . .[57]

Honor included loyalty and devotion to members of one's kinship group but not to one's superiors, for the ancient nomadic system was one of equals. Loyalty and devotion were directed, rather, to one's comrades. This loyalty tended to be concentrated within the kinship group but also extended beyond it in certain cases. Ancient poetry extols those heroes who were willing to sacrifice all that was dear in order to honor a commitment or a relationship, even to the descendant of a dead comrade.[58]

The related term *ʿirḍ* narrows the qualities of tribal men toward honor in battle. Although the term still denotes honor and dignity in modern Arabic, its origin lies in the honor of warriorship. Failure in fighting or the loss of independence was a humiliation, while success in combat was accorded great honor and status. Humiliation was considered the opposite of power because it demonstrates weakness, which brought dishonor. *ʿIrḍ* was a powerful driving force for pre-Islamic nomadic behavior and, as noted previously, is seen by some to have largely upstaged religion as a motivator of attitudes and behavior.[59] Sacred contests of honor known as *mufākhara* or *munafara* tested the mental as well as physical mettle of tribesmen—the men's *ʿIrḍ*. Its near-sacred nature suggests that it was a primary motivator of tribal and intertribal behavior.

Pre-Islamic poets, who were an extremely important institution in Bedouin society, perpetuated the ideals of heroism and manliness in verse. These ideals included the responsibility to reinforce the special worth and qualities of one's own tribe and to devalue those of competing tribes, and it has been suggested by one prominent scholar that poets of the pre-Islamic period probably had more power in their society than the press of modern times has in ours.[60] Because of the great importance placed on honor, such issues as tribal jealousies, insults, and competition all served to encourage fighting between tribes. Even multigenerational wars were attributed to insults given in verse, and poetry occasionally ended bloody conflicts as well. In the latter case, impartial judges were appointed to determine which side was more successful in a contest of boasting against each other (*mufākhara/munafara*). The outcome had nothing to do with impartial justice but, rather, with the poetic accomplishment of the winning side.[61]

Equality

Established by economic necessity for survival in the difficult natural environment and strengthened by the importance of honor, the concept of fraternity among equals was of great importance among the Bedouin. The pastoral economy of the steppe provided very little surplus, and all worked as herdsmen. There was little specialization of skills. Partly because of the need to avoid the retention of material goods that could not be carried easily from place to place, there was little stratification of wealth.[62] The oral arts of singing, reciting poetry, storytelling, and recounting genealogies could distinguish individuals, as could excellence in raiding skills, but these talents were completely portable and were qualities judged among equals. There was more accumulation of wealth and stratification among sedentary populations living around oases, for agriculture was coupled with trade and simple artisanship. The subsistence-level economy of both nomads and agriculturists, however, ensured a nearly undifferentiated society, the importance of which has been eternalized in pre-Islamic poetry.

Tribal Solidarity

Because central Arabia was governed neither internally nor externally by any overarching political organization or state, there was no concept of law in the politico-juridical sense of the term. There was no authority to legislate or enforce universal rules beyond the limits of the kinship group, and even within the kinship group no formal system of law developed beyond that of cultural expectations of behavior. Power relationships were therefore a question of the relative strength of one kinship group in relation to another. The notion of universal justice or an abstract set of legal principles by which an individual was to be judged was not a part of the system. It was probably because of this decided lack of an overarching legal system that tribal solidarity assumed such an important role in daily life. The individual found protection not under the law but, rather, through the family and its extended kinship relations, which could be called on to rally to one's defense. In the absence of law, the strength of the tribe and the threat of retaliation served as the only means of protection.[63]

The basic unit of kinship relation was the family household. A number of households together made up the *ḥayy*, and this or a somewhat larger group constituted the clan, or *qawm*. It is in the clan where solidarity is of the utmost importance, for this is the largest unit for which there can be regular ongoing social interaction in the steppe environment. Each clan led by a chieftain, or *shaykh*, had its own name based on an eponymous ancestor. Several related clans together made up the largest kinship unit, the *qabīla*, or "tribe."[64]

Tribal organization seems to have been the organizing principle of all of Arabia, whether nomadic or settled, in the period leading up to the rise of Islam. Individuals identified themselves in terms of real or supposed association with kinship groups, beginning with the nuclear family and encompassing the larger extended family and clan groupings to the tribe. Nomads, seminomads, settled agriculturists, and urban dwellers all identified themselves according to this system, whether in southern, northern, or central Arabia. The individual felt his primary loyalty to the closest relations and felt less fidelity as the relationship extended out to broader determinants of identification. As a result, different clans or sublineages even within a single tribal grouping might have rivalries or even wars between them, as will be seen. The complicated system of relations between kinship groups promoted a feeling of tribalism, which forced the individual always to be aware of how close one's kinship relation is to the "other" and to determine the quality of interaction and mutual responsibility based on it. Fred Donner summarizes this feeling of tribalism: "Whatever his way of life, the Arabian was first and foremost a tribesman—identified with his tribe, loyal to it, and secured as much as possible against abuse [from outside his kinship group] by it. This was as true of the fully settled populations of South Arabia or the oasis towns scattered through the peninsula, as it was of the nomadic peoples of Arabia."[65]

Because of the adverse natural conditions in most of the peninsula and its subsequently limited resources, the means of sustenance among the Bedouin tended to be insufficient to provide for the natural rate of human increase. Because of the competition for scarce resources, there was a constant tendency for the strong to seize the resources of the weak.[66] Kinship solidarity helped to avoid such divisiveness within closely related groups by subordinating individual interests to those of the kinship group, or *ḥayy*, and to protect its members from the constant threat of predatory raids from outsiders: "I am [of the tribe of] Ghaziyya: if she be in error, then I will err; And if Ghaziyya be guided right, I go right with her!"[67] In fact, when a clan or kinship group went into any kind of military action, no individual was deserted, and none had the right to refrain from participation. Otherwise, the clan had to sever the blood relationship with the members concerned.[68]

The larger the extended kinship group from which support was garnered, the more secure and powerful the group. The meager environment, however, could not support groups beyond a relatively small critical mass except during certain times of the year. Large groups, therefore, broke into smaller units that, given the natural tendency if they were successful, eventually grew to such an extent that they, too, had to divide.[69] The problem with this trend toward increase is that limited desert resources simply could not support the numbers. Too large a population resulted in starvation or epidemic, so the large kinship groups split and eventually separated to such an extent that kinship relationship was eventually unrecognized. Kinship groups vied with one another for limited resources by raiding the assets of unrelated (or not closely related) groups. When circumstances were particularly difficult, they even practiced infanticide within their own group.[70] As a result, stamina, patience, and a fierce toughness were necessary and valued traits.

Although a complex web of obligations and expectations lay within the kinship group, each extended tribal unit considered itself independent of every other and, therefore, considered no inherent obligation to those outside the extended kinship group.[71] Raiding the resources of "unrelated" tribes, therefore, was not only acceptable but also commendable, and raiding has even been termed the "national sport" of the ancient Arabs.[72]

Raiding and Revenge

Raiding (*al-ghazw*)[73] was practiced only against outside groups who were not in close kinship or allied relationship and was an important means of gaining or redistributing resources in pre-Islamic Arabia.[74] Nomadic groups raided each other or sedentary populations or, probably more commonly, extracted what might be called "taxes" or protection money called *khuwwa*, meaning "brotherhood" payments, from weaker tribes. Because the practice of raiding was essentially economic (re)distribution, bloodshed was avoided as much as possible,[75] and the raiders themselves always knew that they, in turn, would also be the victims of counterattacks or independent campaigns.[76] For this reason, a kind of protocol developed, sometimes referred to in Western sources as pre-Islamic chivalry, in which accepted "rules of engagement" were generally honored. The modus operandi was for warriors to appear suddenly and overwhelm the enemy at a moment of inattention in order to acquire their moveable wealth —usually flocks or herds. Raiding was possible especially during certain periods of the year when pasturage supported only small groups.[77] The *sayyid*, or tribal leader, received a fourth part of any spoils taken in raids, but his responsibilities to the tribe were also greater. His duties included ransoming prisoners and seeing that restitution was made for infringements of the accepted "rules of engagement" in intertribal raids and other conflicts. The remainder of the spoils was divided among the male members of the kinship group. As a rule, the closer the kinship relationship between neighboring tribes, the more benign the fighting during a raid. When raids were conducted from a farther distance, however, there was a greater likelihood of more serious violence, and when hostilities deepened, raiding changed its character altogether.[78] Adult males were killed, and women and children were captured and held for ransom or sold as slaves.

Such serious clashes extending over greater geographical and genealogical distances were much rarer and much more dangerous. They tended to be "associated with severe environmental dislocations such as abnormal drought or major political changes that forced one pastoral group to migrate into territories normally claimed by another, and they were sometimes tantamount to battles for the very survival of the groups in conflict, since the resources under dispute could support only one of the groups."[79]

When blood was spilled, the *lex talionis* came into play in the form of tribal retaliation (*qiṣāṣ* or *qawad*), for the basis of tribal unity consisted of the principle that all must act together in war. On the other hand, no one was allowed to protect his own kinsman for the murder of another *within* the kinship group.[80] Because tribal members felt no inherent responsibility toward those outside the kinship group, the system of mutual revenge (*tha*ʾr) served to a certain extent as a preventive to wanton killing across tribal boundaries. Not only was it a matter of individual honor and responsibility for a close relative of the victim to take revenge on the killer, tribal honor was also at stake if the extended kinship group could not protect or avenge its members or those attached to it, and this ideally meant a life for a life. If the killer could not be found, a close relative could be killed as a substitute, although the custom of paying a bloodwit (*diya*) also evolved as a less-honorable substitution.[81]

The payment or receipt of the bloodwit paralleled the distribution of booty among the male members of the kinship group. Inheritance was also shared among the male members of the same group. This practice points again to the importance of tribal solidarity in pre-Islamic nomadic Arabia, since pasturage and other resources were tribal property of which the individual had only usufruct. Blood feud, bloodwit, booty, and even inheritance revolved around male interdependence and sense of responsibility in clan warfare.[82]

A major problem with the combined rules of the *talio* and revenge has been that tribal members tend naturally to value the lives of their own kin greater than those of more distant or unrelated groups. The great warrior and idolatrous opponent of Muḥammad, ʿĀmir b. al-Ṭufayl, is credited with the words, "We slew of them a hundred in requital for an old man. . . ."[83] The pattern of reprisals for blood vengeance, therefore, sometimes escalated to the extent that a full-blown war between tribes might ensue for generations,[84] and even official settlements between extended tribes did not always satisfy the personal need for individuals to avenge the death of close relatives. One example is the feud between the Kināna and the Quraysh in the vicinity of Mecca, where the tribal leaders agreed that the two tribes had achieved a balance of the *lex talionis*. This agreement did not satisfy the brother of the most recently killed, however, who took advantage of an opportunity to avenge his brother, thus rekindling the tribal feud indefinitely.[85] These tribal feuds were complicated by the competing values of kinship solidarity and loyalty to comrades, thereby exacerbating the tensions and raising emotions.[86] In the more centralized state system of South Arabia, an attempt was made to mitigate the problems inherent in blood vengeance by transferring the responsibility for revenge from blood relatives and assigning it to the ruler. Then, only the perpetrator suffered under this system, thereby protecting innocent relatives and reducing the tendency for intertribal escalation.[87] This practice was, of course, only possible in an environment in which a sovereign political organization had the administrative system and power to transcend the individual ties of kinship in adjudicating disputes, which was certainly not the case in central Arabia, where no centralizing authority existed before the genesis of Islam.[88]

The most that we know of the pre-Islamic period from the Arabic sources is about its battles and wars, and the records of these are found in a literature known as *Ayyām al-ʿArab*, meaning, literally, "Days of the Arabs" but more accurately translated as "Battle-Days of the Arabs."[89] Since individual battles tended to be decided in one day, the name of the battle was called "the Day of X." Although the number of "days" recorded in the literature is quite large, it is clear that there were far more battles and raids than are mentioned in the sources because only the interesting ones were recorded or discussed in the ancient literature preserved in the Islamic collections.[90] The reasons for these battles range from blood revenge to competition over pasturage and include cases in which stronger tribes forced weaker units to pay them a tax. The converse situation occurred as well, when tribes battled to free themselves from obligations to a previously stronger tribe.[91]

Traditional Arab as well as modern Western sources all emphasize that fighting among pre-Islamic Arabs was a natural, some even suggest joyous, part of Bedouin life.[92] From an economic and evolutionary perspective, the modus operandi of such fighting seems to have evolved as a means of ensuring survival of the fittest and of distributing scarce resources to those who survived best—at the same time as it contributed to maintaining a limited population in a harsh land. The consistent losers who could not recoup their losses were destined to sell themselves into slavery or clientship to a more powerful tribe that could protect them or else to migrate altogether out of the area in which the system operated, if that was possible.[93]

Religious Factors

A great deal of controversy still lingers over the religious life of pre-Islamic Arabs.[94] Because the Islamic sources sketch out a picture of pre-Islamic Arabia as being hopelessly sunk in the mire of superstitious idolatry, modern scholars have had to read them with great care, and their readings have resulted in a variety of interpretations of pre-Islamic religious realia. It still remains unclear, for example, to what extent indigenous Arabian monotheism (*ḥanīfiyya*) existed before Muḥammad,[95] what kind of polytheistic ritual existed aside from pilgrimages and dedications (including sacrifice), how the people related to their sacred stones and how much influence the religious systems exerted over daily life, the extent of Jewish and Christian influence on indigenous Arabian religious practice, or even what kind of Judaism or Christianity was practiced by the communities living in Arabia.[96] It is clear, despite the uncertain state of our current knowledge, that religio-cultural values and institutions exerted an important influence over the life of the inhabitants of pre-Islamic central Arabia. The extent and nature of that influence, however, cannot yet be determined with any kind of certitude.

Luckily, the factors associated with warring in pre-Islamic central Arabia all appear to be linked directly to the economic and social commodities of pasturage, material wealth, and prestige.[97] No available writings or inscriptions relating to the period describe fighting that we might consider was religiously or ideologically motivated. As might be expected, the pre-Islamic deities may have been consulted before the tribal members embarked on a campaign of war or blood revenge, but this type of action hardly constitutes a form of "holy war." A man seeking revenge, for example, may have consulted divination arrows associated with pre-Islamic idols. According to Ibn al-Kalbī, when the god was consulted through divination, it sometimes appeared to forbid exacting revenge against a victim's killer, which invariably infuriated the would-be avenger.[98]

Despite the lack of any clear reference to holy war in central Arabia, religious wars appear to have been fought between Jews and Christians in southern Arabia during the first half of the sixth century. The most famous of these was a series of battles associated with the last king of Ḥimyar, Zurʿa b. Tibbān Asʿad,[99] known most commonly as Dhū Nuwās, who subsequent to his conversion to Judaism is said to have persecuted and killed Christians living in the Christian enclave of Najran.[100] The conflict was important enough to have entered the oral lore of the Ḥijāz and came to be associated with *sūra* 85:4–7 in the Qurʾān, the verses known as the "people of the trench" (*asḥāb al-ukhdūd*). Early Muslim exegetes associate this reference to the burning of Najrāni Christians, although the qurʾānic passage is likely to be an eschatological reference.[101] In any case, according to the later sources, the Najrāni Christians pleaded to the Abyssinian Christian negus for help.[102] He, in turn, took counsel with his religious ally, the Byzantine emperor.[103] The negus, with Byzantine assistance, then sent troops across the straits into southern Arabia and engaged Dhū Nuwās in battle. Although the first attack was apparently destroyed by the Ḥimyarite army, the second put an end to the kingdom of Ḥimyar and placed the entire region under the control of the Abyssinians.[104] The problem with the entire episode from the standpoint of war is that we can learn very little of the real and purported motivations behind the actions from the incomplete and often contradictory sources. What is most clear is that the affair reflects the influence of the great powers of Byzantium and Persia at that time over the internal affairs of the south Arabian kingdoms. Part of the superpower interest was the control or taxation of trade, both from India and from southern Arabia.[105] The Jewish Ḥimyarites were allied to the Persians, while the Christians of the region were associated with Abyssinia, and despite the major monophysite-duophysite controversy that divided most Semitic Christians from Byzantine orthodoxy, the Arabian Christians inclined toward Byzantium.[106] Abyssinia carried out the policies of its Byzantine suzerain while gaining control of the valuable lands of southern Arabia. It seems, therefore, that although the motivations for warring were perhaps partly religious, religious denomination more likely served as a means of differentiating and dividing the local populations between the influences of the contemporary superpowers of Byzantium and Persia.

Sacred Time and Sacred Space

One of the great economic and therefore survival problems inherent in the pre-Islamic system of tribal exclusivism and intertribal raiding was the resultant difficulty of engaging in trade between separate tribes, exchanging information, and having open social (and genetic) intercourse. This problem was mitigated by the institution of four pre-Islamic sacred months (*al-ʾashhur al-ḥaram*),[107] which served as periods during which fighting between enemy tribes was forbidden. This period of nonbelligerency allowed Arabs of various and unrelated kinship groups to settle claims and debts, arbitrate disputes, and intermingle in other ways as they visited religious shrines and attended the market fairs, where they traded ideas as well as goods.[108] It was during the sacred months that pilgrimage (*ḥajj*) to the sacred sites took place as well, an activity that brought together both nomadic and sedentary populations under the rubric of religious ritual. According to the sources, the Arabs strictly observed the prohibition against both initiating conflicts and exacting revenge during these sacred months.[109]

In addition to the limitations on fighting during sacred time, there were sacred places in which fighting was always forbidden. These were the sacred enclosures associated with local religious cults (*ḥaram*, plural *aḥrām*). Such sacred sites existed in a number of locations besides the most famous pre-Islamic shrines situated in and around Mecca, which continue to function in Islamized form to this day as the *manāsik*, or "sacred sites of pilgrimage." Al-Ṭāʾif boasted a sacred site also within the region of the Ḥijāz, and the territory of al-Yamāma to the east had its own sacred enclosure, probably in the town of al-Ḥajr, in which fighting was strictly forbidden.[110] To respect the sanctity of the sacred areas, particular ritual customs had to be adhered to which varied from location to location, but certain common social and political regulations seem to have been observed in all the sacred enclosures. Killing, for example, was always forbidden in the *aḥrām*,[111] which were known as neutral areas where feuding tribes sent representatives to engage in negotiations. Such sacred enclosures with their special status and restrictions have continued to function in southern Arabia well into the twentieth century.[112]

Warring in Pre-Islamic Arabia

All the evidence suggests that in pre-Islamic Arabia, armed aggression between nomadic tribes and between nomads and settled populations was a normal part of life. War as an activity, however, less defined the relationship between unrelated or distantly related kinship groups than did war as a condition. That is, however often groups within the larger tribal unit engaged in battle, it can be said that a "state of war" existed generally between tribal groupings, even when no actual fighting took place, which was a normal definition of relationship in pre-Islamic Arabia.[113] Battle between unrelated or distantly related kinship groups was a culturally acceptable means for distributing and redistributing the limited commodities of material wealth (in the form of herds and flocks), access to pasturage, and personal and tribal prestige. With regard to the social system as a whole, warring served to keep the population at a survivable level, while in the social Darwinian sense it provided a means for the fittest and most adaptable groups to excel. This warring was nonideological. Intertribal raids served a similar purpose to the hunt in early hunting societies, in that successful endeavors provided sustenance for the tribe while also offering the opportunity for male members to demonstrate skills and excel and rise within the social hierarchy. There is no evidence to suggest that religious restrictions or prescriptions had any significant effect on this aspect of traditional pre-Islamic Arabian life, although it has been noted above that a form of aggression with some similarities to holy war may have been engaged in, at least in one case, by Jewish and Christian tribes of southern Arabia. In central Arabia, however, raiding and intertribal aggression remained nonideological and was not associated in any way with the range of warring defined as "holy war." Martyrdom has little meaning in such a social system, for no transcendent meaning was applied to the act of war, nor was reward in an afterlife a part of the indigenous Arabian worldview. The economic and social (status, prestige) benefits of warring were reason enough for the powerful to engage in the act of war, while the weak had no alternative but to protect themselves through preemptive aggression, alliances, or defense or lose their independent status altogether. Neither religion nor what we today would call "moral consciousness" within this social system had any impact on warring in general, although within certain spheres of kinship relationship, restrictions against excessive violence were at least theoretically in place. This entire system changed significantly, but not easily, with the coming of Islam.

Significance of *Jāhiliyya*

The root *j.h.l.*, which, as we have noted, conveys a general sense of ignorance in Islamic tradition, occurs in the Qur'ān twenty-four times, and the word *jāhiliyya* four times.[114] Goldziher noted that the definition of "ignorance" as opposed to knowledge (*ʿilm*) is actually a secondary and less-important meaning for the root *j.h.l.* in pre-Islamic and early Islamic usage.[115] The much more prevalent usage in the pre-Islamic period itself was a meaning that may be juxtaposed with its Arabic antithesis, *ḥ.l.m.*, conveying the meaning of gentility and civilization. "A *ḥalīm* is what we would call a civilized man. The opposition to all this is the *jāhil*, a wild, violent and impetuous character who follows the inspiration of unbridled passion and is cruel by following his animal instincts; in one word, a barbarian."[116] But this definition is strongly colored by nineteenth-century Western bias by reducing the nature of *j.h.l.* to barbarism. In fact, far from being barbaric, the quality of being *jāhil* was an essential and positive component of pre-Islamic Arabian manhood. Pre-Islamic Arabian culture recognized the importance of both the qualities of *ḥilm* and *jahl* in its society. True *murū'a*, or "manliness," required knowing when *ḥilm* and when *jahl* were indicated. "I am ferocious (*jahūl*) where mildness (*taḥallum*) would make the hero despicable, meek (*ḥalīm*) when ferocity (*jahl*) would be unfitting to a noble."[117]

In Islamic texts, however, the sense of *jāhiliyya* in reference to the pre-Islamic period tends to emphasize only the cruelty, barbarism, and anarchy that Islam wished to associate with Arabia before the coming of Muḥammad and the Qur'ān. Islamic civilization, according to this view, would radically alter Arabian culture. As the Muslim refugee to Abyssinia, Jaʿfar b. Abī Ṭālib, is said to have told the ruler:

> O King, we were an uncivilized people (*kunnā qaum*^{an} *'ahla jāhiliyya*^{tan}), worshipping idols, eating dead [not properly butchered] meat, committing abominations, breaking natural ties, treating guests badly, and our strong devoured our weak. Thus we were until God sent us an apostle whose lineage, truth, trustworthiness, and clemency we know. He summoned us to acknowledge God's unity and to worship him and to renounce the stones and images which we and our fathers formerly worshipped. He commanded us to speak the truth, be faithful to our engagements, mindful of the ties of kinship and kindly hospitality, and to refrain from crimes

> and bloodshed. He forbade us to commit abominations and to speak lies, and to devour the property of orphans, to vilify chaste women.[118]

This classic Islamic attitude toward pre-Islamic days has its own clear agenda. It is profoundly influenced by Islam's claim to have revolutionized the morality and religious behavior of Arabia with the coming of God's revelation and the submission of the region to the religious civilization of Islam. Such Islamic historiography views pre-Islamic Arabian culture as inherently immoral, barbaric, and anarchic. As far as can be discerned, however, its innocent depictions of certain aspects of the social and economic systems of the pre-Islamic period are not significantly distorted by its general devaluation of the ancient days. These systems clearly served as a rational and functional means of survival for nomads living outside of a unified legal framework in the harsh environment of the desert.

It is clear, however, despite our acknowledging the subjective nature of the Islamic worldview, that the coming of Islam does indeed mark a major transition in social, religious, and economic mores from an older time. This transition is noted in Islam as part of the great religious movement, which radically and forever changed Arabian culture for the better, elevating certain values and reducing others.[119] In fact, however, the actual transition may not have been as complete or as sudden as suggested by Islamic historiography, for the coming of Islam simply marked a watershed in a long process of cultural, social, and religious change. Part of this process included a marked revaluation of violence and warring.

PART II

The Qur'ān and Its Interpretation

The Qur'ān as Transition Marker from Jāhiliyya to Islam

Although the Qur'ān is the earliest and most important extant document in Islam, controversy within critical scholarship continues over its provenance and dating. The traditional Muslim view holds that the Qur'ān represents God's most meaningful and perfect Scripture, revealed to the prophet Muḥammad over the nearly twenty-three-year period of his mission from approximately 610 C.E. to his death in 632 C.E.[1] According to the most widely held Islamic view, this long series of revelations was never committed systematically to writing during the lifetime of the Prophet but was known in the community almost entirely in oral form until his death. Approximately two years after Muḥammad's death, and following a battle in which a number of his companions who knew the Qur'ān well in its oral form were killed, one of his closest followers, ʿUmar b. al-Khaṭṭāb, approached the caliph Abū Bakr and suggested that a complete written text of the revelation be assembled so that nothing of God's words would be lost. A written text was established under the leadership of a secretary to Muḥammad named Zayd b. Thabit, who collected all the qur'ānic verses, "whether written on palm branches or thin stones or preserved in the hearts of men." He organized the various fragments on sheets (*ṣuḥuf*), and this written text remained in rough form until it was edited some eighteen years later under the caliphate of ʿUthmān b. ʿAffān. According to this view, the ʿUthmanic text is faithful Scripture, true to the revelation received by the Prophet, and is clearly dated to his lifetime.[2]

Modern critical study of the Qur'ān has, on the whole, accepted the general chronology of this explanation, although mostly by default. There are a great many problems with the traditional view just outlined, many of which stem from the erratic text of the Qur'ān itself as well as from the contradictions among the Islamic sources describing its collection and redaction. However, no alternative has been suggested that has found wide support among critical scholars. The two most important recent suggestions take quite different approaches in their analyses and arrive at nearly opposite conclusions. John Wansbrough submits that the text of the Qur'ān emerged organically from independent traditions over a long period and was not finally collected until the ninth century, more than two hundred years after the death of Muḥammad.[3] John Burton, on the other hand, suggests that the Qur'ān as we have it was collected and edited even earlier than the traditional view claims and by Muḥammad himself.[4]

Given its centrality, it is profoundly problematic to the critical scholar that so little can be considered certain at this time about the provenance, chronology, and setting of the Qur'ān or even its principle of organization, for the great amount of repetition, interpolation, contradiction, and dislocation within it create significant challenges. Seemingly unrelated verses often sit side by side, for example, while duplicate material, exact phrases, or even entire verses may be situated in entirely different contexts. The problem of organization is of great importance because the relationship of verses to one another strongly affects the meaning of individual verses and of larger passages as well.

Significant scholarship has been devoted to the problem of the editing and organization of the Qur'ān, but much more is necessary before the scholarly world will arrive at any consensus regarding it. An independent investigation of the problem extends far beyond the nature and scope of this study, but it is important nevertheless to articulate where I stand in relation to current and traditional ideas on the subject.

The Qur'ān as we have it is an extremely complicated document, which reflects the complexity of Ḥijāzi cultures contemporary to the lifetime of Muḥammad. It is articulated, however, in language and according to conceptual paradigms and cultural realia that reflect generations of pre-Islamic Arabian civilization as well. The core of this civilization could be described as indigenous Arabian, but it had been in contact with and responding for generations to Jewish and Christian religious ideas, Persian and Greco-Roman civilizations, and African traditions that reached Arabia across the Red Sea. Therefore, although the reception of the Qur'ān in its earliest oral stage occurred in relation to the life and mission of Muḥammad, the ideas represented therein reflect a much larger historical epoch.

According to the Islamic tradition, which should not be rejected in its most basic sense, Muḥammad publicly recited a series of revelations shortly after having received them. This early layer of the Qur'ān was therefore produced and immediately "published" orally, in very small pieces or pericopes that were absorbed by a community whose literatures were overwhelmingly oral. This process of oral production and publication occurred erratically over a period of some two decades during Muḥammad's mission. Because of the oral nature of this discourse, the contents of what was later named the Qur'ān were somewhat fluid during this period in that they were inevitably remembered differently by different individuals who were witness to the original public recitation. The various pericopes of material that Muḥammad recited were uttered sometimes in reference or relation to what had been recited previously, and often not. There were, therefore, many possible inconsistencies between the various oral pericopes, depending partially on interpretation and partially on how the material was remembered. Any problems or seeming inconsistencies were verified during the lifetime of the Prophet simply by asking the source of the recitations, who explained the meaning of the material. There is no reason to expect that Muḥammad's own interpretation of the divine revelations should have always been consistent, since the needs of the day varied during his prophetic career. Some of this prophetic interpretive material also entered into the public domain of the early Muslim community but probably at a level that was different from what was remembered as the official scriptural recitation. There was, therefore, a certain fluidity to both the "published text" of the oral Qur'ān and to its interpretation during the lifetime of the Prophet.

After the death of Muḥammad, however, there was no authoritative resolution to seeming inconsistencies among the revealed pericopes, nor were differences between variant remembered versions of the recitations easily reconciled. Neither were differing prophetic interpretations known to the Muslim community settled in the period shortly after the death of the Prophet. After a certain period, the anxiety caused by this problem became so difficult that efforts were made to establish a consistent and authoritative "text" of the Qur'ān. Exactly when anxiety rose to such a level is difficult to determine. Perhaps it occurred according to the traditional Islamic chronology. It is also quite likely that it occurred later, although I cannot subscribe to the view of Wansbrough and his school that the Qur'ān must be dated as late as the early ninth century. The important point is that the text and meaning of Scripture were fluid during the period of Muḥammad's life and mission and, for different reasons, remained so for a time after his death.

Even the redactional process, when it did occur, did not resolve all the problems, because it had to satisfy a relatively wide variety of opinions of subgroups within the community regarding the exact pronunciation, form, internal order, meaning, and relationship of the oral recitational pericopes. This process explains, in general terms, the confusion of the present text of the Qur'ān. Subsequent interpretive mechanisms then had to be employed in order to make sense of the complexities of the redacted Qur'ān, and these include the theories of abrogation, or *naskh.*

To summarize this brief discussion, it was the recitational publication of the Qur'ān in its oral environment, the fluidity of its reception in the minds and hearts of its audience, its interpretation while still in oral form, its subsequent articulation by those who heard it or learned it orally, and the organizational efforts of its redactors that all affected the nature of the Qurʾān in its present form. It should be pointed out, in addition, that this discussion leaves out the additional problem of the primitive nature of the orthographic system of Arabic in the early Islamic period, which, too, extended the range of interpretation or manipulation of what eventuated in the redaction that is generally recognized today as the canonized Qurʾān.

Notwithstanding the many uncertainties in relation to the organization and redaction of the Qurʾān, it nevertheless remains the linchpin linking pre-Islamic Arabia to the period of the first Muslims and serves as the major piece to the complex puzzle that is early Islam. Many of the qurʾānic verses treat cultural realia that are of great importance in the transition from pre-Islamic to Islamic Arabia.[5] There is a good deal of discussion, for example, about the spiritual as opposed to the material gain of fighting in the Qurʾān, a tension that touches directly on transitional issues from pre-Islamic to Islamic Arabia. There are also a number of references to other important transitional issues, such as the shift from a kinship-based to a religion-based system of social organization and the resultant shift in personal allegiance and responsibilities.

As the transition marker from the pre-Islamic to the Islamic period, it is no surprise that the Qurʾān expresses a worldview in many respects significantly different from what we know of pre-Islamic Arabian culture. Some examples of the major changes reflected in the Qurʾān include the view that life was governed by God rather than by such powers as fate and time and that human creatureliness and dependence on God are emphasized in place of living the good life on earth and enjoying simple material well-being. Human behavior is governed by divinely derived moral commandments and the promise of reward and punishment in this world and the next rather than by tribal tradition and tribal and personal honor. So, too, does religion take the place of tribal and other factional interests as the primary basis for human solidarity.[6] On the other hand, the Qurʾān naturally incorporates many ancient Arabian attitudes and beliefs as well as preserving many aspects of pre-Islamic worldviews even in its condemnation or adjustment of certain of the old ways.[7] As Islam continued to evolve after the collection and redaction of the qurʾānic revelations, some of the pre-Islamic artifacts retained in Scripture disturbed later generations. Qurʾānic exegesis attempted, among other things, to mitigate or eliminate some of these in their interpretations of Scripture. Chapter 3 examines a field of qurʾānic interpretation that adjusted the meaning of Scripture in order for it to convey a message more appropriate for an evolving worldview.

THREE

The Qur'ān

The Traditional Reading and Its Inherent Weakness

The Qur'ān has much to say about warring, and, at first sight, its views seem to be quite at variance from what we know of pre-Islamic Arabian views. The most often cited verses express a highly ideological approach to war.[1] They are understood to command unlimited war against non-Muslims, enjoin the killing of idolaters, and refuse to offer peace until Islam is the hegemonic religion.[2] The Qur'ān's message on the topic, however, is actually far from consistent. The verses on warring are numerous, amount to scores in number, and are spread out over more than a dozen chapters. The major challenge for understanding their meaning lies in the problem of verse relationships and the fact that the contexts of many pronouncements remain uncertain. As noted above, for example, it is difficult to know whether a verse is supposed to be read in relation to the verses among which it is currently situated or whether it should be read independently. It is likely, given the relatively large collection of sometimes unrelated verses on warring in *sūras* 2, 3, 8, and 9, for example, that individual statements on war, which had been separated from their context during the oral stage of the Qur'ān, were inserted into larger sections treating the topic because of the obvious similarity of subject matter. The insertion of such verses sometimes confuses the meaning and relationship of the verses into which they had been inserted. Some qur'ānic statements may or may not even refer to war, depending on how one views their context, but are nevertheless considered by post-qur'ānic tradition as articulating divine pronouncements on the subject. The sentiments, ideologies, concepts and attitudes expressed by the many verses cover a wide range of positions.

Some, such as *sūra* 16:125, call for what appears to be nonmilitant means of propagating or defending the faith: "Summon to the way of your Lord with wisdom and good admonition and argue against them with what is better, for your Lord knows best who has strayed from His path and who has been guided."[3] Others, such as *sūra* 22:39–40a seem to sanction fighting for defensive purposes only: "Permission is given to those who have been fought against in that they have been wronged; those who have been wrongly expelled from their homes only because they say, 'Our Lord is Allah,' for God is most powerful for their aid."[4] Still others seem to sanction aggressive warring for the Islamic cause but only within the well-known limits established in the pre-Islamic period (2:194): "The sacred month for the sacred month, but [violation of?] sacred ordinances [only] in retaliation. Whoever transgresses against you, transgress against him. But fear God, and know that God is with the God-fearing."[5] Another category of verses appears to command warring for the Islamic polity without restriction (9:5): "But when the Sacred Months are past,[6] then kill the idolaters wherever you find them, and seize them, beleaguer them, and lie in wait for them in every stratagem [of war]; but if they repent, establish regular prayers, and pay the alms tax (*al-zakāt*) then open the way for them, for God is oft-forgiving, Most Merciful."[7]

A large number of verses portray conflict within the Muslim community over the issue of fighting (2:216): "It is commanded of you to fight, [though] it is disagreeable to you. But it is possible that you dislike a thing which is good for you, and that you love a thing which is bad for you. But God knows, and you know not."[8] So, too, a number of verses promise a great reward for those who are killed on the field of battle (4:74): "Let those fight in the path of God who sell the life of this world for the other. Whoever fights in the path of God, whether he be slain or victorious, on him We shall bestow a vast reward."[9]

Some verses seem to preserve the ancient view that God manipulates the battle or is personally involved in the foray (33:25): "God repulsed the unbelievers in their wrath; they gained no good. God averted their attack from the believers. God is Strong, Mighty."[10] Other verses treat the distribution of spoils and rules of engagement and behavior in war, including the treatment of prisoners and noncombatants.[11] And, of course, verses serve also as encouragement and incitement to combat.[12]

The "Occasions of Revelation" and "Abrogation" Literature

These many statements provide a great deal of information, but, as noted previously, it is difficult to understand their essential meanings because it is usually impossible to reconstruct the context of the utterances from the text of Scripture itself.[13] The order of its chapters, or *sūras*, do not correspond with the presumed chronology of revelation, and the principle or principles behind its present organization remain unknown to this day. As a result of this problem of contextualization, a genre of qur'ānic analysis developed in Islam in order to provide historical contexts for revelations that would help Muslims understand exactly to what the divine pronouncements were referring. This literature is known as *asbāb al-nuzūl*, or "the occasions of revelation," and it attempts to correlate specific verses with actual events in the history of Muḥammad's mission as Muslim prophet.[14] Although the oldest extant example of an *asbāb* work, by ʿAlī b. Aḥmad al-Wāḥidī (d. 1075), is dated only in the eleventh century,[15] many of the earlier standard exegetical works (*tafāsīr*) also suggest contexts for the revelation of certain verses. The problem with relying on them is that they seldom agree and often contradict one another.[16] A second and larger category of Islamic interpretive literature that treats a related problem is *al-nāsikh wal-mansūkh*, or "the abrogating and abrogated [verses],"[17] and similar to the *asbāb* literature, many standard exegetical works include statements about *naskh*, or "abrogation." The reason for the development of this genre is evident from the previous discussion, for the Qur'ān appears to contain a great deal of seemingly contradictory material. In the case of warring, for example, does Islamic Scripture prescribe avoidance of violence in propagating and defending the faith (16:125), defensive wars only (22:39–40), or unrestricted warfare (9:5)? The theological and political implications regarding such seemingly indecisive or scattered divine pronouncements greatly disturbed Muslim religious scholars, and they sought to organize the revelations in a way that would provide clarity to this issue as well as other difficult issues.

The actual text of the Qur'ān is of course inviolable, but an extratextual hierarchy of versification could be established by the *naskh* works, which was done in parallel with the *asbāb* material on the occasions of revelation. The general rule of thumb was to determine which of the inconsistent statements on a topic was the latest to have been revealed. Because of the accepted view that the revelations were given serially in accordance with the specific historical unfolding of Muḥammad's prophetic career, they were understood to have been revealed in response to particular situations faced by the Prophet and the Muslim community. According to the standard Muslim view, Muḥammad was confronted with many different and inconstant predicaments during his evolving mission as *prophete extraordinaire*. God therefore personally guided his apostle by sending Muḥammad revelations to help him through difficult and uncertain times. Conditions normalized, however, as the community grew and its organization became more advanced and secure toward the end of his life. In cases of contradiction, therefore, the earlier revelations were considered to have been given specifically in order to assist with the contingency of the moment, while the later revelations were considered to be normative and eternal. As a rule, therefore, the later the revelation, the more authoritative and more likely it was to abrogate other revelations; the earlier, the less decisive and more likely to be abrogated.

The Classic Evolutionary Theory of War

Using the methodologies developed in both the *asbāb* and *naskh* materials, Muslim scholars came to the conclusion that the scriptural verses regarding war were revealed in direct relation to the historic needs of Muḥammad during his prophetic mission. At the beginning of his prophetic career in Mecca when he was weak and his followers few, the divine revelations encouraged avoidance of physical conflict.[18] Only after the intense physical persecution that resulted in the Emigration (Hijra) of the Muslim community to Medina in 622 were Muḥammad and the believers given divine authority to engage in war and only in defense.[19] As the Muslim community continued to grow in numbers and strength in Medina, further revelations widened the conditions and narrowed the restrictions under which war could be waged,[20] until it was concluded that war against non-Muslims could be waged virtually at any time, without pretext, and in any place.[21]

The scenario of historical development and evolution solved the problem of seeming contradiction in the text of Scripture while it simultaneously linked revelation to specific occasions in the unfolding of early Islamic history. The logic is superb, for this solution demonstrates that divine authority for total war was withheld from the Muslims only until they were ready and organized to properly carry out such a program. The incremental escalation in militancy and its increasing association with ideological rather than material or defense issues were therefore to correspond exactly with the incremental growth and development of the religious community. God was, in effect, preparing and guiding his community for the role of world conquerors and propagators of the greatest and most profound religio-cultural system in history.

This scenario, however, carries with it serious weaknesses, the major one being that the early exegetes who collectively developed this theory disagreed greatly over the occasions of revelation, their dating, and which verses abrogated which. The discussions in reference to the data are spread throughout the early Qurʾān commentaries,[22] and traditional Islamic scholarship on the Qurʾān is extremely conservative, thereby tending to repeat earlier opinions as faithfully as possible and with attribution to the sources of those opinions. We should expect, therefore, a substantial degree of repetition and agreement in the sources over the occasions of revelation and the hierarchy of abrogation. In reading a representative sample of commentaries and *naskh* and *asbāb* works from the first five Islamic centuries, however, we find tremendous disagreement over what occasions inspired the major war verses, when they occurred, and to what or whom they refer. This decided lack of agreement destroys the classic argument of divinely guided evolution and reveals its origin as a theoretical solution to the problem of qur'ānic contradiction. In fact, this classic Islamic "evolutionary theory" of warring presumes from the outset that war against non-Muslims would be essentially unrestricted even before the Muslims engaged in the process because that was the policy of the empire under which the theory evolved.[23]

Qur'ānic Legislation on War: The Traditional Schema

Stage One: Nonconfrontation

> Sūra 15: 94–95
> "Profess openly what you have been commanded, and turn away from the idolaters, for We are sufficient for you against the scoffers."

According to the accepted wisdom expressed in such early exegetical works as *Tafsīr Muqātil b. Sulaymān*,[24] and by Ṭabarī[25] and others, Muḥammad withheld from preaching for two years after having begun receiving the revelation of the Qur'ān in Mecca. *Sūra* 15:94 ("Profess openly what you have been commanded. . . .") is considered by some to have actually initiated his mission. *Tafsīr Muqātil* adds:

> When he [Muḥammad] gave an account of his Lord, the Meccan unbelievers confronted him with annoyance and accused him openly of lying. Therefore, the words [of the second half of the verse]: "and turn away from the idolaters." God commanded him to avoid [them] and [to have] patience in the face of insult.

Another early commentary, *Tanwīr al-miqbās*, attributed to ʿAbdullāh b. ʿAbbās,[26] also considers *sūra* 15:94 to be the verse initiating the mission of the Prophet, except that it suggests that the following verse (15:95), "for we are sufficient for you against the scoffers," was revealed to reassure the hesitant new Prophet.

The context for these two consecutive verses in the latter half of *sūra* 15 (Al-Ḥijr) is one in which Muḥammad is encouraged to act the prophet in his community. He is given comfort with the knowledge that the prophets of old had also been rejected by their people but that those who rejected them were discomfited. This section, however, is placed by Richard Bell and others as not earlier than the end of the Meccan period in 621–622.[27] Moreover, if the literary context of this qur'ānic pericope can be considered trustworthy as a single unit, it appears to be encouraging Muḥammad's mission after his having been treated poorly by those who would not accept his role of prophet. This would suggest that the verse may not be nearly as early as the works attributed to Muqātil and Ibn ʿAbbās suggest.

> Sūra 16:125
> "Invite [all] to the way of your Lord with wisdom and beautiful preaching; and argue with them in ways that are best and most gracious: For your Lord knows best who has strayed from His Path, and who receives guidance."[28]

Wāḥidī dates this verse to an incident after the battle of Uḥud (625 C.E.), some twelve to thirteen years after the assumed revelation of 15:94–95.[29] According to Wāḥidī's placement of the revelation, Muḥammad had learned that his uncle Ḥamza b. ʿAbd al-Muṭṭalib had been killed at the Battle of Uḥud in the month of Shawwāl (roughly March) of 625 and his body horribly mutilated. Muḥammad was so incensed that he threatened to kill seventy Qurayshite men in revenge. The parallel passage in the Sīra, which is cited also by Naḥḥās and Ṭabarī, states that Muḥammad vowed to mutilate thirty Quraysh.[30] This version may be more authentic because it calls for equal treatment in revenge.[31] According to Wāḥidī, it was immediately after the slain of Uḥud were buried that *sūra* 16:125–27 was revealed:

> Invite [all] to the way of your Lord with wisdom and beautiful preaching; and argue with them in ways that are best and most gracious: For your Lord knows best who has strayed from His Path, and who receives guidance. [126] If you punish, then punish with the like of that with which you were afflicted.[32] But if you endure patiently, that is better for the patient. [127] Be patient. Your patience is only through God.

Sūra 16:126–127 does indeed relate directly to physical response in the form of the *lex talionis*, but 16:125 does not relate to the issue. Why 16:125 is cited by Wāḥidī along with 16:126–127 is puzzling, and it seems that the occasion of revelation (*sabab*) he cites for 16:125 cannot be considered to relate appropriately to the meaning of the verse. Ṭabarī, on the other hand, separates 16:125 from 16:126–127 and relates the repeated traditions regarding Uḥud to the latter verses only. In Ṭabarī's fuller exposition, he ties only 16:126–127 to the incident at Uḥud and notes that 16:126 actually abrogated itself. That is, mutilation was first allowed only in response to mutilation: "If you punish, then punish with the like of that with which you were afflicted." But this was soon abrogated by the second part of the verse calling for patience: "But if you endure patiently, that is better for the patient. [127] Be patient. Your patience is only through God."[33]

Without proposing a context, *Tafsīr Muqātil* suggests that 16:125 refers to the Peoples of the Book.[34] This interpretation solves the problem of abrogation because the Peoples of the Book are not to be converted by force but are allowed to live as protected peoples (*dhimmīs*) if they pay a special tax and live in a condition of humility (or humiliation).[35] If 16:125 is directed to the *dhimmīs* only, then it need not have been abrogated by a later more aggressive verse. This interpretation could not construe the verse-string to be an early revelation since it differentiates Peoples of the Book from idolaters, something that could only have occurred after Muḥammad made the Hijra to Medina and came in contact with the Jewish community there.[36]

Only one named tradition on this verse is cited repeatedly in the literature. It is attributed to Mujāhid[37] and glosses *sūra* 16:125 as "Turn away from their wrongs against you (*aʿrid ʿan adhāhum iyāka*),"[38] suggesting a passive or nonmilitant response to harassment. It is the only consistent tradition cited by the exegetes.[39]

Ibn al-Jawzī mentions that "most of the exegetes are of the opinion that this verse was abrogated by the Sword Verse,"[40] although he provides no source for this opinion.[41] Ibn al-Jawzī, however, does not personally consider it to have been abrogated. His reasoning is that arguing and fighting are not mutually exclusive. That is, the meaning of the verse is "Argue with them, but if they refuse, [then use] the sword."[42] Naḥḥās also considers 16:125 to be in force and mentions that those holding this view say that "arguing in a better way is arriving ultimately to what God has commanded."[43]

To conclude here, *sūra* 16:125 does not relate to the verse that follows and must not be associated with it and the incident at Uḥud.[44] The actual message of 16:125, that verbal argument and not physical violence against Muḥammad's detractors is called for, tends to have been largely disregarded. Despite the exegetes' claims that scholars consider it abrogated, not a single tradition is actually cited to this effect. In short, this verse, which prescribes a nonmilitant approach to the spread of Islam, was not formally abrogated but rather ignored.

Stage Two: Defensive Fighting

> Sūra 22:39–40a
> "Permission is given to those who fight[45] because they have been wronged —God is Most Powerful for their aid—those who have been unjustly expelled from their homes only because they say: 'Our Lord is God.'"

According to Wāḥidī, *sūra* 22:39 was revealed during the year of the Hijra immediately after Muḥammad left Mecca. Abū Bakr is reported to have complained that the minute they would leave the limited protection of Mecca, they would be destroyed by their enemies.[46] The verse was therefore revealed to allow them henceforth to defend themselves.

Sūra 22:39 is considered the first revelation allowing the Muslims to engage in fighting.[47] A single unrepeated tradition attributed to Ibn Zayd states that permission to fight was withheld for ten years.[48] Thus, a date for the verse's revelation is established in 622, the year of the Hijra, and ten years after the first revelations were reported to have been received by Muḥammad.

As the first verse sanctioning fighting, it is assumed to have abrogated verses treating conflict through different means, such as 15:94, 16:125, and 29:46. The same Ibn Zayd was attributed to have said that 22:39 abrogated the demand to avoid conflict prescribed by *sūra* 7:180: "Leave the company of those who blaspheme His names."[49] Not all, however, considered 22:39 to have been an abrogating verse. Some suggested that earlier verses still stand, although fighting is also permitted.[50]

The exegetes believed that there existed an actual ban (*nahy*) against fighting before the revelation of this verse. This view is made clear both by reference in *Tafsīr Muqātil*[51] to a ban and by the comment attributed to Abū Bakr that they would certainly be killed if not allowed to fight back.[52] The followers of Muḥammad are reported to have asked him for permission to fight back as well but were presumably not allowed to do so until after having left Mecca.[53]

The early ban against fighting has been explained in retrospect by the tradition as a necessary protective tactic to avoid being destroyed by overwhelming force when the Muslim community was small and weak. It is just as likely, however, that the "ban" against fighting represents a nonmilitant view within the young polity of Muslims—one of a number of different opinions. This view, it is argued, is based on qur'ānic verses such as those we have examined, as well as others calling for verbal argument without physical aggression. It was largely lost to history when a more aggressive stance was taken, but it can be reconstructed in part from the Qur'ān and its early exegesis.

> Sūra 2:190
>
> "Fight in the path of God those who fight you, but do not transgress limits (*walā ta'tadū*), for God does not love transgressors."

According to Wāḥidī's citation of a tradition on the authority of Ibn ʿAbbās, *sūra* 2:190 was revealed in 628 on or just after the occasion of the agreement at al-Ḥudaybiyya,[54] a village bordering the Sacred Precinct (*ḥaram*) of Mecca. According to the agreement, Muḥammad and the Meccan Quraysh agreed that the Muslims would retreat from entering Mecca that year (ostensibly on pilgrimage) but would be allowed to make pilgrimage the following year during which the town would be vacated of its idolatrous inhabitants for three days.[55] Despite the Ḥudaybiyya agreement, the Muslims feared that when they returned to perform the pilgrimage the following year, there would be a battle within the Meccan *ḥaram*, which was strictly forbidden according to pre-Islamic Arabian tradition. The companions of the Prophet were particularly upset about this, he says, so God revealed *sūra* 2:190, which taught that they could fight if attacked.

Muḥammad's decision to enter into a pact with the enemy based on their own terms was so controversial that his stalwart friend and future caliph, ʿUmar b. al-Khaṭṭāb, publicly opposed it.[56] The revelation of 2:190 at this occasion may be seen as providing justification for Muḥammad's controversial compromise. But if this verse were truly revealed for this occasion, was it not already known to the Muslims from 22:39–40, revealed some six years earlier, that defensive fighting was already allowed? If 2:190 were revealed in relation to entering the Sacred Precinct, why would it not be more specific about fighting in that location? The following verse, which will be examined in detail below, does indeed provide the information [2:191]: "Kill them wherever you find them, and turn them out from where they have turned you out, for *fitna*[57] is worse than killing, but do not fight them at the Sacred Mosque (*al-masjid al-ḥarām*) unless they fight you there; but if they fight you, kill them. . . ." As might be expected even from a casual reading of these two verses, the exegetes do not generally associate 2:191 with 2:190 because of the substantial variance between them. *Sūra* 2:191 is not associated with al-Ḥudaybiyya.[58]

The dating of 2:190 at al-Ḥudaybiyya does not correspond with the traditional "evolutionary theory" of qurʾānic war, because that date places it already four years after the Muslim community had passed from a defensive posture to a limited program of aggressive war.[59] The association of 2:190 with al-Ḥudaybiyya can only be because of its proximity to the following verse, which does refer to fighting within the Sacred Precinct in Mecca. But the reason for the adjacent location of the two verses is topical—not historical. Neither modern nor traditional scholars associate them together.[60] In fact, it seems as if their relational placement by the collectors of the Qurʾān was designed in order to make perfectly clear that the limitations suggested in 2:190 were abrogated by the nearly limitless proclamation of 2:191.[61]

Although at first sight, 2:190 seems to be talking about defensive fighting ("Fight . . . those who fight you"), most exegetes understand the verse to be treating an entirely different issue, and very few comments unambiguously treat the issue of defensive fighting.[62] Most understand the words "do not transgress limits" (*walā taʿtadū*) to refer only to the restriction against fighting noncombatants.

Such noncombatants are defined by the exegetes as those "who are not prepared to fight, such as women, children and monks."[63]

Two *ḥadīths* are cited for support of this view. One, on the authority of Ibn ʿUmar,[64] states that Muḥammad was greatly disturbed when he saw a woman killed during a raid and therefore forbade the killing of women and children.[65] The other is more general in nature, in which the Prophet is cited as forbidding even the weak and the oppressed from turning around and oppressing their old enemies.[66]

Ibn al-Jawzī considers 2:190 to remain unabrogated. Although he cites what he considers to be all the opinions regarding its abrogation, there are essentially two:[67]

1. The meaning of the verse is that noncombatant unbelievers must not be fought and killed, but most consider the verse to be abrogated by verses extending the requirement to fight all idolaters whether or not they are capable of fighting.[68]
2. The only part of the verse that is abrogated is "but do not transgress limits." That is, the limits of warfare originally established by the verse no longer apply, and various opinions within this camp refer to those original limits as the killing of noncombatants, fighting during the Sacred Months and in the Sacred Precinct, or fighting those with whom the Muslims had previous pacts.

Like Ibn al-Jawzī, Naḥḥās also considers the verse to be in force (*muḥkam*) and cites a tradition on the authority of Ibn ʿAbbās to the effect that noncombatants must not be fought.[69]

This verse is therefore not considered by most of the exegetes to be an authorization for defensive fighting as is assumed by Rudolph Peters[70] but, rather, a warning to refrain from exceeding the prohibition against fighting noncombatants. As noted above, the relationship between 2:190 and al-Ḥudaybiyya suggested by Wāḥidī does not make sense. If this verse has any relationship with al-Ḥudaybiyya, it would be as the platform of members of the community who would have pointed to it to urge Muḥammad to refrain from engaging in an armed pilgrimage to Mecca. But without additional evidence, we must remain as uncertain of its significance as the traditional Muslim exegetes.

Stage Three: Initiating Attack Allowed but within the Ancient Strictures

> Sūra 2:217
>
> "They will ask you about fighting in the Sacred Month (*al-shahr al-ḥarām*). Say: 'Fighting therein is a grave [offense], but driving [people] away from

> the path of God, unbelief in Him, and expelling His people from the Sacred Mosque is far more grave in God's sight.' *Fitna* is worse than killing. They will not stop fighting you until they turn you away from your religion, if they can. Those of you who are turned away from your religion and die as unbelievers, your acts will come to nothing in this world and in the world to come. You will be companions of the Fire and remain there forever."

The occasion for this revelation is universally acknowledged as the raid to Nakhla led by ʿAbdallah b. Jaḥsh al-Asadī in which a Meccan caravan driver named ʿAmr b. al-Ḥaḍramī was killed. This raid is considered by some to be the first instance of Muslims causing a fatal casualty in battle.[71] The raid is dated in the year 624,[72] two months before the battle of Badr,[73] and the killing took place either on the first day of the month of Jumāda al-Ākhira or the last day of Rajab, one of the four "Sacred Months" during which fighting in the pre-Islamic period was forbidden.[74] The uncertainty of the day is a natural result of the calendrical system of that period, in which the moon was the primary measurer of time, because the beginning of the month was established only by actual observation of the new crescent moon.[75] The traditional narrations of the story of the raid and the killing are quite aware of the issue because of the ancient Arabian prohibition against warring during the Sacred Months and the resulting Qurayshite condemnation of Muḥammad for condoning fighting during the prohibited time. According to one version, for example, the raiders took counsel before their attack and said: "If we let them be this evening, they will [have time to] enter the sacred area of Mecca [the *ḥaram*] and we will not be able to get them. So they decided that they should attack them."[76] When they were explaining the situation later to Muḥammad, they said: "O Messenger of God, we killed Ibn al-Ḥaḍramī as it was becoming evening. We looked at the crescent moon of Rajab, and we did not know whether we hit him in Rajab or in Jumāda."[77]

Because of the overwhelming importance of nonaggression during the Sacred Months in pre-Islamic times, the Quraysh used the issue to try to undermine Muḥammad's authority. They are cited as proclaiming: "You claim to observe the sanctity of the Sacred Month and the sacred city, but you killed during the Sacred Month!"[78] The verse itself alludes to accusations against Muḥammad ("They will ask you about fighting in the Sacred Month"), and the context of the raid seems to fit the meaning of the qurʾānic revelation. It neither disparages the importance of the Sacred Month nor absolutely forbids fighting during it but finds a compromise by extending the permission for defensive fighting to apply against all Meccan Quraysh in every situation and even to allow the expanded prescription occasionally to overrule the ancient prohibition of all manner of fighting during the Sacred Months. It is preferable not to engage in fighting during these months of peace, but, if necessary, the old pre-Islamic tradition may be overruled.

Most of the sources agree that 2:217 was indeed abrogated and that fighting during the Sacred Months was no longer restricted in any way. Most cite the famous "sword verse" (9:5): "When the sacred months are past, kill the idolaters wherever you find them. . . ."[79] This verse was understood by some to mean that with the passing of the current Sacred Months, which must be honored, fighting in God's cause need never again be compromised by time or place. *Sūra* 9:5, however, probably refers to an entirely different set of "sacred months" that represented a period or periods during which certain established pacts between Muḥammad and various non-Muslim groups and individuals remained in effect before they were canceled.[80] It is important to sort out the meaning of "sacred month" in both 2:217 and 9:5. If 9:5 was meant to eliminate the contracted "sacred months," then it would not apply to the institution of the old "peace months" of pre-Islamic Arabia. That it was applied exegetically to the pre-Islamic Sacred Months suggests that this verse was used out of its intended context in order to weaken an old and hoary tradition that was not easily given up by some within the Muslim community.

One occasionally runs across a citation of the view attributed to ʿAṭāʾ holding that 2:217 was never abrogated outright and that fighting during the Sacred Month remained strongly discouraged but not absolutely condemned.[81] Ṭabarsī asserts that fighting remains prohibited during the Sacred Months among Shiʿite jurists but only against those who likewise accept the sanctity of the Sacred Months.[82] In some cases, a *ḥadīth* is cited in which Muḥammad would not fight during the Sacred Month except in self-defense.[83] Other *ḥadīth*s are occasionally cited in support of abrogation of the rule of the Sacred Month. Muḥammad, for example, is said to have ordered attacks against the Hawāzin at Ḥunayn and the Thaqīf at al-Ṭāʾif during the Sacred Months of Shawwāl and Dhū al-Qaʿda.[84]

Rather than representing a spot on a linear continuum moving from avoidance of aggression to all-out aggression, 2:217 appears to represent a faction that existed within the new Muslim community during the lifetime of Muḥammad and perhaps even continuing after his death and that wished to preserve the ancient Arabian custom of the Sacred Months. It recognizes the need to engage in battle during this sacred period but considers it a grave act, which should nevertheless be avoided whenever possible.[85] This view was eventually eliminated by the new and innovative approach of militant Islam, which relied for its authority on a verse (9:5) treating a similar but unrelated issue.

> Sūra 2:191
>
> "Kill them wherever you find them and turn them out from where they have turned you out, for *fitna*[86] is worse than killing, but do not fight them

at the Sacred Mosque unless they fight you there. But if they fight you, kill them. Such is the reward of the unbelievers."

This verse, as has been noted, occurs immediately after 2:190, which Wāḥidī associates with the agreement of al-Ḥudaybiyya. Yet neither Wāḥidī nor any of the other exegetes in our sample associates 2:191 with al-Ḥudaybiyya, despite the fact that by discouraging fighting at the Sacred Mosque, this verse can easily be understood to support Muḥammad's controversial decision to compromise with the Quraysh.

Naḥḥās mentions that *sūra* 9 (al-Barāʾa), containing verses that are considered by most to have abrogated 2:191, was revealed two years after *sūra* 2 (al-Baqara).[87] Since the [Declaration of] Dissociation (*barāʾa*) of *sūra* 9 is nearly universally associated with the pilgrimage led by Abū Bakr in 631, then the date of much of *sūra* 2 would have to be 629, an assumption that places it some six years after the generally accepted date of *sūra* 2.[88] According to Nasafī, the revelation of 2:191 was God's promise that the Muslims would capture Mecca, which places it shortly before 630.[89]

The exegetes concentrate on the second part of the verse, treating fighting at the Sacred Mosque. Most state in their own words, and without citing supportive exegetical traditions, that the purpose of the revelation was to restrict fighting at the Sacred Mosque and, by extension, throughout the Sacred Precinct except in self-defense.[90]

Naḥḥās sums up the view that 2:191 restricts within sacred space what outside that space would be allowed as unlimited fighting, just as 2:217 restricts within sacred time (the Sacred Months) what outside of that time would be allowed as unlimited fighting. He adds that 2:194 defines when fighting within these restrictions of time and space is allowed, namely, whenever the enemy "exceeds limits" against the believers. When this occurs, the believers may in turn exceed the normal rules of military behavior defining the limits of what is allowable in fighting (2:194): "Whoever exceeds the limits against you, you may exceed the limits against him likewise."[91]

Tafsīr Muqātil suggests that there are three levels to the meaning and, by extension, revelation of this verse: "When 'and kill them wherever you find them' was revealed, God restricted this rule from application in the Sacred Precinct of Mecca ('but do not fight them at the sacred mosque.')." But this restriction was relaxed by the words "unless they fight you there," meaning that fighting in self-defense is allowed without restriction even in the Sacred Precinct.[92] In other words, the third part of the verse relaxed the second part, which restricted the first part.

The "sword verse" (9:5) is cited most often as the verse abrogating 2:191. *Sūra* 2:193, however, is also cited: "Fight them until there is no *fitna* and the religion becomes God's, but if they cease, let there be no hostility except against the oppressors."[93]

Some felt that 2:191 remained in force based on the view that fighting may be allowed in the Sacred Precinct as a defensive measure but should be avoided if possible. This view, of course, was a logical response of those who were uninclined to liberalize the ancient taboo against fighting in the Sacred Precinct, even in the name of Islam. Naḥḥās points out that 2:191 is "one of the most difficult among the abrogating and abrogated verses" and that adherents of each view used *ḥadīth*s from the canonical collections for support.[94] Yet both he and the encyclopedic commentary of Ṭabarī cite only Mujāhid as an authority for traditions claiming that the verse is not abrogated.[95]

Stage Four: Unconditional Command to Fight All Unbelievers

> Sūra 2:216
> "Fighting is commanded upon you even though it is disagreeable to you. But it is possible that you dislike something which is good for you and that you love something which is bad for you. God knows, but you know not."

Sūra 2:216 is not generally tied into an occasion of revelation, although *Tanwīr al-Miqbās* links it with the following verse (2:217) and gives its occasion of revelation as the raid of ʿAbdullāh b. Jaḥsh.[96] The item of greatest import for the exegetes is the problematic phrase in the first sentence, *kutiba ʿalaykum*, meaning, literally, "*written* for you," which is invariably paraphrased as *furiḍa ʿalaykum*: "is commanded upon you." The major issue discussed by the commentators is whether the requirement to fight is prescribed on every individual Muslim male who must go out to war (*farḍ wājib*) or whether it is technically required but may be ignored by many if enough others are willing to fight (*farḍ kifāya*).

One opinion, ultimately rejected by al-Shāfʿi and others, is that the requirement to fight was incumbent only on the Companions of the Prophet.[97] Another opinion, which is also rejected, suggests that fighting is recommended (*ʿalā al-nadab*) but not required (*lā ʿalā al-wujūb*) and, for support, cites the exclusion of war from the five pillars of Islam.[98] Some early commentaries consider the ordinance required (*farḍ*), although they do not specify whether it be *farḍ wujūb* or *farḍ kifāya*.[99] Later commentaries make it clear that the obligation to fight is *farḍ kifāya* unless an emergency requires that all able-bodied males bear arms.[100]

The issue of abrogation is spelled out most clearly by Ibn al-Jawzī,[101] who considered the verse to be abrogating but also qualified, based on his view that the requirement to fight evolved in three stages:

> The first is prevention from fighting, which is understandable from verse 4:77: "Have you not seen those unto whom it was said: 'Withhold your hands?'"[102] Then this [withholding of hands mentioned in verse 4:77] was abrogated with this verse [2:216], and the obligation [to fight] was imposed upon all. The verse [9:41] "Go forth lightly [armed] and heavily [armed]" supports this.[103] Then the matter became established that when a group engages in *jihād* (*idhā qāma bil-jihād qawm*[un]), [the obligation] falls away from the remainder (*saqaṭa ʿalā al-bāqīn*) according to the verse [9:122] "The believers should not all go forth; if only a group from every contingent go forth. . . ." The correct view (*al-ṣaḥīḥ*) is that the verse [2:216] "Fighting is commanded upon you . . ." is in force and that the requirement of *jihād* is necessary for everyone, except that this [requirement is in the category of] collective obligations (*furūḍ al-kifāyāt*). If a group engages in it, [the obligation] falls away from the remainder and there is no reason for abrogation.

In short, according to Ibn al-Jawzī's schema, stage one referred to by 4:77 was the prohibition against fighting.[104] In stage two, every individual (male of fighting age and fitness) was required to fight (*farḍ wujūb*); but in stage three, although technically required, one was not always obliged to respond to the call unless needed (*farḍ kifāya*).

Ibn al-Jawzī's discussion centered on whether 9:122 ("The believers should not all go forth") actually abrogates 2:216. *Sūra* 9:122 is often cited to support the view that fighting for religion is *farḍ kifāya*, although those who object state that considering 9:122 an abrogating verse would forever keep fighting from being a *farḍ wājib*, even in time of crisis. Thus, according to this view, 9:122 is not abrogated but merely qualified, in that not every individual need go off to war in most cases, although the technical requirement remains in effect.[105]

The commentary on this verse, too, displays an obvious lack of consistency. A variety of opinions is expressed, and no real consensus may be found. It is interesting to note that the good (*khayr*) or bad (*sharr*) of war is measured in these sources according to material rather than ideological standards. Fighting is good "because following the fighting is victory and triumph over the enemy and the capture of their towns, wealth, progeny and children."[106]

> Sūra 9:5
> "When the sacred months are past, kill the idolaters wherever you find them, and seize them, besiege them, and lie in wait for them in every place of ambush; but if they repent, pray regularly, and give the alms tax, then let them go their way, for God is forgiving, merciful."

Although Wahidī does not include the first eleven verses of *sūra* 9 (al-Barāʾa) in his book, the overwhelming consensus considers the "Declaration of Dissociation" (*barā'a*, the first word of the *sūra* and the general subject for the first twenty-nine verses) to have been revealed to Muḥammad in the month of Shawwāl and publicly declared in Mecca by ʿAlī during the pilgrimage led by Abū Bakr in 631.[107]

The exegetes treat four issues presented in this, the classic "sword verse": (1) the meaning of the "Sacred Months," (2) whether or not unbelieving prisoners must be killed, (3) why only three of the five pillars of Islam may be construed from the verse, and (4) the purpose of fighting. Only the first and last issues relate to the current discussion.

Ibn Kathīr and Ṭabarī record the differences of opinion regarding the definition of the sacred months.[108] The question centers on whether these sacred months are the four honored in the pre-Islamic period[109] or whether they represent a special period of nonbelligerency established by Muḥammad with the Declaration of Dissociation (*barā'a*), after which all prior pacts with idolaters would be broken and fighting would commence against all non-Muslims.

Tanwīr al-Miqbās and *Tafsīr Muqātil* conflate the two by defining the special time period set aside by Muḥammad after *barā'a* as the remainder of the Sacred Month of Dhū al-Ḥijja and the entire following Sacred Month of al-Muḥarram. Since according to the prevalent view, the announcement of *barā'a* was declared on the tenth day of Dhū al-Ḥijja,[110] and the following month of al-Muḥarram is thirty days, that special period lasted exactly fifty days.[111] This view is also provided in Ṭabarī.

The second and majority view is that the "sacred months" referred to in 9:5 are the four stipulated earlier in 9:2: "Go throughout the land, then, for four months." During this period, according to the interpreters, all the old pacts and obligations established between Muslims and idolaters would be honored as a kind of limited "grandfather clause." After those four months had passed, however, all previous treaties and arrangements with non-Muslims would become null and void and the relationship between Muslims and idolaters would be one of belligerency as defined by 9:5. Since the day of the announcement of *barā'a* was Dhū al-Ḥijja 10, the sacred months of protection for those having pacts included twenty days of Dhū al-Ḥijja, all of al-Muḥarram and Ṣafar, and ten days of Rabīʿ al-Ākhir.[112] Although the first interpretation, which conflates the two concepts of sacred months, is only a small minority view among the sources, 9:5 is nevertheless cited regularly and without attribution to a named source as the verse abrogating the *pre-Islamic tradition* of Sacred Months during which all manner of fighting was forbidden.

According to the exegetes, the purpose of fighting in this verse is to bring people to witness God's unity (the definition of the word "repent"—*tābū*—in the verse), to pray, and to give the alms tax. This definition provides some insight into the justification or goal of fighting beyond the propagandistic goals of material gain noted previously. The verse itself establishes the criteria for refraining from fighting: "but if they repent, pray regularly, and give the alms tax, then let them go their way." These criteria are made explicit only in later works—for example, by Ṭabarī and, following him, Ibn Kathīr,[113] in which repentance is defined as renouncing idols and worshipping God and that performing regular prayer and giving the alms tax can be observed immediately as outward manifestations of Muslim observance. The verse is therefore seen as calling on the Muslims after the end of the four sacred months stipulated earlier in the *sūra* to kill or seize idolaters everywhere unless or until they bear witness to the three requirements mentioned above, which are made explicit through the citation of a *ḥadīth* attributed to Ibn ʿUmar that Muḥammad said: "I was commanded to fight the people until they gave the witnessing: 'There is no god but God, and that Muḥammad is the Messenger of God,' and that they establish prayer and give the alms tax."[114] Somewhat different criteria are cited in a *ḥadīth* attributed to Anas: "[Muḥammad] said: I was commanded to fight the people until they witnessed that there is no god but God and that Muḥammad is the Apostle of God, and they turn to our direction of prayer and eat of our sacrifices and pray our prayers. Then their blood is forbidden to us except by law."[115]

Ibn Kathīr further understands from this verse that all unbelievers must be systematically fought until killed or until they become Muslims (or, presumably, they pay the poll tax [*jizya*] if Scriptuaries).[116] He stresses, however, that one must not be overwhelmed with "naked passion" against them in a burst of fighting during, for example, the height of the Islamic Conquest, when blood is hot and passions are high. The phrase "besiege them, and lie in wait for them in every place of ambush" is understood as the systematic subjection of all non-Muslims.[117]

Ibn Kathīr's late and systematized view holds that four qurʾānic "sword verses" refer specifically to four types of people against whom the Muslims are obligated to fight: 9:5 refers to fighting the idolaters; 9:29 refers to fighting the Scriptuaries until they pay the poll tax; 9:73 ["O Prophet, fight the unbelievers and the hypocrites"] refers to fighting those who outwardly appear as Muslims but who actually oppose Muḥammad and the community of Islam; and 49:4[118] refers to fighting Muslims who unjustly oppress other Muslims. *Sūra* 9:5, which is cited more than any other verse as abrogating less-aggressive qurʾānic revelations, is said to have abrogated 124 verses of the Qurʾān.[119]

> Sūra 9:29
>
> "Fight those who do not believe in God or the Last Day, and who do not forbid what has been forbidden by God and His Messenger, nor acknowledge the religion of truth from among the People of the Book, until they pay the poll tax (*al-jizya*) out of hand (*ʿan yad^{in}*), having been brought low (*wahum ṣāghirūn*)."

The revelation of 9:29 is associated with the raid on Tabūk in 630 (after Rajab 9 A.H.).[120] This verse is acknowledged as the first command specifically for fighting Scriptuaries, and all acknowledge that Muḥammad's decision to send a raiding party to fight the Byzantines occurred after having received 9:29. The Muslims had by this time subdued the Ḥijāz and were expanding, so the decision to move into Christian areas was an understandable next step.

Sūra 9:29 is cited by Naḥḥās as abrogating virtually all verses calling for patience or forgiveness toward Scriptuaries.[121] It was also suggested that 9:29 even abrogated 9:5, although it is seen more as qualifying 9:5 in that the latter required the killing of idolaters (*mushrikūn*) (a term which often includes Scriptuaries), while 9:29 specifically excluded the killing of Scriptuaries if they paid the *jizya*.[122]

The commentators devote most of their interest to defining the difficult terms: *jizya*, *ʿan yad^{in}*, and *ṣāghirūn*, but the standard view of abrogation in relation to war is summed up by Naḥḥās in his discussion of this verse: "It is clear that some of the [verses] are abrogated, including [2:109] 'Forgive and be indulgent,' because the believers were in Mecca at the [early] time and were being beaten (*yuḍribūna*) and were released from fighting the idolaters. They were . . . commanded to be forgiving and indulgent until God brought His command. God then brought His command and abrogated that."[123]

It may be observed from the exegesis of the nine verses examined here that the commentaries preserve little consistent tradition associated with the qurʾānic ordinances on fighting but, rather, express differing views and faithfully cite contradictory traditions preserved from earlier periods. Despite the lack of consistency, these verses are cited by the legal literature (and, following them, Western scholars) in such a way as to suggest a historical development in the qurʾānic conception of holy war. The schema, as has been noted, suggests an evolution of qurʾānic pronouncements from the earliest period of revelation, when fighting opponents of Islam was forbidden, to the latest period, when it was aggressively encouraged. We have observed, however, that the chronology of revelation as established by the exegetes, their association of verses with supposed events in the mission of the Prophet, and the reasoning behind their associations are far from consistent.

The fact is that the conflicting qurʾānic verses cannot prove an evolution of the concept or sanction for religiously authorized warring in Islam from a nonaggressive to a militant stance. To suggest that they do is nothing more than an interpretation applied to the obvious problem of disparity in the qurʾānic revelations treating war. As Morton Smith has argued with regard to the Bible, every statement in favor of a particular position suggests the existence of counterpositions as well.[124] It is just as likely that the conflicting verses of revelation articulate the views of different factions existing simultaneously within the early Muslim community of Muḥammad's day and, perhaps, continuing for a period after his death. Each faction would refer to different scriptural sources available from the oral and as yet unedited and uncanonized compendium of revelation for support of its views. It is now to this possibility that we turn.

FOUR

The Qurʾān on War
A New Reading

It should be expected, based on our knowledge of human social behavior, that a variety of factions would have organized within the early Muslim community over various issues.[1] The biographies of the Prophet, Islamic histories treating his mission, qurʾānic exegesis, and the Qurʾān itself support this view by reporting that Muḥammad had his detractors within the community and that factions formed over several issues. Among these factions was a group that is described in the Qurʾān as refusing to go out to battle (4:95):

> Not equal are those believers who sit [at home], except those disabled and those who strive and fight in the cause of God with their goods and their persons. God has favored in status those who strive and fight with their goods and persons over those who sit [at home]. Unto all [believers] has God promised good. But those who strive and fight has He distinguished above those who sit [at home] by a great reward.

Those refusing to fight are portrayed elsewhere in the Qurʾān as selfish and liable for punishment.[2]

A number of other qurʾānic passages suggest that certain groups or individuals were not prone to militancy.[3] Moreover, the very large number of exhortations calling Muslims to engage in battle against their enemies suggests that significant portions of the community were not inclined to do so. Those refusing to set out on the expeditions are portrayed as being cowardly, selfish, or simply uncommitted to God's religion, but these criticisms were naturally directed toward opposition groups or factions taking an opposing stand from that which was eventually adopted. The qur'ānic evidence suggests that the Muslim community was not of one mind regarding fighting during the period of Muḥammad's leadership. More militant and less-militant factions competed for the support of the Prophet and/or the community, and these factions cited divine authority for their views by referring to the words of God as revealed in the Qur'ān. Militant groups promoting aggressive behavior toward opponents of Islam eventually won the day. Their program is supported by militant scriptural passages, especially in what are dated as the "later" revelations according to the "evolutionary theory" examined in the previous chapter, and this faithful ammunition exceeds the number of scriptural supports that would have been cited by their opponents. But because Scripture cannot be "erased," something had to be done with the contradictory divine words. The theory of *naskh* ("abrogation") accounts for the problem. That a winning militant faction was not entirely successful in burying the views of less-militant or nonmilitant approaches is clear from the retention of nonmilitant views in the early exegetical literature as well as in Scripture, not to mention the general confusion that we have noted is associated with these scriptural verses and their exegesis. Some traditions, such as those stating that the Muslims used to hate fighting,[4] refer to the prominence of nonmilitant groups that temporarily epitomized the sentiments of a large segment of the community or perhaps even the community altogether.[5]

In a similar vein, the qur'ānic verses and exegetical views expressing support for the ancient prohibition against fighting during the Sacred Months represent a conservative view advocating retention of this pre-Islamic custom.[6] The Sacred Months had been a moderating institution, which prevented even the hottest of blood feuds from enabling one Arabian faction to dominate the others. It forced a truce at strategic periods every year, during which each tribe had the opportunity to recover, thereby preventing any single tribe or confederation of tribes from overwhelming the others.[7] The problem of the institution of the Sacred Months for militant Islam was that it hindered the new socioreligious affiliation of Muslims from completing the goal of mastery over all the Ḥijāz. It therefore had to abolish the institution, which it did through the support of divine revelation and its own particular exegesis. But not all divine revelations on the subject were consistent, and some were understood to support the continued sanctity of the Sacred Months, as has been noted previously. Those groups upholding the traditional view on the Sacred Months were defeated by innovators desirous of establishing a break with what came to be defined as the evils of the pre-Islamic period. The major scriptural source for their platform is *sūra* 9:5, which, as has been noted from early Islamic exegesis as well as its purported context given in the Qur'ān, seems to refer to an entirely different institution of "sacred months." Nevertheless, just as less-militant factions within the early Muslim community were defeated on the issue of warring against the detractors of Islam, so were those upholding the old institution of the Sacred Months also defeated by the innovative and militant factions of the growing Muslim community.

The War Verses: A New Organization

Given Islam's overwhelming acceptance of the traditional "evolutionary theory" of war, it is difficult to avoid the traditional dating of revelations when we examine the war verses, but it is nevertheless necessary to do so in order to avoid being misled by old assumptions. The verses to be studied below are, therefore, examined without regard for traditional views of chronology except where indicated, and they are analyzed, on the whole, independent of the verses among which they are situated. This method sometimes creates a rather awkward situation in which verses seem to be taken entirely out of context, but it is necessary in order to avoid prejudging the analysis because of proximity to possibly unrelated verses or because of preconceived ideas of historical context based on late interpretations. Rather than categorize verses according to where they fit in the traditional "evolutionary theory" of warring in the Qur'ān, I group them according to the following division:

1. Verses expressing nonmilitant means of propagating or defending the faith
2. Verses expressing restrictions on fighting
3. Verses expressing conflict between God's command and the reaction of Muḥammad's followers
4. Verses strongly advocating war for God's religion

The Nonmilitant Verses

It would be excessive to claim that these four categories represent an entirely accurate division of all the war verses of the Qur'ān. Some of the verses could arguably be placed into one or another of the categories, depending on how one understands and interprets their meanings, and arguments could be made for including other verses not listed here or for excluding some included in this schema. These divisions therefore represent my own reading of the relevant material, based on an approach to the text of the Qur'ān that is as independent of traditional Muslim assumptions as possible. I try to let the verses speak for themselves, but I also note opinions of early commentators wherever their suggestions might be helpful. By selecting which comments to include here, I may be accused of using only those that support my own readings, while rejecting others that might present persuasive but contrary opinions; and, in fact, any critical study of Scripture taking account of traditional exegesis always begs the question of influence and manipulation. On the other hand, because the Qur᾽ān provides virtually no historical contexts for its own messages, the varied suggestions of the traditional exegetes must be made available to examination in order to allow for any and all possible meanings, but these suggestions must be subject to the same critical scrutiny as any other. When opinions of the ancients support a modern critical thesis, they should most certainly be cited but without distorting their relative importance and without neglecting to examine or offer contrary opinions.

Of the eight verses in this category of "nonmilitant revelations," half appear to fit a Meccan context, suggesting that they were revealed before the Hijra, or "Emigration," of the Muslim community to Medina in 622.[8] The other half refer to Peoples of the Book, suggesting, therefore, that they were revealed after the beginning of Muḥammad's ongoing contact with the Jews of Medina in 622. Of the first group of "Meccan verses," two refer to idolaters and two use the old rhyming scheme (*saj*ʿ) so typical of Meccan material.

> Sūra 6:106
> "Follow what has been revealed to you from your Lord; there is no God but He; and turn away from the idolaters (*al-mushrikīn*)."

The referent of this verse is idolaters, which Muḥammad is commanded to avoid. This revelation appears relatively early, since it suggests that there remained a possibility for Muḥammad to retrench into idolatrous ways.[9] The tenor of this verse is in stark contrast with that of other verses such as 9:5, which relates to idolaters quite differently: "kill the idolaters (*al-mushrikīn*) wherever you find them."[10]

> Sūra 15:94
> "Profess openly what you are commanded, and turn away from the idolaters."

This verse also appears as an early Meccan revelation, since it calls on Muḥammad to make known or evident (*᾽iṣda*ʿ) God's teachings, which had presumably remained secret before that command.[11]

> Sūra 16:125
> "Invite [all] to the way of your Lord with wisdom and beautiful preaching; and argue with them in ways that are best and most gracious: For your Lord knows best who has strayed from His Path, and who receives guidance."

This is a difficult verse because of its lack of context. It is sandwiched between two verses that, although employing the same standard *saj*ʿ scheme,[12] are unrelated thematically. No referent is given for the command to the Prophet to "invite/call" (*ʾidʿu*). Whether the verse can be assigned as Meccan or Medinan[13] and whether those to be invited are idolaters or Jews, the command is for Muḥammad to bring the non-Muslims into Islam in a nonmilitant manner while assuring him that both those who refuse as well as those who accept will be recognized by God.

> Sūra 50:39
> "So bear with what they say, and give glory to your Lord before sunrise and before sunset."

This verse, too, is vague with regard to context, although its use of the old *saj*ʿ style supports the possibility that, as is claimed by Islamic tradition, the context is Meccan. The verse calls for patience (*ṣabr*) in the face of opposition and has no hint of an aggressive response to conflict.

Three of the above verses clearly differentiate unbelievers from believers, while the fourth presumes the differentiation. Kinship is a nonissue, while ideology (belief) becomes the determinant of identity. The sentiment expressed throughout is to avoid conflict and certainly not to be aggressive.

The next four verses refer to Peoples of the Book as opponents. This fact suggests, following the almost universally accepted macrodating of the revelations, that these are "Medinan" verses, since Muḥammad did not have regular contact with monotheist communities until after his Emigration to Medina in 622.

> Sūra 2:109
> "Many of the People of Scripture would love to turn you back from your belief to unbelief because of their envy when the truth has been revealed to them. But be forgiving and pardon until God gives His command (*ḥattā yaʾtī Allah biʾamrihi*), for God is able to do all things."

This verse refers to the attempt of Scriptuaries (most likely Medinan Jews) to weaken the growing Muslim polity.[14] God's advice in the face of this threat is to remain steadfast and refrain from responding, although different future options remain open ("until God gives His command").

> Sūra 5:13
> "Because of their breaking their covenant, we cursed them and hardened their hearts. They change words from their contexts and forget some of

> what they were taught. You will continue to uncover treachery from all but a few of them, but be forgiving and pardon, for God loves the kindly."

The verse just before this one refers to the Children of Israel, but the treachery (*khāʾina*) mentioned here represents a transition of reference to Jews.[15] The command here is the same as 2:109: Forgive and pardon (*faʿfū waṣfaḥū*)[16] but without the reservation of 2:109 ("until God gives His command"). Rather less ominous, it calls for tolerance, "for God loves the kindly."

> Sūra 29:46
> "Only argue nicely (*illā bil-latī hiya aḥsan*) with the People of the Book, except with the oppressors among them. Say: We believe in what has been revealed to us and revealed to you. Our God and your God is one, and it is Him to whom we surrender."

The sentiment expressed in this verse suggests that it may be associated with the early Medinan period when, as both traditional and most critical scholars believe, Muḥammad expected the Jewish communities of Medina to accept the version of monotheism he preached.[17] Its clear reference to monotheist opponents certainly suggests a Medinan dating.

> Sūra 42:15
> "Therefore call [to the faith] and be upright as you have been commanded. Do not follow their desires, but say: I believe in what God has revealed from a book and have been commanded to be just among you. Allah is our Lord and your Lord. We have our works and you have yours. There is no argument between us and you. God will bring us together, for the journey is to Him."

This verse also suggests a trend toward rapprochement with monotheists, who, given the history of Muḥammad's prophetic career, were Jews living in Medina.

To summarize thus far, 29:46 and 42:15 suggest a period when Muḥammad welcomed the Jewish community of Medina to Islam. These verses are mostly positive and optimistic. Verse 2:109, on the other hand,[18] represents People of the Book attempting to undermine the status and authority of Muḥammad and his new religious community. Even the latter two verses, however, despite the bitterness they express, remain committed to nonaggression. In each of these verses, the monotheists referred to are not formal members of the Muslim community of Medina. They are neither related by kinship nor by religion.[19] As nonmembers of the in-group, they were not expected in the pre-Islamic cultural environment to have value to the Muslims. That they do in these verses suggests their potential for becoming members of the new Islamic community, and the mode of alignment to the group is ideological. We note, then, that relationship with outsiders, at least as expressed in these verses, is ideological and not genealogical or economic—clearly a transition from the pre-Islamic world.[20]

The attitude of these verses toward opponents to Muḥammad's program, whether idolaters or Jews and whether at the earliest period of his mission in Mecca or after the transition to Medina, remains constant. Muḥammad is commanded to argue with his opponents kindly but effectively and to have patience. Hints are provided suggesting that his opponents might receive punishment at the hand of God, but it was not the role of Muḥammad or the Muslim community to inflict punishment or to escalate the conflict. The consistency of the program in these disparate verses suggests that they represent a point of view that remained intact over a significant period. This scenario is clearly at variance with the traditional one in which God provides dispensation to the Muslims to engage in defensive fighting during or immediately after the Hijra to Medina.

Restrictions on Fighting

The common thread in this group of verses is the restrictions on fighting expressed within them. These restrictions correspond closely to the old pre-Islamic cultural strictures applied to intertribal raids and wars, which eventually were repealed by Islam. The persistence of the old norms of engagement in war or raiding was a serious issue during the transition period to Islam, as may be understood from the repeated scriptural references, especially to limits on violence and to the Sacred Months. In some verses (2:194, 9:36), the issue of pre-Islamic restrictions is raised as a major question to be addressed, while in others (2:190, 2:217), the old rules seem to be referenced in order to stress the importance of their abrogation. Verses in which pre-Islamic restrictions are raised as legitimate questions are included in this category of restrictions on fighting, while those highly militant qur'ānic expressions in which the old rules are mentioned only for rhetorical purposes are listed below in the category of verses strongly advocating war for God's religion.

> Sūra 2:190
> "Fight in the path of God (*fī sabīl Allah*) those who fight you, but do not transgress limits (*walā ta'tadū*); for God does not love transgressors."

This verse advocates defensive fighting, but the importance of this verse lies in the understanding of the word *ta'tadū*, the root meaning of which is "to pass beyond something." The particular form of the verb found in this verse signifies "passing beyond the proper limit," which corresponds semantically with the

English equivalent, "to transgress." The obvious question raised by the verse is exactly what transgression is referred to, and the answers provided by the traditional commentators all relate to pre-Islamic strictures on fighting. Early suggestions center on the restriction against fighting within the Sacred Precinct (*ḥaram*) of Mecca[21] or the killing of women and children and other noncombatants.[22] The restriction against fighting in the Sacred Precinct is overruled, say the commentators, if the Muslims happen to be attacked there, but they are not to initiate hostilities within the sacred space.[23] This verse appears to retain pre-Islamic views of warring. It articulates the requirement to refrain from those excesses that must have been so familiar to the listener that it was not even necessary to enumerate them. Or perhaps it is only expressing a general caution against transgressing the well-known traditional "rules of engagement." One major innovation in the tradition of warring is expressed in this verse, however, and that is the use of the term "in the cause of God" (*fī sabīl Allah*). This new idiom in the vocabulary of warring represents a critically important change. It occurs seventy times in the Qur'ān in a variety of contexts, but many occur in the context of fighting. In the pre-Islamic period, kinship responsibility required that one go off to battle to protect the viability or honor of one's kinship group. In the new and evolving system, which becomes that of classical Islam, religious responsibility required that one go off to battle to protect the viability or honor of the new community of believers by fighting in the path of God.

This change from a kinship-based system to one of trans-kinship religious identity is reflected in the Qur'ān a number of times, perhaps most clearly in 3:103: "Hold fast all together to the cord of God and do not separate. Remember God's favor to you when you were enemies [with one another]. He bound your hearts together and you became, with God's grace, brothers."[24]

> Sūra 2:194
> "The Sacred Month for the Sacred Month, but [violation of?] sacred ordinances [only] in retaliation. Whoever transgresses against you, transgress against him. But fear God, and know that God is with the God-fearing."

The obscure phrase initiating this verse has been understood by most Muslim commentators to refer to the Sacred Month of Dhū al-Qaʿda in the year 628, when, according to tradition, Muḥammad was prevented by his Meccan opponents from performing the ʿUmra pilgrimage. According to a compromise arrangement, he would return to Mecca the same month of the following year with his entourage, during which the Meccans would vacate their town and allow the Muslims to perform the pilgrimage without interference.[25] Thus, one Sacred Month (of Dhū al-Qaʿda) is substituted for one the following year in the performance of the lesser pilgrimage. Others, however, suggest that the verse implies that fighting during the Sacred Month was allowed only if the Muslims were attacked.[26] The original meaning of the verse remains obscure, but it clearly places value on the ancient institution of the Sacred Month while also advocating keeping the sacred ordinances (*al-ḥurumāt*) except as a retaliatory measure. These sacred ordinances are not explained in the verse or in adjacent verses, but Ṭabarī describes them as three: the Sacred Month (*al-shahr al-ḥarām*, during which fighting was forbidden), the sacred city (*al-balad al-ḥarām*, in which fighting was forbidden), and the state of ritual consecration of the pilgrim (*al-iḥrām*, during which the pilgrim was forbidden to bear arms), all of which correspond with pre-Islamic custom.[27] The caution to avoid transgressing these limits, however, is couched now in religious language rather than in the language of tribal honor. Success in no longer determined by the strength and solidarity of the kinship group but, rather, by the overwhelming power of God. The old restrictions remain sacred, but the authority for them is now expressed in new Islamic terms.

> Sūra 9:36
> "The number of months in the sight of God is 12 [written] in God's Book the day He created the heavens and the earth. Of them, four are sacred. That is the right religion, so do not wrong each other during them; but fight all the idolaters just as they fight all of you,[28] and know that God is with those who are God-fearing."

Most of the commentators agree that this verse emphasizes the importance of the old institution of the Sacred Months and the abolition of warring during them but allows the Muslims to fight even during them if in defense.[29] The verse therefore supports the old prohibition against fighting during the Sacred Months aside from the exceptional case of being attacked during that period of safety, but the authority for this position now rests in the divine will rather than ancient custom. This suggests an attempt to "Islamize" the old institution of the Sacred Months and to retain them even in the new Islamic age.

> Sūra 22:39–40
> "Permission is given to those who fight[30] because they have been wronged—God is Most Powerful for their aid—those who have been unjustly expelled from their homes only because they say: 'Our Lord is God.' If God had not warded off some people by means of others, then monasteries and churches and synagogues and mosques in which the name of God is often cited would have been destroyed. God most certainly helps those who help Him. God is Strong, Mighty."

These two verses appear to belong together syntactically as well as with regard to meaning. The major message of the first section is that those who have been victimized have been granted sanction to fight by God. Such a messasge presumes that before this revelation, fighting was not considered an option, and the commentators indeed tend to consider this the first revelation allowing Muslims to fight.[31] What is particularly noteworthy with regard to this verse is that a relatively long explanatory justification (certainly long by qur'ānic standards) is provided for the permission to engage in fighting. The need to cite this long justification reveals some ambivalence about fighting in general and clearly restricts combat to those against whom wrongs have been committed. Thus, a good deal of speculation was encouraged among the exegetes over exactly to whom this verse was referring.[32] The second part of the combined verses provides a new rationalization for engaging in war, and it clearly expresses a universal concern for monotheistic practice.[33] Whatever the position resting behind this revelation, it certainly does not support the classic view that Islam has been an extremely aggressive and militant religious expression almost from the outset. On the contrary, it expresses a strong reticence toward fighting and may very well articulate the nonmilitant view of a faction within the community paralleling nonmilitant positions of early Christianity and Rabbinic Judaism.[34]

The first three selections in this section represent a point of view that was highly influenced by the norms of pre-Islamic practice. The sanctity of the old Sacred Months retained great importance according to this point of view. Other sacred institutions (*ḥurumāt*) also carried weight but are not explained by the verses, although the old pre-Islamic restrictions of the Sacred Precinct (*al-ḥaram*) are articulated in other verses to be examined below. The position represented by these verses appears to be one in which the pre-Islamic standards of military behavior must be retained in Islam. The ancient restrictions may be violated only in self-defense—only if they are currently being violated by the enemy that is attacking. Justification for the old norms, however, has been updated through the new religious vocabulary of Islam. The old system continues to apply but, now, within the context of the new religious dispensation rather than old Arabian custom.

As will be demonstrated below, this traditional position was eventually overruled by a more militant approach, which disdained any restrictions to warfare against non-Muslims. It is nevertheless noteworthy that the pre-Islamic sensibilities are supported by the very language of revelation from the Qur'ān itself, thereby demonstrating that holding to them was an honorable position among some factions of the Muslim community.

The last selection of this category is particularly interesting because of the need it expresses for justifying militant behavior, even in self-defense. It clearly expresses some discomfort with fighting altogether and justifies it on the basis of defense and the protection of foreign monotheistic as well as Islamic religious institutions. These verses justifiably can be considered as an articulation of universal concerns and as not just particular to the needs and problems of the fledgling Muslim community. Following Morton Smith, these verses clearly articulate a position in the Muslim community that did not survive, yet, like all the others examined here, they express divine authority in support of its point of view.

Conflict between God's Command and the Response of the People

This category holds the greatest number of verses, which of course suggests that the Muslim community was far from unified in its view on warring on behalf of religion and the religious community. As will become evident, the issues presented by these verses and the lacunae contained within them invited attempts by interpreters to suggest scenarios in which such verses would have been revealed. These explanations are of great interest for determining opinions and attitudes of later times, but little can be certain about their descriptions of purported incidents during the mission of Muḥammad. The qur'ānic verses, therefore, are taken to speak for themselves—and are themselves enough to reveal deep divisions within the Muslim community over the issues related to raiding and war.

> Sūra 2:216
> "Fighting is commanded upon you even though it is disagreeable to you. But it is possible that you dislike something which is good for you and that you love something which is bad for you. God knows, but you know not."

God is depicted here commanding fighting (*al-qitāl*) in response to the lack of action among Muslims, who appear to have complained or at least refrained from responding positively to prior calls for military action. Early statements relate the command in this verse to apply to embarking on raids,[35] but this verse has become the source for the protracted discussion over whether the legal obligation to engage in warring on behalf of religion is an obligation for the community as a whole (*farḍ kifāya*) or the personal obligation of every individual Muslim (*farḍ ʿayn*).[36]

> Sūra 3:156
> "O you who believe! Be not like the unbelievers who said of their brethren who went abroad in the land or went on raids: If they had been [home]

> with us they would not have died or been killed; that God may make it anguish in their hearts. God gives life and causes death; and God is Seer of what you do."

This verse depicts a natural response of those who lost loved ones in war. Such a response, according to the verse, is attributed to unbelievers (*al-ladhīna kafarū*). The implication, of course, is that such behavior is typical of unbelievers, whose kinship ties have not been superseded by loyalty to the Muslim community. It is clearly unacceptable for believers. The underlying issue here is the conflict between the old kinship affiliation of pre-Islamic days and the new religious affiliation through the community of Muslims (the Umma), and some were clearly hesitant and uneasy in making such a radical change in the basis for individual and group identity. The verse is then followed by one teaching that, if that transition is made, then even dying while warring in the path of God (*fī sabīl Allah*) brings great benefit to the believer.[37]

> Sūra 3:167–168
> "And that He might know of the dissenters, unto whom it was said: Come fight in the path of God or defend. They answered: If we knew anything of fighting we would follow you. On that day they were nearer disbelief than faith. They utter with their mouths a thing that is not in their hearts. God is most aware of what they hide. Those who said to their brethren while they sat [at home]: If they had only listened to us, they would not have been killed. Say: Then repel death from yourselves if you speak the truth!"

This passage is part of a longer section treating "the day the two armies met,"[38] and later Islamic tradition associates that section with the famous and nearly disastrous battle at Uḥud.[39] The "dissenters" (usually translated as "hypocrites")[40] mentioned here and in many other verses of the Qur'ān refer to Muslims who dissented from within the community, sometimes openly and sometimes in secret. Dissenters are condemned for not joining up to fight at the battle of Uḥud,[41] but they are condemned in many disparate verses of the Qur'ān for being apostates (63:1–3; 9:73–74, where they are paralleled with *kāfirūn*—"unbelievers"), the enemy (63:4), reprobates (63:6), and so on. As a result, they should be killed (4:88–89).[42] The derision and anger leveled against them in the Qur'ān and in so much post-qur'ānic religious literature have obscured the fact that the term, "dissenters," refers, at least in part, simply to individuals or factions within the community that opposed some or many of the decisions and policies of the leadership represented by Muḥammad and his closest associates. The dissenters depicted in the Qur'ān represent the classic historical losers, who are portrayed by surviving texts (texts written or edited by the winning factions) as opaquely evil. The real situation, however, is far more complicated. It is much more likely that these dissenters represent a number of individuals and factions within the community, each of which had the strength and support to oppose policies or decisions of the Muslim leadership, thereby threatening that leadership in various ways. The dissenters in this passage are accused of offering a poor excuse for not joining in battle. They claim lack of fighting skills, while the passage accuses them, rather, of wishing to save their own lives even at the expense of the community as a whole. Although much has been written in the traditional literature to fill in the gaps of this qur'ānic passage, the exegetical material is so self-contradictory that it cannot be relied on as historically accurate. We must remain content to note that, for whatever reason, a large and powerful enough segment of the Muslim community refused, at least for an important period, to engage in fighting. The qur'ānic condemnation of those refusing to engage in war is considered by some early commentators to be the strongest divine rebuke to the dissenters.[43] The problem was certainly great enough to invoke the powerful and repeated condemnation of God.

> Sūra 4:72–74
> "Among you there is he who tarries behind, and if disaster overtook you, he would say: 'God has been gracious unto me since I was not present with them.' [4:73] And if a bounty from God befell you, he would surely cry, as if there had been no friendship between you and him: 'Oh, would that I had been with them, then should I have achieved a great success!' [4:74] Let those fight in the path of God who sell the life of this world for the other. Whoever fights in the path of God, whether he be killed or be victorious, on him We shall bestow a great reward."

Here, again, we observe a rebuke against those who are accused of withdrawing from the community of fighters embarking on a raid. Those who tarry are accused of withdrawing when the material benefit of raiding is not certain and of being sorry that they did not join in when spoils are gained. The sentiment of the "tarriers" expressed by this passage is that of pre-Islamic times, when raiding was a source of material resources. The culprits are condemned, in effect, for not taking on two new requirements of the Islamic system. On the one hand, they are not taking on the responsibility to fight for their religious community as they would fight for their own kinship group. In other words, these Muslims have not replaced the kinship solidarity of pre-Islamic Arabia with the religious solidarity expected of believers. On the other hand, they remain too narrowly interested in the material gain of spoils, which is not to suggest that the new system disdained spoils in war. History has proved the opposite to be the case, for spoils of war became a major factor in the success of the great Islamic Conquest, but the message of this passage is that those who fight for religion demonstrate through their actions that their horizons have been broadened. Muslims should not be concerned merely for the material gains of the ancient system. Religious kin (*ikhwān fīl-dīn* to use a qur'ānic term)[44] are willing to trade the limited benefits of this life for the eternal and unlimited benefits of the Hereafter. The ultimate message is that the real fighter in the path of God—the ideological warrior—will gain in either case: either from the spoils of war in this world or, if killed in battle, the far greater reward of a future world. This message that the new Muslim fighters will gain great rewards in either event is common in the Qur'ān,[45] and it is clearly an enticement to those who for whatever reasons, whether materialistic, ideological, or for fear of their own lives, hesitated or outright refused to engage in warring and raiding alongside their new brethren of believers.

> Sūra 4:75
> "What is wrong with you that you do not fight in the path of God when weak men, women and children are crying: 'Our Lord! Bring us out of this town of evil people and give us from Your presence a protector! Oh, give us a defender!'"

This verse offers an additional incentive for encouraging those refusing to fight to engage in battle. The implicit assumption of the passage is that some followers of Muḥammad remained in Mecca after the Hijra and were being persecuted by the Meccan populace. The atrocities perpetrated against them should serve to incite the hesitant to fight on behalf of their persecuted religious kin. *Tanwīr al-Miqbās* does indeed supply a metahistorical explanation for the verse, but it does not seem to correspond with the simple meaning of the passage.[46] It is more likely that 4:75 was simply appended to the previous verses because of its similar message of incitement to war. For our purposes, it adds more support to the view that a significant segment of the community refused to follow the command to fight at various times and that further qur'ānic passages employing a variety of arguments to encourage fuller participation in military actions were revealed in response to the problem of disunity over the issue of warring.

> Sūra 4:77
> "Have you not seen those unto whom it was said: Withhold your hands, observe prayer and pay the alms tax, but when fighting was prescribed for them, a group of them fear people as much as the fear of God or even more. They say: 'Our Lord! You have commanded fighting for us, but if You would only put it off for us for a while!' Say [to them]: The comfort of

> this world is scant; the Hereafter is better for the God-fearing, since you will not be wronged even the slightest bit."[47]

This passage appears to describe the negative reaction of some Muslims to an early command to engage in fighting. The commentators contend that the phrase "Withhold your hands" (*kuffū aydiyakum*) refers to former requirements of the Muslims during the Meccan period to refrain from responding physically to the harassment of the Meccan idolaters.[48] According to this view, the Muslims were satisfied in Mecca to obey God's commands to observe the prayers, pay the alms tax, and refrain from physical aggression, but when the command was later given in Medina to engage in fighting in God's cause, a faction balked. This group is depicted simply as being cowardly, and it is possible that some were indeed unwilling to obey the command to fight for that reason. On the other hand, fighting for group solidarity in pre-Islamic Arabia was such a common cultural norm and tied up so closely with personal and tribal honor that it seems unlikely any respectable Arab would volunteer such a reason for his unwillingness to engage in battle. It is now known as a commonplace among ancient (and often modern!) documents written by the "winners" of history that the motivations posited in the documents are often manipulated by the writers. The motivation suggested by the verse may therefore be suspect, but the passage describes a very real problem confronted by the leadership of the community when a faction (*farīq*) protested the command to engage in fighting.

> Sūra 4:95
> "Those believers who sit [at home], other than the disabled,[49] are not on an equal level with those who strive in the path of God (*al-mujāhidūn fī sabīl Allah*) with their possessions and their lives. God prefers those who strive with their possessions and their lives to those who sit [at home]. God has promised good to each, but God distinguished those who strive above those who sit with a great reward."

This brief passage distinguishes fully three times between those who engage in war or support it materially and those who withhold all support from the campaigns. It demonstrates equality between those who physically engage in a campaign and those who remain behind but outfit the campaign materially, but it also clearly indicates that there were those who refused to support the campaigns altogether, and it condemns them.

> Sūra 9:38–39
> "O believers! What is the matter with you that when it is said to you: 'March out in the path of God,' you are weighed down to the ground. Are

> you so satisfied with the life of this world over the Hereafter? The enjoyment of the life of this world is but little [when compared] to the Hereafter. [9:39] If you do not march forth He will afflict you with a painful punishment and will substitute another people instead of you. You cannot harm Him at all, but God has power over everything."

This passage is generally considered to have been revealed in relation to the march to Tabūk to engage the Byzantines in 630,[50] which, according to the commentators, was during the oppressive heat of the desert summer. It cannot be certain, as has been noted above, whether this is true, nor can it be determined exactly what the motivations were for those who tried to avoid marching off to battle. It is clear, however, that the threat of dissidents was great enough to engender a strong response in this revelation. It is particularly noteworthy that 9:39 not only threatens the dissident individuals or factions with divine punishment but also threatens the entire community of believers if they cannot achieve solidarity in battle: "[God] will substitute another people instead of you." This again lends support to the importance of replacing the old kinship solidarity with the new solidarity of religious affiliation.[51]

> Sūra 9:42
> "Had the gain been nearby and the journey easy, they would have followed you, but the distance seemed too great to them. Yet they swear by God: 'If we could, we would have set out with you.' They destroy themselves. God knows that they are liars."

This verse is considered by the commentators to be a continuation of the passage referring to the Tabūk expedition. The problem of Muslims refusing to set out for battle was serious enough that it elicited a large number of responses to the problem in revelation. The fifteen verses that follow 9:42 continue to focus on the theme of those who refrain from going out on expedition and on dissenters in general. Muḥammad himself is criticized in 9:43 for giving in to those who refused to fight,[52] and the following verses express a deep bitterness over this problem.

Many more verses treat the conflict between the qurʾānic command to fight and the lack of response among segments of the community. We cannot treat all of them here, but some general comments are of interest. Some seem to repeat the basic themes of verses treated above, such as 47:20, which accuses otherwise good Muslims of balking at the command to engage in war.[53] Others mention specific groups, which were not inclined to participate in the Muslim raids and battles. Given the contentious nature of the revelations over this issue, it cannot be taken for certain that specific religious or political factions simply were not lumped together into named groups such as "the wealthy" or "the nomads," for the identities of losing opposition groups tend to be lost to history. On the other hand, logical reasons may also be suggested to explain why the wealthy or the Bedouin might wish to refrain from full participation in military expeditions. Verses 9:86–87 condemn the wealthy (*ūlū al-ṭawl*)[54] for asking special dispensation for staying at home. Nomads (*al-aʿrāb*) are repeatedly portrayed as being less than willing to go out to battle (9:90, 120; 33:20; 48:11, 16). In other passages, the nomadic Arabs (in contrast to agriculturalist or urbanized Arabs) are portrayed as less willing or able in a number of other ways to make the transition from the old way of life to the new system of Islam. They are accused of tending toward disbelief and dissent and do not know (or accept) the new restrictions imposed by Islam (9:97, 101; 49:14), and they are accused of going along with the new system only unwillingly (9:98).[55] This resistance is fully consonant with observations of Bedouin, which have described the nomadic culture as traditional and conservative, not prone to adopting new cultural or religious norms.[56]

According to the commentators, 33:9–27 treat the famous Battle of the Trench (*al-khandaq*) in Medina at which the Muslims were very seriously threatened by an attack of a large allied force.[57] In these verses, dissenters are accused of questioning the divine promise and the leadership of Muḥammad (33:12). Different factions (*ṭāʾifa, farīq*) are said to have attempted to convince the Medinans to abandon their defenses or to have sought to remain at home rather than join forces with the defenders (33:13). Some are accused of being ready for treachery (33:14) and trying to evade their sworn responsibility to defend Medina (33:15). It is clear that some who refrained from fighting were not Muslims themselves (33:26–27), although all Medinans, whether Muslim or not, were required by the "Constitution of Medina" to engage in defense of the town from the attack of outside forces.[58] The overall condemnation of those who did not join in battle focuses on the fear and cowardice of those who did not come to the defense of the Muslim community under attack. As mentioned earlier, however, the accusations preserved for history do not tell the entire story. It is clear from the passage that there were several different factions of dissenters (*munāfiqūn*) who resisted joining the battle for different reasons. The exact identity and motivations of these dissenting groups cannot be reconstructed, but their existence is clear.

These verses expressing conflict between God's command and the response of large segments of the community demonstrate the lack of unity regarding the issue of war. Various factions are mentioned in the verses, and two are even labeled. Criticism focuses on the problem of old kinship ties hindering the unity and strength of the Umma and the narrow concern among some for spoils of war rather than solidarity in fighting for religious cause. As is expected in any transitional community, the adaptation of new cultural norms occurred at different rates among various segments of the population, and it is not surprising that dissenting factions arose over such important issues as kinship relations, spoils, and the new demands of membership in the Muslim community. In addition to the general problem of cultural transition, it must be remembered that a number of revelations were explicitly against militancy in the community's dealing with non-Muslims. The aggressive, even bellicose revelations must have been problematic for some Muslims who had been strongly influenced by the layer of revelations condemning any actions beyond discussion and argumentation on behalf of the new religious system and its adherents.

Verses Strongly Advocating War for God's Religion

The verses in this section are considered by post-qur'ānic writings to be abrogating verses, which have come to override earlier revelations with less-strident messages about war. These are the latest revelations according to the traditional Muslim understanding of the "evolutionary theory" of war in Islam, and as such they represent the most valid and timeless commands regarding war. Although we have shown that the traditional "evolutionary theory" cannot stand up to critical analysis, these verses nevertheless have been understood by most traditional Muslim legalists and religious policymakers to express the most important and eternal divine message with regard to war in the path of God. They carry the highest authority in all discussions of war and have been cited most often from the days of the earliest exegesis until the present. We have noted previously that they do not stand alone in the qur'ānic presentation but must be read in conjunction with other revelations taking different positions on the issue so that we may understand the full range of thinking on war in the early formative period of Islam. Nevertheless, they have come to represent classic post-qur'ānic thinking on holy war and serve as proof texts for the codification of the legal traditions on war in all the legal schools of Islam.

> Sūra 2:191
> "Kill them wherever you find them and turn them out from where they have turned you out, for *fitna* is worse than killing,[59] but do not fight them at the Sacred Mosque unless they fight you there. But if they fight you, kill them. Such is the reward of the unbelievers."

The root *q.t.l.* appears in this verse six times but is read in some instances in the first form (kill) and in others in the third form (fight). The lack of the consonantal *alif* in some renderings of the word in the verse makes a definite reconstruction of the earliest reading impossible. The reading in the standard version of the Qur'ān is that of the Meccan and Medinan Qur'ān reciters, according to Ṭabarī, but a minority reading has "but if they kill you, kill them."[60] This minority reading suggests concern with the *talion* and lessens the harshness of the command. That is, the verse may be read to mean that killing the enemy is forbidden in the Sacred Mosque even in defense, unless a Muslim has been killed, although limited defensive fighting would presumably be allowed. The issue must remain only theoretical, however, for we cannot reconstruct the original intent of the verse.

The qur'ānic context of 2:191 is the war verses of 2:190–195 and perhaps 2:216–217, which present interesting difficulties because of the contradictory messages contained within them.[61] Verse 2:190, as has been observed, commands defensive fighting only and calls for moderation (*walā ta'tadū*).[62] Verse 2:191 then commands anything but moderation when it calls on Muslims to kill the enemy wherever they may be found (or caught—*ḥaythu thaqiftumūhum*). A restriction is then placed on this command in the following sentence, when the Sacred Precinct is protected from fighting except in defense, but this restriction is in turn abrogated, according to some exegetes, by a statement found only two short verses later (2:193).[63] This confusion lends strong support to the suggestion that unrelated verses treating war were sometimes joined together in the editing process.

The command to turn out the enemy just as they turned out the Muslims is the reason that some traditionists associate these verses with the conquest of Mecca,[64] but of primary concern in this verse is the statement that "*fitna* is worse than killing." The base meaning of the word *fitna* is testing or purifying through testing.[65] Most exegetes define the word in this and the other major war contexts in which it occurs (2:193, 217, and 8:39) as *shirk*, or "idolatry"—that is, the trial or temptation of associating partners with the one God.[66] In a few cases, however, the word is defined in conjunction with its later historical meaning as the common term for sedition, a meaning derived from the temptation to rebel against the leadership of the community.[67] With regard to either definition, the justification for killing on the ground that it is less onerous than *fitna* is clearly an ideological statement. As will become clear in the continuation of this section, the use of the term *fitna* in four major war verses most clearly establishes the ideological as opposed to materialistic nature of Islamic holy war. Both aspects make up the full Gestalt of the canonical Islamic holy war.

> Sūra 2:193
> "And fight them until there is no more *fitna* and religion becomes God's (*wayakūn al-dīn lillāh*). But if they cease, let there be no hostility except to the oppressors."

Whether *fitna* carries the meaning of idolatry or sedition, the community is commanded to fight the enemy until Islam becomes the hegemonic power (*wayakūn al-dīn lillāh*).[68] This goal, of course, represents a classic expression of holy war: the promotion of a specific religious ideology. The meaning of religion ("and religion becomes God's") according to Ṭabarī is not simply generic monotheism but, rather, the particular monotheism of Islam as known by "worship and obedience to God according to His command and prohibition."[69] Islam, therefore, must be the religion of dominion. Nevertheless, a famous *ḥadīth* is often cited to show that adherents of other forms of monotheism may be allowed to practice their religion without undue molestation:

> The Prophet said: "I was commanded to fight the people until they say, 'There is no god but God,' establish [regular] prayers, and pay the alms tax. If they do this, then they will have preserved from me their lives (*dimāʾahum*) and their property aside from what is legally acceptable, and their debt to God."[70]

What is important in this *ḥadīth* is not what is in it but what is left out. The standard statement of the Islamic creed is the *shahādatayn*—"the double witnessing"—a credal statement in two parts affirming that there is no divinity but God and that Muḥammad is God's apostle. The first part may be considered "universal monotheism," while the second defines the particular case of Islam. It was not lost on the legalists that some versions of this authoritative *ḥadīth* include only the first part, and it is this version that is cited by Ṭabarī.[71]

"But if they cease" is understood by the exegetes to refer either to the practice of idolatry or to sedition against Muslim power,[72] and "the oppressors" are defined simply as those who continue to practice idolatry or engage in sedition.[73] That is, although the term "cease" (*intahaw*) may have originally referred simply to the cessation of hostilities against Muslims and the term "oppressors" (*al-ẓālimīn*) may have referred to aggressors in the verse's plain meaning, the exegetical literature has understood this revelation as a condemnation of non-Islamic practice rather than a moderating statement encouraging a peaceful response to the cessation of hostilities.[74]

> Sūra 2:217
> "They will ask you about fighting in the Sacred Month (*al-shahr al-ḥarām*). Say: 'Fighting therein is a grave [offense], but driving [people] away from the path of God, unbelief in Him, and expelling His people from the Sacred Mosque is far more grave in God's sight.' *Fitna* is worse than killing. They will not stop fighting you until they turn you away from your

> religion, if they can. Those of you who are turned away from your religion and die as unbelievers, your acts will come to nothing in this world and in the world to come. You will be companions of the Fire and remain there forever."

As noted previously, this verse raises the issue of the pre-Islamic practice of ceasing all hostilities during the Sacred Months, but it is considered in general to have overruled the custom. Although fighting during this period is indeed wrong, the wrongs done to the Muslims justify abrogating the old rule. The verse may even imply that initiating hostilities during the Sacred Months would therefore be condoned, perhaps because of earlier transgressions by the enemies of Islam against the Muslim community. As noted in the previous section, the exegetical literature associates the revelation of this verse with the raid on Nakhla led by ʿAbdallah b. Jaḥsh, in which a Meccan was killed by a Muslim on the last day of the Sacred Month of Rajab. The Meccans accused Muḥammad of violating the sanctity of the Sacred Months by sending out the expedition, and they expected his prestige to be reduced in the eyes of his fellow Muslims for his having disregarded the sanctity of the ancient rules. According to the exegetical (and perhaps historical) narrative, both the Muslims and the Meccans involved in the incident presumed that the old pre-Islamic customary rules about fighting were in force. When the Muslim raiders realized, however, that they would miss their opportunity if they waited one more day to the end of the Sacred Month, they decided to attack without regard for the restriction. They succeeded in gaining the intended spoils but killed one man in the process. When they returned to Medina, Muḥammad chastised them and denied having ordered them to fight during the Sacred Month (*mā amartukum biqitāl fī al-shahr al-ḥarām*). In response to Muḥammad's disavowal, the raiders thought that they would be killed for having broken the rule and causing a fatality during the restricted period. Even their fellow Muslims condemned them, perhaps also for having tainted the honor of the Muslims or for endangering them all as well. It was only at this point, at the height of tension in the narrative, that 2:217 was revealed.

Although the narrative cannot be relied on as accurate historically, it does provide important information about cultural values. First of all, it establishes the great importance of the institution of the Sacred Months in the pre-Islamic period, and it notes that the ancient system was functional during the early Islamic period as well. The context it establishes for the Qurʾān verse also makes it quite clear that the pre-Islamic sanctity of the Sacred Months was indeed abrogated, and it also suggests that raids or fighting might be initiated without regard for the ancient restrictions. The Muslim community would henceforth play by its own rules, and the authority for these rules transcends any authority that the Arabs of pre-Islamic times could muster. God abrogates the old system because the evils of idolatry and all that is tied up with it are more grievous than violating the rule of the Sacred Months. In other words, the temptation of idolatry and all that is associated with it are more grievous than killing ("*fitna* is worse than killing"), even during the Sacred Months.

The enemy is portrayed in this verse as persistent and insidious ("They will not stop fighting you until they turn you away from your religion, if they can"). They must be overcome because of who they are (idolaters) and what they represent (the absence of belief). The ideology of Islam must overcome the evils of the *ancien régime.*

> Sūra 8:39
> "And fight them until there is no more *fitna*, and religion becomes God's in its entirety. But if they cease, God is aware of what they do."

This verse is a near duplication of 2:193, and the exegetes provide little additional insight here than was given in relation to 2:193.[75] The exegetes provide no historical context to explain the repetition of thought. Its twofold appearance may be a result of two slightly different versions of the revelation preserved among the collectors and/or redactors of the text, or it may be a result of the emphasis on the idea they express.

> Sūra 9:5
> "When the sacred months are past, kill the idolaters wherever you find them, and seize them, besiege them, and lie in wait for them in every place of ambush; but if they repent, pray regularly, and give the alms tax, then let them go their way, for God is forgiving, merciful."

This verse, as has been noted above, is cited most often by the exegetes as an abrogating verse. Often referred to as "the sword verse," it is understood to represent the final qur'ānic statement regarding relations with idolaters. According to most traditional commentators, the "sacred months" referred to here are not the Sacred Months of the pre-Islamic system. They refer, rather, to the four months mentioned earlier in *sūra* 9 (al-Barā'a), during which the old pacts and obligations established with idolaters before Muḥammad and his community became hegemonic would still be honored. After those four months had passed, however, all previous treaties or arrangements would become null and void and the state of relationship between Muslims and idolaters would be determined by 9:5.[76] This understanding becomes clear from the text of the Qur'ān itself. The exegetical literature then fills in and adds the details. The tenor of the relationship between Muslims and idolaters after the grace period had passed is clear. It is a relationship defined by total war—a war defined by religion and fought for religion. If, on the other hand, idolaters established the minimum religious requirements of Islam as authorized in this as well as other verses,[77] they may not be disturbed, for they will then have moved into the community and will have become one with the believers. It is this "sword verse" (*āyat al-sayf*) that has given rise to the idiom "Islam or the sword."

The commentators provide many more details. Verse 9:5 abrogates any restrictions to fighting based on the old Sacred Months, the sacred area of the Meccan *ḥaram*, or the state of ritual sanctity taken on by religious pilgrims (*al-ʾiḥrām*).[78] It serves as the unconditional command to fight all nonbelievers at any time and any place.

> Sūra 9:29
> "Fight those who do not believe in God or the Last Day, and who do not forbid what has been forbidden by God and His Messenger, nor acknowledge the religion of truth from among the People of the Book, until they pay the poll tax (*al-jizya*) out of hand (*ʿan yad^{in}*), having been brought low (*wahum ṣāghirūn*)."

This is a difficult verse because, as noted in the previous chapter, it is not clear exactly what are the original qurʾānic meanings of *jizya*, *ʿan yad^{in}*, and *ṣāghirūn*. Later interpretive and legal literature understand the last two terms to legislate a ceremonial humiliation as part of the payment of the poll tax, although most modern scholars believe that the Qurʾān itself does not require such an act.[79] In addition, the reference to Peoples of the Book not believing in God or the Last Day seems odd since both Rabbinic Judaism and Christianity hold these two beliefs as essential to their religious systems. This reference leads me to suggest that an early version of the verse may not have included the phrase *min alladhīna ūtū al-kitāb*[80] but may have represented a lenient position with regard to idolaters that became unacceptable to a later more militant Islam.[81]

Despite the difficulties raised by critical readings of the verse, it has come to be read by Muslim scholars in conjunction with 9:5 and serves as a qualifier of the latter with regard to those groups having received a prior revelation. Verse 9:5 is understood to command unqualified war against all idolaters until they are killed or become Muslim. Verse 9:29 is understood to command unqualified war against Scriptuaries until they acknowledge the hegemony of Islam by paying the poll tax and living a second-class status (*wahum ṣāghirūn*) as "People of the Poll Tax" (*ahl al-jizya*) or "Protected Peoples" (*ahl al-dhimma*). The concept of "Islam or the sword" never officially applied to

Scriptuaries, despite the Western myth to the contrary. The two verses together are often referred to nevertheless, even in Arabic parlance, as "the sword verses" (*āyāt al-sayf*).

A few additional verses provide the same militant and self-confident expression of ideological war against non-Muslims. They are less-popular source texts among the exegetes and legalists than those examined above, but they nevertheless reinforce the tenor of the operative revelations on war in classical Islam. These will be translated below.

> Sūras 9:73/66:9[82]
> "O Prophet! Strive (*jāhid*) against the unbelievers and the dissenters (*al-munāfiqīn*), and be ruthless with them. Their refuge is Hell, a bad destination."

> Sūra 9:123
> "O you who believe! Fight the unbelievers (*al-kuffār*) who are near to you and let them find ruthlessness in you, and know that God is with those who fear Him."

This command to fight those nearby is reminiscent of Deuteronomy 20:15–18, which commands the utmost severity in fighting nearby peoples.[83] As in the other verses in this category, the command is for a ruthless ideological war of religion against those labeled as unbelievers. Divine assistance will be forthcoming to the true believers.

> Sūra 47:4–5
> "When you meet the unbelievers, then [let there be] slaughter (*faḍarb al-riqāb*) until, when you have routed them, bind [them] fast. Afterward, [free them by] grace or ransom until the war lay down its burdens. That [is the rule?]. If God had wished, He would have taken vengeance on them, but He is testing some of you with others. The deeds of those killed in the path of God are not in vain. [47:5] He will guide them and improve their situation."[84]

These four categories of verses on the subject of conduct toward non-Muslims reveal some interesting patterns. The fourth category contains the classic militant qur'ānic war verses calling for the destruction of idolaters and the surrender of non-Muslim monotheists, but the first category shows how, contrary to the classical Muslim "evolutionary theory," nonmilitant instructions appear to range from early Meccan through at least the early to middle Medinan periods.

The second category demonstrates how, at least among certain Muslim factions, the traditional pre-Islamic Arabian restrictions on fighting remained of great importance and were hard to uproot. The third category shows just how divided the Muslim community was over the command to wage war and suggests that different groups took opposing stands for a variety of reasons.

Taken together, the verses among the four categories reveal how the transition from pre-Islamic to Islamic systems of personal and community identity, social structure, governance, and conduct toward outsiders was a painful process. Pre-Islamic fighting was nonideological and was conducted either for material gain or to retaliate or exact revenge on unrelated or distant kinship groups. Responsibility to engage in war was a necessary component of kinship responsibility and tribal solidarity. Fighting in the fully developed Islamic system, on the other hand, became a highly ideological issue despite the added benefit of material gain in the form of spoils.[85] Motivation to engage in war moved from economic incentive and kinship commitment to the ideological responsibility of religious commitment, and it created the awkward situation in which new Muslims were commanded to fight against members of their own intimate kinship groups because of their new religious affiliation. Religious affiliation replaced kinship affiliation as the religious community replaced the tribe, but the transition was difficult and, as will be noted below, never entirely successful.

What we have seen in these qur'ānic verses are signposts along the way of that difficult transitional path from old Arabian to Islamic norms of war in the passage from *jāhiliyya* to Islam. We can be assured that such a major transition was not smooth but, rather, suffered the rough effects of bumps and potholes found in the path of any major journey. Once the excursion was completed, the story associated with it became enriched in the telling. Many of the old bumps were smoothed over and potholes filled in, but the continued existence of the ancient qur'ānic signposts always offers the possibility of critically reexamining the exegetical filling. We have observed how the Qur'ān may be read to suggest a different narrative regarding the evolution of ideological war in the religious civilization of Islam. The transition was not smooth but, rather, tumultuous as the old and new systems collided and clashed. Now that a fuller portrait of that transition has been begun, it remains to flesh out the picture and explain why and how it developed as it did.

PART III

The Oral Tradition

The Ḥadīth, which is sometimes likened to the "Oral Torah" of Judaism,[1] represents the "words, deeds, and tacit approvals attributed to the Prophet, as well as descriptions of his person, developed through a number of stages."[2] After the death of the Prophet, scriptural revelations ceased, and along with them, Muḥammad's personal interpretation as well as his personal guidance. The Qur'ān—the record of those revelations that had been recited by Muḥammad to the community—remained as a guide, but the fixed text of the Qur'ān could not answer all the questions that naturally arose within the new Muslim community with regard to proper religious ritual, personal behavior, and law. No more direct divine guidance was forthcoming, so Muḥammad's surviving companions tried to understand the meanings of Scripture as best they could. Without a direct scriptural answer to the many queries that were made regarding a wide range of issues, early Muslims naturally looked also to the acts and statements of their recently deceased prophet as models according to which Islamic behavior could be molded. This practice was no Islamic innovation, for the inclination to look toward a tribal leader's person and behavior for guidance was a common aspect of pre-Islamic culture. Sunni Islam, however, eventually narrowed the concept down almost exclusively to the sayings and acts of Muḥammad.[3]

Muḥammad had made a powerful impression on his contemporaries, and his followers naturally spoke about him as they engaged in conquest and governance far beyond the confines of the Ḥijāz. It was quite natural that new followers and conquered peoples wished to learn about the Prophet under whom the new world power began, and it was equally natural that the conquerors wished to tell of their great founder and leader. *Ḥadīth* means "a piece of information," "narrative," or "account," and the brief accounts about the Prophet that make up the stuff of the literature known as Al-Ḥadīth, or "the Tradition," are likewise called *ḥadīths*, or "traditions."[4] These traditions remained largely in oral form for well over a century until they were reduced to writing in official collections. The Ḥadīth par excellence, as known today, represents the *sunna*, "the 'beaten track'—the custom and practice"[5] of the prophet Muḥammad. The *sunna* refers to Muḥammad's acts and statements, which are considered authoritative for the determination of proper Islamic behavior. These prophetic acts and teachings were remembered in the form of short narratives and anecdotes (*ḥadīths*) preserved in the hearts and minds of Muḥammad's surviving contemporaries and their descendants and students.[6]

These human vessels of the prophetic *sunna*, the "traditionists" (*muḥaddithūn*), were soon spread beyond Mecca and Medina, the cities of Muḥammad's religious mission. They spread throughout most of the Fertile Crescent; so seekers of religious knowledge and behavior traveled in search of traditions in order to learn from them.[7] As the demand for traditions among the seekers grew, the supply of traditions grew to meet it, and the huge growth in the number of *ḥadīths* is exactly the problem that has come to plague both traditional Muslim and modern Western scholars, although not in the same way, in their reading and use of the Ḥadīth. Different schools of thought and practice authorized their various and sometimes contradictory positions by citing dicta that were purported to have originated in the prophet Muḥammad himself.[8] When no prophetic traditions (*ḥadīths*) could be found to support their positions, they were not infrequently created.

With the passing of time, the legendary status of the Prophet naturally increased, even to the point that his acts and teachings were considered inherently infallible or protected from error,[9] and the authority of the *sunna* grew in conjunction with his increasing status in the hearts of believers. The practice of forging traditions thereupon grew along with the increasing authority associated with the prophetic Tradition. The problem became so acute that a system of authentication had to be developed in order to determine which of the vast number of traditions could be relied on as genuine. The test of authenticity came to be that a *ḥadīth* about Muḥammad must have derived from an eyewitness companion of the Prophet himself, who passed the material through an unbroken chain of reliable transmitters until it was accurately recorded and preserved.[10]

The actual process of establishing a system of authentication and the overall function and flaws of that system do not concern us here,[11] but we must nevertheless extend the discussion somewhat in order to treat the problem of historical accuracy from the perspective of critical scholarship. The method that came to be accepted by Muslim scholars to determine authentic traditions centered on an analysis of the chain of authorities who relayed them. For a tradition to be acceptable, it had to be anchored by a chain of authoritative "*ḥadīth* tellers" (*muḥaddithūn*), which could demonstrate that the tradition derived without interruption directly from the Prophet. Every single authoritative tradition, therefore, consisted of both the actual information conveyed and its chain of authorities. The actual message (*matn*) of the tradition was irrelevant without a list of reliable tellers who could be determined to have transmitted it straight from the Prophet himself. A typical *ḥadīth* reads, "*D* related to me that *C* related to him on the authority of *B*, who said that he had heard *A* say that he was with the Prophet and heard him say (or saw him do). . . ." If adjacent members of the chain of authorities[12] personally could not have met together in order to pass on the information because of chronological or geographic irregularity, or any of the authorities cited were considered unauthoritative or irresponsible for any number of reasons, the tradition was deemed suspect, weak, or absolutely inauthentic, depending on the nature of the problem.

The actual message (*matn*), as opposed to the chain of authorities (*isnād*), of acceptable traditions was not usually open to criticism, however. The reason for this lack of investigation into the composition of the tradition is most likely that it was nearly impossible to establish effective universal criteria for critique. Once the message itself was open to legal or historical criticism, the entire corpus could be suspect.[13] As a result, a wide range of statements was possible as long as the chain of authorities was considered reliable and trustworthy. On the other hand, once highly credible chains of authorities were universally accepted, it was not difficult to fabricate "proper" or "sound" traditions that led all the way back to the Prophet.[14]

The Ḥadīth remained largely in oral form until the ninth century, when tens of thousands of individual traditions were collected and reduced to writing in dozens of collections. Committing the oral literature to writing marked a definitive stage in the evolution of the tradition, for it finally established those traditions in fixed forms, thereby slowing if not stopping the long process of change and embellishment that naturally occurred as they were told and retold in oral form. Six of these collections of prophetic traditions from the ninth century eventually took precedence over all others in classical Sunni Islam. Of these, the most authoritative works of *sunna* are the Ṣaḥīḥayn—the two most credible or authentic—of Muḥammad b. Ismāʿīl al-Bukhārī (d. 869 C.E.) and Muslim b. al-Ḥajjāj (d. 873 C.E.). Of slightly lesser importance are the four collections called *sunan* (plural of *sunna*)—the works of Abū Dāwud (d. 888), al-Tirmidhī (d. 892), al-Nasāʾī (d. 915), and Ibn Māja (d. 886). In addition to religious ritual, law, rules of commerce, and aspects of public and private behavior, they (and especially the collections of Bukhārī and Muslim) contain Qurʾān commentary and biographical information about the Prophet.

As indicated by the foregoing discussion, the problem of identifying authentic versus forged traditions was clearly recognized by Muslim scholars, and they attempted to solve the problem through a critique of the traditions' chains of transmitters. The result of their efforts, however, was uneven at best. The Muslim scholars themselves have noted that forged traditions managed to creep into the collections of even "sound" traditions. This intermixing did not create a major problem for Islamic law and practice in the long run, for only those traditions consistent with the developing positions of the major schools of law and behavior could have been integrated successfully into the mass of tradition in the first place, whether or not they represented the true words or acts of Muḥammad. Western scholars, however, when confronted with the obvious fact that many traditions were fabricated and yet fully integrated into the most valued collections of *ḥadīth*s, have tended to suspect the entire corpus.[15]

Western skepticism has centered on the traditions that are chiefly legal in character, in which both the motives and the signs of falsification are sometimes quite apparent. But Peters and others have raised the question whether that skepticism should be applied as rigorously to the nonlegal material, which describes, often as an aside, other aspects of the history of the earliest period of Islam.[16] Since the issues over which the fabricated traditions were invented seem to have been restricted largely to legal and political controversies, even those inauthentic traditions would have had to be couched in terms consistent with early Muslim society and its worldview in order to be accepted into the corpus of traditions making up the Ḥadīth. That is, even the spurious material would faithfully exhibit aspects of Islamic culture that could be deemed authentic from a historical or anthropological perspective. In the worst-case scenario, such material would reflect the realia of ninth-century Iraq. In the best-case scenario, it would reflect the realia of seventh-century Arabia during the obscure period of transition from the pre-Islamic to the early Islamic eras.

The same type of raw material, the individual *ḥadīth*s or building blocks that in particular form became the *sunna* of the prophet Muḥammad, also was formed into other genres of early literature such as the *maghāzī*—the expeditions and raids of the early Muslim community—and the *sīra*, or "biography" of the Prophet. The *maghāzī* resemble the form and content of the pre-Islamic accounts of tribal battles and manliness (the *ayyām al-ʿarab*) discussed previously[17] but modified as it was influenced by the cultural and religious overlay of early Islam. Both the *maghāzī* and the *sīra* contain traditions that treat the history of Muḥammad's military forays, and it is not always clear how to differentiate between the two types of collections.[18] Thus, the problem of terminology in general is raised, for such terms as *maghāzī* and *siyar* (plural of *sīra*) are sometimes used interchangeably, while at other times they are used to differentiate between types of warlike expeditions. Bukhārī, for example, has separate chapters entitled "Jihād"and "Maghāzī" in his *Ṣaḥīḥ* while the other major collections do not. Some collections call their chapters on war *jihād wasiyar*, while others title them simply *jihād*. It is most likely that the terms *maghāzī*, *sīra*, and *sunna* had a good deal of semantic overlap when they were used in different locations and periods to label collections or types of traditions, as the *ḥadīth* literature went through its own internal development from primitive to more highly developed stages.[19]

It is clear that legendary (i.e., not only legal) material about Muḥammad in the literature was also forged, which can be discerned in its most obvious form among the many descriptions of miracles ascribed to him. Such a problem of forgery does not concern us here, for we are not concerned about whether a miracle actually occurred, whether a certain raid took place at a certain date or time, or even whether it took place at all. Neither are we concerned with the numbers of fighters or even, in most cases, with the actual conduct of battle during war. We are, rather, seeking attitudes and visions about fighting in the Tradition. For our purposes, there is no need to differentiate between traditions found in collections labeled *sīra*, *maghāzī*, or *sunna*,[20] as long as they may be considered fairly representative of what, for lack of better terminology, we consider emerging "classical" or "orthodox" Islam.[21]

FIVE

The Prophetic Sunna

It should not be surprising, given the history of early Islam during the lifetime of Muḥammad, that the canonical collections of prophetic *sunna* contain a great deal of material on warring. Most of the material, however, tends to treat actual warfare rather than ideas about war. It naturally focuses on the behavior and discourse of Muḥammad through his own involvement in the political and military as well as religious affairs of the young Muslim polity. Most of the material, therefore, is irrelevant for our purposes. It tends to center on the treatment of prisoners and noncombatants, rules of distributing spoils, the role of female believers in the enterprise of war, the treatment of riding animals and equipment used in battle, the practice of praying or calling out to God during or before battle, and many individual incidents associated with specific raids and expeditions. On the other hand, the tradition literature also provides some information about the value of warring in the path of God, furnishes the beginning of a definition for the idiom "in the path of God," and provides some incidental information about attitudes toward warring in general.

The Merits of Warring in the Path of God

The prophetic *sunna*, in a quite unsystematic way, provides hierarchies of value for specific activities that may be considered religious acts or acts of devotion (*ʿibādāt*). Such hierarchies are found throughout the various collections of tradition literature, and they are inconsistent in their conclusions. The term *jihād* finds a prominent place in many of these hierarchical statements, and this *jihād* invariably means fighting in the path of God. The opening *ḥadīth* of the chapter "The Book of Jihād" in the most highly respected collection of traditions, for example, starts off with a faithful follower of the Prophet asking, "What is the best deed (*ayyul-ʿamal afḍal*)?" Muḥammad's answer here is, "Prayers at their proper times." The question is then asked, "And then what?" to which the reply is given, "filial piety." The third item is "*jihād* in the path of God."[1]

Another tradition slightly further along in the same collection raises the status of fighting to the top of the list: "A man came to God's messenger and said: 'Show me an act equal to *jihād*.' [Muḥammad] replied: 'I cannot find one.'"[2] In other traditions, raiding or *jihād* is considered "better than the world and all that is in it."[3] Ascribing exceptional merit to engaging in raids or war on behalf of the Umma may be found throughout *ḥadīth* literature.[4] The large number of traditions ascribing great merit for engaging in warring acts on behalf of the community has virtually no dissenting traditions to temper it. It seems to reflect a view that had become universal by the time that the oral traditions were committed to writing.

Reward for Those Engaging in War

Those who engage in sanctified war receive great rewards for their involvement. They will gain deserved material spoils and rewards when successful in the campaigns, and if they are killed or even wounded while warring in the path of God, they will be admitted to paradise.[5] "Any slave [of God] whose feet get covered with dust in the path of God, the Fire will not touch him."[6] The reward for martyrdom while engaging in war in the path of God is stressed greatly, even if the victim dies while not actually engaged on the battlefield,[7] and as many as seventy members of one's family who would have been doomed to hellfire will be ensured entry into paradise because of the intercession of the martyr in the path of God.[8] "The Prophet said: No slave [of God] who dies and has goodness with God wants to return to the world, even if he would have the world and all that is in it, except the martyr (*illā al-shahīd*), for when he sees the greatness of martyrdom (*faḍl al-shahāda*), he will want to return to the world and be killed again."[9] Muḥammad is also cited as having said, "By the One in Whose hand is my soul, I would love to be killed in the path of God and be resurrected, then be killed and then resurrected, then be killed and then resurrected, then be killed."[10] A well-known idiom teaches that "Paradise lies under the shade of swords."[11] Angels shade martyred warriors with their wings, and all who die in battle automatically enter paradise.[12]

The historical-political underpinning of these traditions is impossible to ferret out with any sense of accuracy. They clearly provide solace for fighters and their dependents for the dangerous job of making war, thereby serving as incentive and encouragement for the necessity of warring on behalf of Islam. On the other hand, such encouragement also suggests a certain (and not unnatural) resistance to fighting among Muslims who, for whatever reason, preferred not to engage in combat.

Resistance to Fighting

The tradition literature indeed records that not all were willing to engage in warring, but such traditions are few. "He who dies without fighting or believing in [the merit of] fighting dies as a kind of dissenter."[13] "One who does not fight, supply a warrior, or look properly after a warrior's family while he is away, God will bring upon him a sudden calamity."[14] It is clear that these traditions were responding to a certain lack of enthusiasm for warring. The community was clearly not all of one mind on the matter. However, the number of traditions in this category are quite small, suggesting that by the time of their collection there was little open dissent from the mainstream view about the merits of engaging in military campaigns in the path of God.

Deferments

While the Ḥadīth universally advocates warring in the path of God, it does note that certain individuals have deferments. The most famous case is that associated by the Tradition with the occasion of the revelation of *sūra* 4:95: "Those believers who sit [at home], other than the disabled, are not on an equal level with those who strive in the path of God (*al-mujahidūn fī sabīl Allah*) with their possessions and their lives. God prefers those who strive with their possessions and their lives to those who sit [at home]. God has promised good to each, but God distinguished those who strive above those who sit with a great reward."[15]

According to the nearly universal interpretation found in the Qur'ān commentaries, the Ḥadīth, and the *asbāb al-nuzūl* literature, this verse was originally revealed lacking the words "other than the disabled (*ghayr ūlīl-ḍarar*)." Muḥammad was immediately approached by a blind man by the name of ʿAmr (or ʿAbdallah) Ibn Umm Maktūm who was present when the verse was revealed and who complained that his disability, through no fault of his own, would keep him from attaining the highest rewards. Thereupon, Muḥammad immediately received the additional phrase of the revelation, which provided for physical deferments from warring.[16]

Sūra 24:62 is similarly taken to provide for certain deferments from warring: "The believers who [truly] believe in God and His Messenger [are those who], when engaged in an issue of common concern with [Muḥammad], do not leave until they ask permission of him. Those who do ask permission of him [truly] believe in God and His Messenger. So when they ask permission of you for some reason of theirs, grant whomever among them desires [to leave], and ask God to forgive them, for God is Forgiving, Merciful."[17] Bukhārī associates this verse with Muḥammad's giving permission to a newlywed to avoid battle and return home.[18]

In a fascinating *ḥadīth*, Muḥammad is cited as telling a story about a prophet (*nabiyy^{un} min al-ʾanbiyāʾ*) who, before going into battle (*ghazw*), forbade anyone who had not consummated his marriage, finished building his own house, or seen the offspring of his own flocks to follow him into battle.[19] Muḥammad also sends home a young man to be with his parents rather than engage in *jihād*. When asked permission by the young man to accompany him, Muḥammad asks whether he has parents. When he answers in the affirmative, Muḥammad tells him, "Strive on their behalf."[20]

These traditions, along with many others restricting certain behaviors associated with war, demonstrate a certain maturity with regard to the complexities of policy regarding war. The issue of deferments does not appear in any way as a response to organized factions resisting war or its engagement. On the contrary, the tone of the Tradition in general is one of near universal agreement regarding the need to engage in war in the path of God and the merit for doing so. It exhibits almost none of the ambiguity apparent from the Qurʾānic material on warring.

Motivation for Fighting

A number of traditions, however, exhibit disappointment with the motivations of many warriors for engaging in battle.

> Muʿādh b. Jabal reported on the authority of the Apostle of God: There are two kinds of fighting. One [in which the warrior] seeks out the face of God, obeys the leader, gives one's prized possessions [presumably on behalf of warring], is obliging toward one's companions, and avoids iniquity. There is great reward [for him], whether asleep or awake. As for the one who fights for glory and to be seen and heard, who disobeys the leader and is immoral (*waʿafsada fīl-arḍ*), he will not return with much [reward].[21]

Similarly, if one fights "in the path of God" only for material reward, he will receive no reward at all.[22] A great deal of material centers also on the problem of those who misappropriate the spoils of war.[23] Such discussion suggests that, while warring seems to be universally acclaimed, a significant number of fighters went out to battle for reasons that were consistent with pre-Islamic times—not with Islam. They sought individual glory, prestige, and material advancement. These motivations became unacceptable for fighting "in the path of God," and it is through such traditions that we may begin to define what "holy war" means in early Islam according to the tradition literature. "Fighting in the path of God," whether the term used is "striving" (*jihād*) or "warring" (*qitāl*), is fighting for the right purpose and with the right motivation:

> A man came to the Prophet and asked: "One who fights furiously, one who fights valiantly, one who fights in order to be seen; which of these is in the path of God?" He answered: "One who fights so that God's word will be superior is in the path of God."[24]

The old purposes and motivations of the pre-Islamic period are no longer acceptable when fighting "in the path of God."[25]

The traditions in the canonical Ḥadīth on war (those six collections referred to previously) can be summarized simply. Great merit is ascribed to fighting in the path of God. Those who engage in such combat are guaranteed entrance into paradise. Not all Muslims of warrior age and fitness were willing to engage in such combat despite the great personal advantages ascribed to doing so. However, the overwhelming majority, it seems, were quite amenable to engage in warring, but their motivations often reflected the old pre-Islamic interest in advancing personal prestige and gaining material wealth rather than the religio-spiritual benefit of warring in the path of God.

This assessment does not contradict the general conclusions reached from our analysis of the qur'ānic evidence. The major difference lies in the consistent and nearly universal stance of the traditions in the canonical collections promoting warfare in the path of God. This stance, in turn, corresponds with the militant school evidenced also in the Qur'ān, which platform became that of Islam as a whole.

In conclusion, the traditions in the canonical collections tend to confirm the victory of militant Islam over the non- or less-militant factions of the earlier period reflected in the verses we have examined from the Qur'ān. Aside from this, the material of the Ḥadīth does not add much information to our study, despite the fact that it often treats specific incidents or prophetic statements associated with individual campaigns, such as the ample material in the long chapter on *maghāzī* by Bukhārī. But these traditions simply treat acts of warfare per se, adding little to our quest for material shedding light on conceptual views of warring. It will be left to the *sīra* material—the traditions carefully organized in chronological relation to the history of Muḥammad's mission—to clarify some of the historical issues that must be fleshed out in order that we can make sense of the development of the concept of holy war in early Islam.

SIX

The Sīra

The *sīra* literature is a genre of *ḥadīth* literature that was edited into the form of a biography of Muḥammad. The building blocks of tradition that make up this literature were transmitted according to the same general processes as that of the Ḥadīth, except that the various traditions were, in the case of the biographical literature, arranged chronologically—according to what the compilers determined (or decided) was to have been the outline history of Muḥammad's life and mission. Rizwi Faizer is critical of the chronological accuracy represented by the literature, suggesting that the pool of traditions from which the biographies were crafted were uncontextualized, thereby allowing the compilers to place individual traditions in chronological relation to one another in ways that promoted their own particular bias.[1] The surviving biographies nevertheless agree on a basic chronology of the prophetic mission, which is followed here. There can be no question that some of the material was forged in order to fill gaps in his biography, provide appropriate historical contexts for certain qur'ānic revelations, extol the miracles associated with the Islamic Prophet par excellence, and promote certain partisan ideas or views by associating them with Muḥammad himself.[2] Traditionists felt freer about relating *ḥadīths* of dubious authority about the biography of Muḥammad than they did about relating Muḥammad's utterances in the form of prophetic *sunna*. By the time that stringent measures were taken at least a century after Muḥammad's death to eliminate problematic biographical material by applying the rules of Ḥadīth criticism, it was too late to identify, separate, and do away with it.[3]

Notwithstanding the problematic nature of the biographical literature for reconstructing the history of Muḥammad's mission, some material—such as that describing the setbacks, failures, and humiliation of Muḥammad and his community and the detailed information about his opponents and loyal allies—suggests the preservation of actual historical data. The difficulty is in devising a consistent methodology that can successfully extract historical information from the embellishments of the imagination and the agendas of the many different parties that received, transmitted, and recorded the traditions. Our purpose is not to reconstruct historical occasions but, rather, to establish ideas as expressed, often innocently, by the literature. Although the *sīra* has been considered to be "a record of the life of [Muḥammad's] contemporary society,"[4] because of the fluidity of the material's oral nature until it was reduced to writing sometime in the eighth century and because of all the *tendenzen* just mentioned, we cannot rely on it as an accurate representation of the ideas of Muḥammad's generation on warring and warfare without confirmation from other sources, such as the Qur'ān.

The biographical literature on the Prophet was first collected by compilers in the early eighth century under the title *maghāzī*.[5] The earliest extant collection is that of Muḥammad b. Isḥāq (d.768), whose original *Kitāb al-Maghāzī* has disappeared but can be found essentially intact in the recension by ʿAbdul-Malik Ibn Hishām (d. 833–834) known as *Sīrat [Muḥammad] Rasūl Allāh*.[6] It is Ibn Isḥāq's work known through Ibn Hishām that is relied on here,[7] with occasional cross-references from the somewhat later collections of Muḥammad b. ʿUmar al-Wāqidī (d. 823),[8] his student Muḥammad b. Saʿd (d. 845),[9] and the canonical Ḥadīth.

Muḥammad at Mecca

When Muḥammad first began preaching in response to receiving divine revelations, the Meccan populace, all of which is portrayed as belonging to the extended Quraysh tribe that controlled and populated Mecca, did not oppose him until he began berating their gods and insulting their ancestors who died as unbelievers.[10] Quite early on, says Ibn Isḥāq, Muslims and idolaters came to blows. One occasion was when a small band of Muḥammad's followers was rudely interrupted in the midst of prayer. The result was more serious than merely a pushing match, for one of Muḥammad's companions, Saʿd b. Abī Waqqāṣ, struck one of the idolaters with the jawbone of a camel and drew blood.[11] This Saʿd is described as hotheaded in the *sīra*, for not only is he distinguished for being the first Muslim to shed blood, he is also credited as the first Muslim to shoot an arrow on an expedition.[12] He was proud enough of his actions that he composed a poem distinguishing his act.[13]

Muḥammad, on the other hand, although he is harshly criticized by his Meccan opponents for insulting their idolatrous way of life, is described even during the most heated argument as refraining from any kind of physical violence. This description is significant, given the fact that all the available accounts of Muḥammad's career were written and redacted by the winning Muslims, whose very success was predicated by their willingness (or desire) to engage actively in war. Muḥammad is invariably portrayed as steadfast in his refusal to respond to insult with violence. One of his most violent opponents in the heat of argument berated him as not being *jahūl.*[14] The *sīra* describes him as remaining silent in the face of humiliations and terrible insults hurled at him by his opponents in the early period.[15] Similarly, his famous companion and Qur'ān reciter, ʿAbdallah Ibn Masʿūd, is said to have recited some of Muḥammad's revelations to the idolatrous Quraysh, knowing that he would be beaten for doing so. He does, according to the tradition, recite, and is indeed beaten in the face. There is no discussion of violent reprisal or even defense with regard to this incident.[16]

The Muslims are portrayed in this early period as being regularly beaten and occasionally even tortured by their Meccan opponents, with virtually no recourse for the injurious treatment they received. They assuredly are not portrayed as pacifists, as the case of Saʿd b. Abī Waqqāṣ demonstrates, but they most certainly refrained in most cases from violence in reaction to such harmful treatment. In at least one case, a person is killed simply for belonging to the new followers of Muḥammad.[17] This was an exceptional case, however, because kinship responsibility for the *lex talionis* generally prevented such excesses. In this early period, non-Muslim clansmen of Muḥammad's followers continued to protect their kin from killings.[18] The harassment and beatings continued, nevertheless, until a large group of followers fled Mecca for Abyssinia. It is revealing that, according to the poem preserved by Ibn Isḥāq, one of those who fled recited:

> My heart refuses, I will not lie, to fight them.
> So too, refuse my fingertips [to fight].
> How can I fight a group of people who educated you
> About truth, that you not mix it with falsehood. . . .[19]

After it became clear to the Meccan opponents of Muḥammad that the Abyssinian negus was protecting Muḥammad's refugee followers, a Meccan delegation was sent to appeal to him to withdraw his protection. The pretense for the request was that the refugees had forsaken traditional religion for a newly invented one, thereby rejecting both their own custom and the Christianity practiced in Abyssinia. The negus agreed to consider withdrawing his protection but only after having an audience with the refugees. After hearing the refugees recite a section of the Qur'ān and noting its similarity to his own Scripture, the New Testament, he refused to rescind his protection. When the Muslims were asked by the negus to describe their religion, they distinguished themselves from the old pre-Islamic system in a number of ways. Their representative, Jaʿfar b. Abī Ṭālib, is made to say in the Sīra,

> We were an ignorant [pre-Islamic] people (*kunnā qawm ahlal-jāhiliyya*), worshipping idols, eating improperly butchered meat, committing abominations, breaking kinship relations, treating guests badly, and our strong devoured our weak. We lived that way until God sent us a messenger whose lineage, truth, trust, and modesty we came to know. He called us to God, to acknowledge His unity, worship Him, and to give up the stones and idols that we and our fathers had been worshipping. He commanded us to be truthful in speech, trustworthy, to honor ties of kinship, be hospitable, and refrain from forbidden things and bloodshed. He forbade us to commit abominations, speak falsely, devour the property of orphans, and slander the unblemished reputation of women. . . .[20]

The distinctions made in this monologue between the ways of Islam and those of the *jāhiliyya* are revealing, for it considers the early ways to be full of lies and violent behavior in association with idolatry. Muslims, as opposed to Meccans of the *jāhiliyya*, honored kinship ties but refrained from violence. Because these earliest Muslims fled to Abyssinia before the Hijra to Medina and the creation of the new Muslim Umma, they remained organized purely according to the old pre-Islamic system of kinship ties. One of the very traits they cite to describe their difference from their idolatrous brethren was refraining from bloodshed. This may also be an oblique critique of the violent Qurayshite behavior directed to their own fellow tribesmen who followed Muḥammad, for as we shall observe below, one of the most important social-moral traits of the pre-Islamic period was fidelity to one's kinship ties.

On the other hand, the *sīra* celebrates when ʿUmar b. al-Khaṭṭāb became Muslim because he was so strong and powerful. As a new Muslim, ʿUmar fought the Quraysh until he and the Muslims were allowed to pray at the Kaʿba.[21] Different reports provide conflicting stories of his conversion, but he is invariably depicted as a powerful and confident man who easily wielded his sword both before and after becoming a Muslim. He was considered a serious threat to Islam and even somewhat of a bully before his conversion but also a good potential convert. According to one narrative, ʿUmar, before becoming a Muslim, once approached the home in which Muḥammad was staying with his sword girded. Muḥammad's powerful companion and uncle Ḥamza suggested that he be allowed in and that if he threatened the Prophet's life they would grab ʿUmar's own sword and kill him with it.[22] In another narrative, ʿUmar is depicted as single-handedly fighting a group of Quraysh after announcing that he had become a Muslim.[23] With the two powerful men, Ḥamza and ʿUmar, now both Muslims, the followers of Muḥammad were less physically threatened by their opponents, although they continued to be persecuted through boycotts and other nonphysical means.

From Restraint to Defensive Fighting

The immediate danger of physical threats was mitigated by the conversion of ʿUmar, but Muḥammad's official protection was significantly eroded soon after with the death of his influential wife, Khadīja, and his powerful uncle Abū Ṭālib, both of whom died in the same year.[24] Muḥammad attempted to procure protection from tribal units outside the immediate influence of Mecca, such as the Thaqīf from al-Ṭā'if, the Banū Ḥanīfa, and the Banū ʿĀmir b. Ṣaʿṣaʿa, but to no avail. Shortly after that, however, some residents of the oasis town of Yathrib (later known as Medina) met Muḥammad at the trading fairs near Mecca and a few joined his following. Twelve of these Medinans, the first of the so-called helpers, or *anṣār*, pledged themselves to follow him and his religion at a place just outside Mecca known as al-ʿAqaba. This occurrence is known as the "First ʿAqaba," and it is clearly indicated that the duty of warring was not included among the responsibilities of the pledge.[25] At the "Second ʿAqaba" the next year, many more Medinan *anṣār* returned and committed themselves to support and protect Muḥammad physically, even through fighting, against any of his enemies.[26] As one of them, an al-ʿAbbās b. ʿUbāda, told Muḥammad, "By God who sent you in truth, if you wish, we will fight against the people of Minā tomorrow with our swords."[27] This marks the first mention in the Sīra of organized fighting by followers of Muḥammad. It is noteworthy that it is mentioned in conjunction with Muḥammad's upcoming Hijra, or "emigration," from Mecca to Medina and that it is the Medinans (the *anṣār*) who are the first to demonstrate their willingness as a community to go to war.

This willingness to engage in warring is then immediately confirmed, according to the Sīra, by a revelation commanding the permissibility of war. In the words of the Sīra:

> Before the pledge of al-ʿAqaba, the Messenger of God had not been given permission for war or allowed to shed blood. On the contrary, he was commanded to call [people] to God, to be patient in the face of offense, and to turn away from the ignorant. The Quraysh had persecuted those Meccans [*muhājirīn*] who had followed him to such an extent that they had seduced them away from their religion and expelled them from their

> town. They were either seduced from their religion, tormented at their hands, or had to flee as fugitives from their own homes either to Abyssinia or to Medina. In any case, when the Quraysh were insolent against God, rejected the dignity that He asked of them, called His prophet a lier, and tormented and expelled those who worshipped Him, proclaimed His unity, believed in His prophet, and clung to His religion, God gave permission to His prophet to engage in fighting and be victorious over those who tyrannized them and oppressed them. The first verse revealed that permitted war for him and allowed fighting and the shedding of blood against those who oppressed them, according to what I have received from ʿUrwa b. al-Zubayr and other religious scholars, is [*sūra* 22:39–41]: "Permission is given to those who fight because they have been treated cruelly, for God is indeed able to give them aid—those who have been expelled from their homes without justification only because they say: Our Lord is God. For if God had not warded some people off by means of others, then hermitages, churches, and places of worship and prostration in which God's name is often mentioned would have been destroyed. God helps those who help Him—God is strong, almighty—those who, if We empower them, observe prayer, pay the poor tax, command right and forbid evil, God is eternal." This means: I have allowed them to fight because they have been treated cruelly. They have committed no sin against others simply by worshipping God. When they gain the upper hand, they will observe prayer, pay the poor tax, command right and forbid evil—this is in reference to the Prophet and his companions. Then God revealed [*sūra* 2:193]: "Fight them until there is no more temptation (*fitna*)"—that is, until a believer is no longer tempted away from his religion—"and religion is God's"—that is, when God is worshipped and nothing other than Him is worshipped.[28]

According to the Sīra, the Meccan Quraysh had a different perspective on the matter than that expressed here, for they were of the opinion that Muḥammad had decided to wage war against them (*waʿarafū annahum qad ajmaʿa liḥarbihim*).[29] When the Qurayshite leaders realized that Muḥammad had gained a power base in the settlement of Yathrib (Medina) located outside their range of influence, they met together to decide how to respond. They acknowledged that once the conflict with Muḥammad was no longer an internal tribal affair (Muḥammad was also a member of the tribe), the situation had become dangerous to all the extended kinship groups within it. From their perspective, therefore, Muḥammad was not at all restricted to defensive engagements. As it in fact turned out, it was Muḥammad and not the Meccan Quraysh who initiated the battles that subsequently ensued between them.

At the point at which the Qurayshite leaders considered Muḥammad to be a major threat to the stability of Mecca, they decided to solve the problem in a manner consistent with pre-Islamic norms. A representative of every kinship group of the larger tribe (aside, of course, from Muḥammad's immediate kinship group) would participate in his murder. Because his own clan could not possibly take revenge against all the various groups in Mecca for the killing, the *talion* would be averted and Muḥammad's kin would be forced to accept blood money compensation, thereby putting an end to Muḥammad's threat and avoiding a long and protracted kinship war.[30] That they were not successful, according to the Sīra, was due to miraculous powers vouchsafed to Muḥammad so that he could flee the Qurayshite plot.

Muḥammad at Medina

The Sīra notes within the context of discussion about Muḥammad's immediate arrival in Medina that he prepared for war "in response to God's command to him for *jihād* against his enemy and fighting (*qitāl*) those nearby Arab idolaters whom God commanded him to fight, this occurring 13 years after God called him."[31] However, the first time Muḥammad actually went out to raid, according to the Sīra, was fully twelve months after his arrival.[32] A number of forays were launched at this time, but no actual fighting occurred. It is noted that only those believers who followed Muḥammad from Mecca to Medina, the so-called *muhājirūn*, or "emigrants," were engaged in these outings, and the Sīra makes it a point to state this clearly.[33]

The first successful raid was the infamous raid led by ʿAbdallah b. Jaḥsh during which a Meccan was killed on the last day of the Sacred Month of Rajab.[34] The attackers knew, according to the Sira, that they were breaking an ancient taboo by fighting on that day, but they realized that they would lose their prize if they waited another day before the attack.[35] They therefore decided to attack despite the ancient prohibition, and succeeded, but not without killing one of the Meccan defenders. This incident caused a major crisis in the young Muslim community in Medina. Muḥammad denied having ordered them to fight during the sacred month, "and their own Muslim brothers rebuked them severely for what they had done." Their Qurayshite opponents, of course, used the transgression to their political advantage and condemned Muḥammad and his followers for violating the ancient taboo against warring during the Sacred Months. The crisis was averted only after Muḥammad received a new revelation allowing fighting during the Sacred Months [*sūra* 2:217].

According to the traditional view of the evolution of the Islamic concept of warring, this incident marks an acceleration in the consistent and divinely guided linear development from no war to unrestricted warfare. The incident must be understood differently however. The raiding party was clearly caught in a bind unforeseen by Muḥammad when he sent them out, and the raiders argued over what to do until they eventually decided to attack. Once the decision was made, however, they are depicted as trying to kill as many of the enemy as possible even though it was during the Sacred Month.[36] Such a conclusion does not appear to be a compromise but, rather, a confident position completely disregarding the sanctity of the old pre-Islamic institution of the Sacred Months. The majority of the raiders must have held this position, and their view prevailed over those whose did not. It should be noted that the raiders' willingness not only to set out on an expedition (and during the Sacred Month of Rajab!) but also to engage the Meccans head on in battle certainly distinguished the type of man who volunteered or was sent by Muḥammad to participate in such an action in the first place. Such a person was more likely to advocate violent action than those who did not volunteer to participate or those who were not chosen to do so.[37] Their position on the Sacred Months, however, was clearly in conflict with that of Muḥammad and most of their Muslim brethren in Medina at that time. Muḥammad's view changed only after receiving the new revelation, which was given, according to the tradition, in response to the raid of ʿAbdullah b. Jaḥsh. This evidence suggests that the community was not of one view and that some were clearly willing to stretch the old pre-Islamic restrictions to warring more than Muḥammad himself. Those in this category were the most likely to volunteer or be chosen to join raiding parties, for their very willingness to engage the enemy encouraged such a view. That many Muslims were greatly distressed by the breaking of the ancient taboo is stated clearly in the *Sīra*, for the new revelation was said to have dispelled the fear of those who still adhered to the ancient tradition of honoring the Sacred Months.[38]

Immediately following the story of this raid in the biographical sources is the narrative of the great expedition of Badr (*ghazwat badr al-kubrā*). This victorious expedition brought Muḥammad and his followers great distinction and success in the acquisition of spoils and prestige. When the Prophet called his followers to set out, however (and in this expedition the *anṣār* were included), some quickly complied while others were sluggish in their response. The reason given for the unevenness in response to Muḥammad's call was that the people did not think that the Messenger of God would actually go out to war.[39] The Quraysh, however, who had learned of his impending attack, were anxious to engage the Muslims and exact revenge for the successful raid of Ibn al-Ḥaḍramī's caravan.

When Muḥammad learned that the Quraysh were prepared for his attack, he asked his warriors' advice and was assured by the *muhājirūn* among them that they would stick with him. When he heard no response from the *anṣār*, which made up the majority of his community and his fighters, he specifically asked them as well. According to the Sīra, he was less assured of their faithfulness because they had pledged at ʿAqaba to protect him in defensive war but not necessarily to remain with him if he initiated an attack outside their territory in and around Medina. The spokesman for the *anṣār* assured him that they would not abandon him: "We are not against going with you to meet our enemy tomorrow, for we are patient in war, trustworthy in engaging [in battle]."[40]

Nevertheless, when the two parties met and the customary individual skirmishes began, the Quraysh refused to fight against the Medinan *anṣār* because in true fidelity to the pre-Islamic norm, they said, "We have nothing against you."[41] Only after both sides engaged fully in combat, did the *anṣār* have the opportunity to fight.

Until Badr, there were two distinct classes of Muslims with regard to fighting.[42] It is unlikely that the *anṣār* took part in any raids before Badr, but they made up some three-quarters of the Muslim fighting force at Badr.[43] The *muhājirūn*, on the other hand, did go out on expeditions, though largely unsuccessful before that time. This situation seems to represent the opposite from that which obtained at the Second ʿAqaba, where the *anṣār* were made to express perfect willingness to go into battle on behalf of Muḥammad while his Meccan followers were largely passive in the face of physical abuse and intimidation.[44] Although it is possible that the statements attributed to the *anṣār* at the Second ʿAqaba may be forged, they should not be dismissed so easily. In fact, the early situation in Mecca shows Muḥammad's followers refraining from organized defense or even any kind of aggressive behavior aside from certain exceptional individuals such as Saʿd, Ḥamza, and ʿUmar. As we may recall, Muḥammad himself refrains from responding physically, even to aggressive forms of public humiliation.[45] Their lack of response has been explained traditionally as a logical reaction of the powerless to physical threat. On the other hand, when aggressive believers such as Saʿd, Ḥamza, or ʿUmar physically responded to intimidation in Mecca, they were not harmed but, in fact, left alone. This fact suggests that it was more than practicality that governed the behavior of the early Muslims. As we have noted above, the Qurʾān itself is witness to a school of thought that sought to avoid physical aggression and solve issues purely through reasoned discussion or avoidance.[46] This view finds inadvertent support in the Sīra as well.

The change in attitude among Muḥammad's Meccan followers seems to have occured in relation to the Hijra to Medina. Any number of factors may have exerted an influence on the *muhājirūn* to begin engaging in warring behavior, including the realization of safety in a location far from Mecca, the willingness of the *anṣār* to defend Muḥammad and his followers, and the economic necessity of engaging in raiding once the *muhājirūn* found that they had no source of income in Medina. A likely contributing factor was the omnipresent element of kinship. While in Mecca, the early believers were to a large extent persecuted by their own tribal relations within the Quraysh, both from close and more distant kin. Given the pre-Islamic system of kinship solidarity prevalent even in the disturbed urban environment of Mecca, the believers had little choice but to adopt an ascetic view and be willing to suffer on behalf of their religion. It was, after all, their own kinship relations that were persecuting them, and it was almost inconceivable to define one's own kinship group as the enemy. Only certain individuals were willing or able to forgo the social and psychological need for kinship association. Once the community moved to Medina and was confronted with the immediacy of its new sociopolitical situation, however, the old Meccan kinship relations began to have much less impact. This diminished effect is evidenced by the Medina Agreement (see below) and perhaps even earlier by the institution of *mu'ākhāt*, or "brothering," in which members of different kinship groups were paired and thereafter shared mutual responsibilities.[47]

It was only later, at Badr, that Muḥammad is depicted in the Sīra as inciting his warriors with the promise that martyrs slain in battle will enter paradise. Following this promise are stories of exceptional cases of martyrdom, including the story of ʿAwf b. Ḥārith, who, purportedly because Muḥammad told him that God loves martyrdom, removed his armor and fought until he was killed.[48] A number of mythic stories entered into the narrative of the great battle of Badr. For example, Muḥammad turned the tide of battle by throwing a handful of pebbles at the enemy, angels descended from heaven and fought by the side of the Prophet, and Muḥammad handed a fighter whose sword broke a wooden cudgel, which turned miraculously into a gleaming sword. A great deal of information about the conduct of war, treatment of prisoners, and so on, may be found in the Badr material and in the narratives describing subsequent raids and battles.

My reading of the Sīra confirms that it arranged the disparate qur'ānic war verses in the traditional manner in order to conform to the then accepted theory of warring. This arrangement should not be surprising in a text reflecting the views of normative eighth- or ninth-century Islam. Prophetic biographies remained in fluid oral form for much longer than the Qur'ān, which was reduced to writing within a generation or two after Muḥammad's death, so that the former tend to reflect the views of eighth/ninth-century Islamic society. We have noted, however, that the Sīra nevertheless provides enough raw material not fitting into the traditional scenario to cause one to pause and reflect on the traditional model. Because we have reached the point after Badr where, according to the tradition, warring in the path of God was now required virtually without restriction, the material following Badr will not occupy us. The one area that must be examined in greater detail, however, is the transition from Mecca to Medina.

From Mecca to Medina: The Hijra as Transition Marker

Once translated as "flight" but today more accurately translated as "emigration," the term *hijra* involves more than a simple change of location. To the Muslim, *hijra* connotes a significant change in status transcending the mere geographical. On one level, it means a change of relationship to one's tribe. In the classic sense, "to make *hijra* was to leave one's tribe and attach oneself to the *ummah*."[49] On another level, the changed status may signify a religious or spiritual awakening as well. The prophet Abraham's *hijra*, for example, which because of his important role as the first monotheist assumes exceptional symbolic and paradigmatic significance in Islam, takes on mythic proportions as the first religious journey. According to Islamic tradition, Abraham's geographical *hijra* from the land of the East to Syria[50] also marked his spiritual journey from pagan to prophet.[51]

Muḥammad's Hijra to Medina also provides meaning at a multitude of levels. It assumes such importance in Islam that it marks the beginning of the counting of sacred time. The Islamic calendar begins with the beginning of the year in which Muḥammad moved to Medina,[52] and the transition of the Hijra marks a striking number of significant changes in the development of early Islam, from religious ritual to social legislation, even the quality and content of divine revelation, and, most certainly, concepts of warring.

Muḥammad was invited to Medina to mediate a bloody and irresolvable blood feud between the two main subgroups of the tribe of Banū Qayla, known as the Aws and the Khazraj. The root of the problem was probably competition over limited arable land under the stress of population growth, but, according to Watt, once violence entered the equation, the old pre-Islamic system of blood revenge that developed within and for the nomadic tribal system of the Arabian steppe caused havoc in the confined area in and around Medina. There were no vast expanses of desert in Medina to separate the kinship groups in conflict, so members were forced to be on constant guard against sudden attacks and were likely to be killed if they happened simply to wander into the wrong place at the wrong time.[53] This situation was making life in Medina virtually untenable, since most of the population groups of the settlement were allied with one or other of the two groups in conflict.

When some Medinans met Muḥammad at a trading fair outside Mecca, they recognized from what they had learned from the Jews of their town that he seemed to be a prophetic or perhaps even messianic figure. Ibn Isḥāq gives two reasons for their interest in joining up with Muḥammad. As the story goes, the Jews had been known to threaten their idolatrous neighbors when conflict arose between them by saying, "A prophet is being sent [to us] at any moment. His time is approaching. We will follow him and kill you with him [with his help] just like the killing of ʿĀd and Iram."[54] So when those Medinans recognized Muḥammad as a holy man, they believed him to be the prophet spoken about by the Jews and decided to join with him before he could come and lead the Jews against them. The second reason given in the Sīra is that Muḥammad offered hope to solve the terrible blood conflict dividing Medina. Those same Medinans who wished to join the early followers of Muḥammad are cited as saying: "We have left our people (*qawm*), for there is no people divided by hostility and wickedness as they. Perhaps God will unite them through you, so we will approach them and invite them to your leadership and propose that they join this religion, for if God unites them in it there can be no man more powerful than you."[55]

These Medinans returned to the fair the following year with more adherents to pledge their support at the First ʿAqaba, and a much larger contingent returned a year later for the second pledge at the Second ʿAqaba. With the support of these *anṣār* and with God's express permission given to fight immediately thereafter, Muḥammad told his followers to emigrate to Medina and followed them shortly afterward.[56]

What is both interesting and problematic about this key point in the narrative is that Muḥammad is granted protection by the entire Medinan community after only seventy-five Medinans pledged themselves to him at the Second ʿAqaba.[57] While the Sīra does claim that Muḥammad's followers promoted him in every kinship group within the settlement, and Ibn Saʿd cites a tradition in which a Medinan disciple calls on his nonbelieving kin to defend Muḥammad in order to maintain tribal honor,[58] that would hardly result in a strongly divided community suddenly embracing the presence of such a controversial Meccan taking authority in Medina. His few Medinan followers would certainly welcome him, and it could perhaps be argued that the Jews might withhold judgment until evaluating his prophetic claims, but feud or no feud, it is hardly reasonable to expect Medinan clan leaders and other traditional authorities to give up their positions voluntarily to an outsider whose only claim was prophethood believed in by a small and beleaguered following.

The Ḥadīth suggests that Muḥammad was known as a wise and honest arbitrator,[59] but his arrangement with Medina was not simply to come and arbitrate a dispute. The deal, rather, was for him to assume a position of significant political authority over most of the tribal groupings of the settlement, and this major innovation must have had some kind of grounding beyond merely his claim to prophethood. A reasonable answer to this puzzle has been suggested by R. B. Serjeant, who indicates that Muḥammad's Hijra, his establishing a formal Medina Agreement (see below), and the nature of his authority and office all point to a largely overlooked institution of the holy man (or *manṣab*) who establishes a sacred enclave (*ḥaram* or *ḥawṭa*), judges or arbitrates disputes between disparate and often conflicting tribes, and derives exceptional authority over broad tribal groupings in the process.[60] As Serjeant notes, such practice existed in Arabia with slight permutations from pre-Islamic times into the twentieth century. Muḥammad's authority for coming to Medina, establishing the formal Medina Agreement, and declaring Medina a *ḥaram*, or "sacred enclave,"[61] would thus derive not only from his claim to prophethood but also from his heritage as a son of the holy family of Mecca, which ran its own *ḥaram* from ancient times. Such a person, if successful, could establish a new *ḥaram* serving to link self-governing tribes not yielding their own sovereignty or the management of their own affairs but, nevertheless, committed to bringing disputes to the holy man and otherwise offering him protection to carry out his centralizing function. The status of the holy man in this arrangement has aspects that are both secular and religious. He is neutral enough to be accepted by disparate tribes, whether practicing traditional (idolatrous) Arabian religious traditions or following monotheistic practice.

We cannot yet establish a confident chronology for either the Medina Agreement or the date of his declaration of Medina as a sacred enclave. It is almost certain that Muḥammad could not have established such monumental changes immediately upon his arrival. The point, however, is that traditional pre-Islamic practice had already established a precedence for the acceptance of his position in Medina. His innovation, from the historical point of view, is in what would become of the institution of the central "holy man," the nature of the responsibilities to adhere between the disparate tribal groupings centralized by the system, and the development through such a system of a polity (for lack of a better term) that would begin to function in a unique manner in relation to the ancient system. These subtle innovations in traditional Arabian social structure would have an overwhelming impact on the nature of war in Islamic civilization.

The Medina Agreement

The "Constitution of Medina," as it has come to be called in most Western sources, is a document outlining the formal responsibilities that governed the relationships between the inhabitants of Medina after Muḥammad's arrival.[62] Because it was to serve as the legal basis for communal life in early Muslim Medina, some early form of it apparently was written down immediately. The Medina Agreement is a primary document of considerable importance but is also associated with a great deal of controversy. Its earliest provenance is in Ibn Isḥāq's Sīra, where it is placed chronologically immediately after Muḥammad's Hijra.[63]

Ibn Isḥāq gives no date for it, and Western scholarship is divided over whether it belongs to the earliest Medinan period or whether it represents the situation obtaining after the exile and destruction of the Jews of Medina or at least after the battle of Badr in 624.[64] Although presented in the Sīra as a single document, the repetitive nature of certain of its content, the linguistic variations in its descriptions of identical objects, and its particular organization strongly suggest that it is a composite document.[65] This likelihood explains the difficulty in its dating, for it probably includes aspects reflecting both pre- and post-Badr Medinan realia. Despite the continuing controversy over these points, critical scholarship overwhelmingly accepts its fundamental authenticity, based on its archaic style and certain peculiarities, which strongly counter any claim for an Umayyad or ʿAbbasid forgery.[66]

The major, and indeed revolutionary, contribution of the agreement is that it begins the process of creating a single community out of disparate kinship and religious groups under the authority or supervision of Muhammad. Although he probably did not intend it exactly as such in the first place,[67] it became the basis for the powerful institution of the Muslim Umma, which eventually unified diverse Arabian populations into an extremely effective and powerful religious, political, and military force.

The initial purpose of the agreement was to mediate the tribal conflicts raging in Medina: "Whenever you disagree about a matter, it must be referred to God and to Muḥammad."[68] This requirement is completely consistent with the system referred to by Serjeant's study of similar Arabian agreements, wherein tribes participating in such a pact retain most of their independent autonomy. In the case of the Medina Agreement established by Muḥammad, however, the goal evolved from the traditional purpose of mediating tribal conflicts to eliminating them entirely, and the mechanism for doing so was the creation of what has sometimes been called a "supertribe," in which a new determinant of relationship was to replace the old kinship ties: "A believer may not kill a believer on account of an unbeliever, and may not help an unbeliever against a believer. The security of God is one; the protection granted by the least of them is binding on [all] of them. The believers are in relationship with one another to the exclusion of [other] people."[69]

Despite the theocratic tone of this statement, the agreement established a single, common, political community made up of Muslims, Jews, and idolaters. It detailed no religious requirements but, rather, outlined political and military responsibilities ranging from the payment of blood money to mutual defense against outside aggression. As Peters describes its nature, "[T]he contracting parties did not embrace Islam: They did agree to recognize the authority of Muhammad, to accept him as the community leader and to abide by his political judgments. In so doing they were acknowledging, as was the Prophet himself, that they were one community, or *umma*, under God, Muhammad's God, not yet uniquely composed of Muslims, but committed to defend its own joint interests, or what was now newly defined to be the common good."[70]

The *muhājirūn*, along with the various kinship groups making up the residents of Medina (whether *anṣār*, Jews, or idolaters) were all parties to the agreement. It cannot be overstressed, therefore, that the original agreement did not strictly define the religious followers of Muḥammad. Although the community is referred to in the agreement as *umma*, it is not the same Umma that became the universal community of Muslims.[71] All the parties were nevertheless responsible to one another in certain ways, while individual subgroups had separate responsibilities in other ways. Old kinship responsibilities were not abandoned by the agreement initially. The various kinship groups, for example, paid their own blood money and ransomed their own captives (articles 2–10). Believers, however, often seem to be singled out (e.g., articles 11–15). On the other hand, Jews are joined with believers in a variety of common responsibilities (articles 16, 24–31, 37–38). And, finally, all parties to the document, presumably whether Muslims, Jews, or unbelieving Medinans, must agree to the status of Yathrib/Medina as a sacred compound,[72] and none may go to war without Muḥammad's permission.[73] None may give protection to the Meccan Quraysh (article 43), and all must help each other against outside attack (article 44).

As far as can be discerned, most but not all identifiable groups of the Medinan populace were represented in the agreement.[74] Although we may never know the exact context and meaning of the intricate interrelationships established by the agreement, it is clear that a major intent of the document was to avoid renewal of old intertribal intrigues based on kinship and previously contracted alliances and to prevent the establishment of new alliances with foreign elements not represented by the agreement. Each represented group had certain restrictions and responsibilities that cemented its relationship with the community and its leader. Any infringement would isolate the individual group, since all previous alliances and kinship relationships would have been severed. The result was not only to discourage alliances between any Medinans and Muḥammad's enemies in Mecca or their allies but also to prevent internal alliances from forming within the Medinan *umma* against the leadership of Muḥammad.

When individual subgroups within the political *umma* broke the agreement, they naturally became isolated because of the lapse of their prior independent ties. Watt suggests that the isolation of the Jewish tribes of Medina demonstrates how delicate the entire situation was, because old ties remained influential, even if not determinant. Even as late as the destruction of the tribe of Banū Qurayẓa, for example, prior alliances had a major impact on the situation. In the case of the Qurayẓa, when it became clear that Muḥammad would prevail after nearly a month of besieging them in their fortified settlements, their old allies among the

Aws pleaded on their behalf to the Prophet. He acceded to the Aws' intercession by asking them if they would be satisfied with a member of their own tribe passing judgment on the fate of their erstwhile allies, the Qurayẓa. The case of the Banū Qurayẓa is revealing since, according to Watt, Muḥammad himself could not decree the shedding of blood against the Qurayẓa because of the likelihood of the old relationships automatically reasserting themselves. Therefore, "[t]he decision about the punishment was left to the chief of the clan of which they had been confederates."[75]

One interesting side of the final struggle with the Qurayẓa is a statement attributed to the tribe in reference to Muḥammad. According to the story in the Sīra, Muḥammad's cousin ʿAlī had reported to Muḥammad that the Qurayẓa were insulting him behind his back. When, as a result, Muḥammad approached them in their forts, he said: "O brothers of monkeys, Has God shamed you and brought down His vengeance upon you?" They replied: "O Abūl-Qāsim,[76] you are no *jahūl* (*mā kunta jahūl^an*)."[77] This, as may be recalled, is the same word used to describe Muḥammad at Mecca, when he refrained from responding physically to insults hurled at him by the Quraysh. As noted previously, *jahūl* derives from the same root as *jāhiliyya*, meaning "ignorance," the common Arabic term for the pre-Islamic period. According to the classical dictionaries, one who is *jahūl* ignorantly engages in foolish or wrong conduct.[78] Muḥammad, who was known as a steady and thoughtful man not prone to rash or impulsive behavior, was the opposite of *jahūl*, and this was known to the Qurayẓa. When he came against them, they hoped that he would not engage in such vengeful violence as was common in the pre-Islamic period, and, as members of the agreement, the Qurayẓa hoped that they would be protected. As it turned out, however, they were accused of breaking the agreement by aiding the enemy Quraysh, so were excluded from the protection normally accorded to its signatories.

Despite the political nature of the document and the resultant secular nature of the early *umma*, Muḥammad's status as religious as well as political leader must not be underestimated. The reason for the successful projection of his authority in Medina resulted from the coalescence of a number of sources of authority in his person. Part of his genius lay in the successful manipulation of multiple sources of status in his prophethood, his personal charisma, and his clan status as a holy family assigned to the famous sacred enclave of Mecca, thereby affording him the opportunity for establishing a new sacred enclave also in Medina. The last pillar of his authority has a religious component that nevertheless crosses religious boundaries, for the institution of the holy man of the sacred enclave seems to have been universally respected.[79] Its significance for our purposes is that it provided a universal status as holy man for Muḥammad, even among those who were not his direct followers, thus opening the way through continued contact and persuasion for non-Muslims who were party to the agreement eventually to cross over to becoming his full followers.

As his power in Medina grew, as the revelations continued to descend, and as more and more Medinans became believers, the nature of the *umma* began to evolve from a political association designed to mediate tribal conflicts to a religiously defined community taking over the all-important social and political role of the old kinship group. This narrowing of definition and the increased social pressure encouraged those not naturally inclined to be actual believers to throw in their lot eventually with the Prophet. When the organized Jewish opposition was eliminated from Medina, Muḥammad's last internal threat was the dissenters or hypocrites (*munāfiqūn*), those nominal believers who could not be completely trusted to follow his leadership. This evolution from the Medinan *umma* to the Muslim Umma was critical in terms of building solidarity and, ultimately, creating a large and cohesive population from which fighters could be recruited for warring. The same powerful emotional attachment to kinship was being transferred to religion, so that as the community became more religiously defined, the old centrifugal ties of kinship had less of a divisive effect. War and revenge could therefore be motivated more out of a sense of common identity through the brotherhood of believers, the supertribe of Islam.

Warring in the Medina Agreement

The opening phrase of the agreement defines the members of the community governed by the document as "the believers and Muslims from the Quraysh and Yathrib and those who follow them, are attached to them, and strive (*jāhada*) along with them."[80] Given the context and parallel terminology, the term *jāhada* here must not indicate warring but, rather, something akin to its generic English translation of "striving." Rather than describe an activity, therefore, the term describes a relationship. The term in the full sentence helps to define the members of the agreement: all those individuals and groups that are engaged in a positive formal or informal relationship with the *muhājirūn* or the *anṣār*.[81] This sentence, therefore, has nothing to do with warring in its simple meaning.[82]

Article 14: , "A believer may not kill a[nother] believer on behalf of an unbeliever and may not help an unbeliever against a believer." As mentioned above, this article is meant to establish the new mode of relationship responsibility and most likely refers to revenge killings. Such killings, which were so much a part of pre-Islamic life, continued to function also in the Islamic period, with the major difference being in the network of relations responsible to exact revenge or pay the bloodwit. It adds nothing new conceptually to pre-Islamic motivations or notions of warring, but it radically redefines the network of relationships for which blood responsibility applied. No longer is kinship the determinant factor.

Article 17 employs the phrase "fighting in the path of God:" "The peace of the believers is one (*wa'inna silm al-mu'minīn wāḥida*). A believer may not make peace apart from a[nother] believer when there is fighting in the path of God (*fī qitāl fī sabīl Allāh*), unless [it is done] on the basis of equality and justice between them [the believers]." The qualifying phrase here is "in the path of God." The article presumes that independent conflicts may arise between believers and those outside the agreement. However, in conflicts defined as being in the path of God, there can be no diminution of the solidarity between believers. This article seems to portray a middle step between the complete severing of the old kinship ties and the rigid establishment of the new association of the Muslim Umma.

The idiom "in the path of God" appears a second time in article 19, which requires believers to take revenge on behalf of any other believer whose blood has been spilled "in the path of God." These two articles seem to make a distinction between fighting in the path of God for which there must be absolute solidarity between believers—but no responsibility from nonbelievers who are party to the document—and fighting in defense of Medina and the *umma*, for which all signatories to the document, whether believers or unbelievers, must be responsible.

Article 24: "The Jews must spend their resources along with the believers so long as they are at war (*mā dāmū muḥāribīn*)." This article is an extension of the qur'ānic injunction to spend resources in the path of God.[83] It defines the network of relationships by which members of the community must support each other in time of war. Here, very specifically, Jewish nonbelievers who are party to the agreement must contribute to the cause of the Medinan *umma*.

Article 36: "No one may go out [to fight] without the permission of Muḥammad (*wa'innahu lā yukhrij minhum aḥad illā bi'idhni Muḥammad*), but one may not be prevented from taking vengeance for wounds. . . ." This article clearly establishes Muḥammad as the authority for the community with regard to organized fighting, but it (perhaps grudgingly) accedes to the powerful pre-Islamic requirement for revenge, presumably based on old kinship relations.

Article 37: "The Jews must spend their [own] resources and the Muslims must spend their [own] resources, but between them there must be assistance [i.e., they must help one another] against anyone who wars against the people of this document.[84] There must be friendly counsel and mutual guidance between them, and right behavior, not treachery. . . ." This article is seen by some as a reference for each group paying their own taxes,[85] but it may refer to a wider definition of expenses for which there is no mutual responsibility between Jews and Muslims aside from mutual protection in war. In any case, it reinforces the mutual responsibility between believers and nonbelievers in defense of the Medinan *umma*.

Article 38: "The Jews must spend their resources along with the believers so long as they are at war." This article is an exact repetition of the first part of article 24.

Article 44: "Between them [the signatories of the agreement?] there must be assistance against whoever suddenly attacks Yathrib." This article largely repeats the intent and language of part of article 37,[86] except that it extends the parties responsible for defense from Jews and Muslims to all signatories of the document; the article further extends the requirement of defending only the parties to the document to defending all of Medina.

Article 45: "When they are called to make a peace treaty and accept it, they must indeed make the treaty and accept it (*wa'idhā du'ū ilā ṣulḥ yuṣāliḥūnahu wayalbisūnahu fa'innahum yuṣāliḥūnahu wayalbisūnahu*). And if they are called to the like of that [or if they call to the like of that], then they have [a right?] against the believers, except for those who make war in the name of religion (*wa'innahum idhā du'ū, or da'ū, ilā mithli dhālika fa'innahu lahum 'alāl-mu'minīn illā man ḥāraba fīl-dīn*). To each man is his share from the side which is toward him." It is not clear who is referred to in the various sections of this article, which remains obscure. Does the first line refer to the Jews or to all parties of the agreement? Is the repeated verb *d.'.w.* in the active or passive form? Do the assumed conflicts refer to fighting between different groups *within* the Medinan *umma*, which must cease whenever any party to the conflict calls for a truce, or do they refer to fighting outside groups? Whatever the references, it is clear that both believers and nonbelievers who are signatories to the document must be willing to accept cessation of hostilities when called on, although it is not at all clear who might be the one calling on them to do so. It also appears from this article that nonbelievers have certain rights with regard to such agreements, perhaps even to the disadvantage of believers. The exception is those who fight on behalf of religion, but it is not clear whether such exception is a privilege or a burden. Here, the term *ḥāraba fīl-dīn* is different from the more common *qitāl fī sabīl Allah*. Does it refer to the same thing, or do the different idioms denote different types of warring? These questions cannot yet be answered, given the available data.

The Medina Agreement is a complex set of articles, some of which seem repetitive, and some of which appear even contradictory. These traits suggest that it is indeed a composite document that conflates material representing different realia of post-Hijra Medina. Nevertheless, some general conclusions may be drawn from the document as it is. Its delineation of kinship and cross-kinship responsibilities clearly marks a transition from pre-Islamic kinship affiliation to the later Islamic institution of the Umma. The old kinship responsibility of paying previous blood commitments is not abandoned (articles 3–10), but, henceforth, believers must be mutually responsible for blood commitments across kinship lines (articles 11, 19). In some areas, believers are mutually responsible, in others Jews are included, and in others all parties are responsible for one another. These distinctions clearly are not kinship-based, despite the fact that the listing of parties to the document are sometimes given according to kinship groups (articles 3–10, 25–34, 46) and sometimes given according to their identity as *muhājirūn*, *anṣār*, believers (or Muslims), or Jews. Blood vengeance is not eliminated, but the network of relationships responsible for exacting revenge begins to be redrawn from the old kinship system to the new one of religious alliance.

The fact that fighting is described in such disparate terms complicates the sense of the document. There is "fighting in the path of God," "warring," assisting parties to the document who are being fought, assisting against sudden attack on Medina, and "fighting for religion." On the one hand, the difference between fighting "in the path of God" and fighting "for religion" is not clear and may in fact represent synonymic meaning among different layers of the document. On the other hand, the complex interrelationship between believers, Jews, and unbelieving Medinans reflects different levels of responsibility to engage in war. All must assist in the defense of Yathrib/Medina (article 44), and no one may initiate hostilities without express permission from Muḥammad (article 36). Jews, however, are also expected to assist the believers as long as they are at war, although they are not specifically told to engage in combat (articles 24, 38).[87] But it is only the believers who engage in fighting "in the path of God," who are forbidden to make a separate peace if there is fighting "in the path of God" (article 17), and who are mutually responsible to avenge blood spilled "in the path of God" (article 19).

The Institution of the Umma

It should now be clear that the Medina Agreement marks the transition from the old pre-Islamic kinship system to the new Muslim Umma. It actually represents a middle position between the two institutions, in that it exhibits a certain fluidity between kinship relations and religious alliance. In fact, as a composite document, it most likely represents a number of stages on the continuum. Unfortunately, we do not yet have the tools to distinguish accurately between different sections of the document in order to deliniate these stages. In any case, the Medina Agreement defines an early *political umma* of Medina in which Muslims, Jews, and idolaters all had certain mutual responsibilities under the pact. As Muḥammad's religious, military, and political success increased his prestige and power within the community and in the extended region, the parties to the agreement who were Jews or unbelievers either merged with the believers or were eventually eliminated from the system. This narrowing occurred in conjunction with the success of militant Islam, and the two reinforced each other. The membership of the *umma* of Medina was eventually narrowed to believers only, thereby creating the nucleus of what became the great Muslim Umma or religious fellowship of Islam. This Umma represents the religious and political consolidation of Arabia through the unification of disparate tribes, nomadic and settled peoples, and even the small urban population of the peninsula under Islam.[88]

A number of traditions emphasize the feeling of kinship associated with the Umma and to such an extent that even the old common kinship terminology of the pre-Islamic period came to be applied to the religious community: "A believer is the brother of a believer. He protects his losses and guards his flank."[89] Similarly, "A Muslim is the brother of a Muslim. Do not opress him or betray him. Whoever attends to the needs of his brother, God attends to his own needs, and whoever relieves the pain of a Muslim, God will relieve him of his pains on the Day of Resurrection. And whoever shields a Muslim, God will shield him on the Day of Resurrection.[90] In the famous address of his farewell pilgrimage near the end of his life, the Sīra depicts Muḥammad as declaring, "Know that every Muslim is a Muslim's brother, for the Muslims are brothers. Nothing is permissible [to be taken] from one's brother unless he gives it to him willingly, so do not wrong yourselves."[91] The old kinship rules now apply to religious brethren of the Umma. One has no right to the property of one's religious brethren, whether or not they derive from close kinship relationships. Also in parallel with the pre-Islamic system, Muslims are forbidden from taking vengeance on another Muslim, even if that Muslim is not a blood relation, unless he transgresses the most odious of crimes: "The blood of a Muslim is forbidden except in three cases: The adulterer who is stoned, one who kills another, and one who apostasizes."[92] The analogue of kinship responsiblity in the pre-Islamic system could not be clearer in the following tradition: "Help your brother whether he is an oppressor or one who is oppressed."[93]

When the disparate tribes of Arabia were consolidated into a single, massive, and basically united sociopolitical group, the tremendous energy that had previoiusly been expended in tribal feuds, raids, and attempts at dominating other groups could no longer be released. Most of the pre-Islamic criteria for determining success—honor, manliness, strength, and prowess in fighting—would also naturally be suppressed in such a state. This tremendous energy, therefore, needed release, and the only way possible was outward, against the outsider, the nonmember of the now extrakinship affiliation of the Islamic Umma. This release of energy, channeled as it was through new definitions of self and other and through a religious framework of solidarity based on a unifying God and prophet, became the power that drove the holy war enterprise that takes shape in the great Islamic Conquest.

SEVEN

Conclusion

From Mundane War to Holy War

The transition from the mundane or materially driven fighting of pre-Islamic Arabia to the sacred, divinely sanctioned warring of Islam occurred within a surprisingly short period. It represents a jump rather than a slow evolutionary change from the standpoint of cultural evolution. Although earlier factors undoubtedly had some influence on this change,[1] the watershed can be isolated to the few years following the Hijra in 622 C.E. It was during this period that Muḥammad's—and his followers'—sense of personal identity came increasingly to be felt in terms of religious rather than kinship affiliation, and it is this change, in conjunction with the particular history of the conflict between the Meccans and the early Muslims, that stimulated the transition.

In the following paragraphs I will attempt to summarize and explain this transition, with the caution that the very process of summarization tends to smooth over the many bumps represented by the data. In other words, the data do not suggest that the transition was smooth, without its detractors, or even total. Despite the fact that the community as a whole indeed came to view warring in a new way, that community, like any community, was made up of many factions and subgroups holding contradictory views and perceptions. The discussions in the previous chapters attempted to demonstrate how the community of believers was made up of a variety of factions, each pressing for its own ideas and perceptions to represent the community as a whole. Those that did not succeed in dominating the community with their particular views became lost to history along with the views they represented.

Luckily, however, the nature of Scripture sometimes ensures that even losing positions remain part of the historical record. Once identified as Scripture, the words contained therein cannot be obviously tampered with, for, by definition, Scripture represents the word of God. Therefore, even when antedated or antithetical material or positions are articulated within the canon of Scripture, they cannot simply be eliminated by the ideological victors in intercommunal conflict. Contrary views represented by Scripture are retained, but their continuing existence causes anxiety and dissonance within the community of believers, which, like any community, is pulled by centripetal as well as centrifugal forces that tend toward disunity. The lingering scriptural views that are contrary to the views of the normative community must, therefore, be explained in ways that do not detract from the dominant position, and it is this exegetical process that ensures that the dominant view remains ascendant.

Oral literature likewise, but for different reasons, may retain old views and ideas representing opinions that were not accepted by the normative community. The fluid nature of living oral literature makes elimination and manipulation through redaction impossible, for the repository of living oral literature is the minds of the people. The process of reducing oral literature to writing is, by definition, of course redactional and involves sorting, editing, and elimination, for every part of that process involves decisions by the redactors about what should be recorded in the expensive and necessarily limiting endeavor of writing. Luckily, the transition from orality to literacy has always been a long process spanning generations, and even an attempt at canonization cannot immediately stop the continuation of orality. Perhaps the most obvious case of such a failed attempt at redactional canonization was the creation of the Jewish Mishnah under the auspices of Judah the Prince at about 200 C.E. The reappearance of previously unrecorded traditions (*baraitas*) in the Jerusalem and Babylonian Talmuds centuries later demonstrates how the simultaneous existence of orality and literacy ensured the retention of positions that were not deemed worthy of saving by the officials engaged in the redactional process. Moreover, even the redactional process itself does not eliminate all the vestiges of early and nonnormative ideas in the final edited product, for innocent information nevertheless slips by.

As approaches and methodologies in the study of Scripture and Tradition continue to develop, more data can be extracted from ancient literatures that may provide clues about the development of ancient ideas and practices that have been blurred by the disinterest or the exegesis of centuries. The previous chapters have attempted to do just that with regard to the topic of the origin of holy war in early Islam, and the data may now be summarized.

In Mecca before the Hijra, Muḥammad and his followers tended to be quite moderate with regard to war or any kind of physically aggressive behavior against their detractors, even in the face of aggression committed against them. As noted above, aside from a very few individuals, they avoided physical aggression at almost any cost and suffered physical and emotional abuse as a consequence. Although purely religious factors may have been influential in this regard, these Qurayshite Muslims could not conceive of relating to their own kinship group as the enemy. The Qurayshite establishment or tribal leadership, on the other hand, had no difficulty either conceptually or in practical terms with isolating an aberrant subgroup of the tribe and treating it with severity. This unidirectional relationship changed radically after the establishment of the Muslim community in Medina and the creation of the *umma.*

The institution of the *umma* originated, as I have indicated in the previous chapter, as a formal expression of political relationships and responsibilities obtaining among the disparate religious and kinship groups populating the heterogeneous oasis settlement of Medina. Believers, Jews, and idolaters among the various factional kinship groups were nominally unified as these parties took on a series of mutual responsibilities—which differed between certain categories of these groups—with regard to defense, taxes, and other forms of communal commitment. This formal unification of the Medinan community evolved into an increasingly powerful sense of commitment to the *umma* as a result of the social-spiritual leadership of Muḥammad and certain serendipitous historical events. As a result of these factors, the believers and their non-Muslim associates in the *umma* felt a growing sense of solidarity, which transcended traditional kinship boundaries. Because kinship no longer functioned exclusively in defining mutual relationships within the innovative political *umma,* the members of the new community were able to—indeed were forced to—define relationships increasingly in ideological terms. The boundaries between "believers" and "idolaters" were not always clear in this transitional period, as the ubiquitous references to "dissenters" (*munāfiqun*) in the texts makes so clear; thus it would be rash to define the sense of relationship early on as religious. But as Medinans, as defenders of the community, as followers of Muḥammad's leadership of the political *umma,* and as observers of the abuse that Muḥammad and his followers received at the hands of the Quraysh, the members of the *umma,* whether *muhājirūn* or *anṣār* (and as either official believers or those tending in that direction), could easily view themselves as ideological comrades, even ideological "brethren." Concomitant with the growth of this ideological solidarity in the face of Meccan threats and the eventual attacks of the Meccans and their allies, the traditional kinship divisions between members of the political *umma* were weakened. As Muḥammad's leadership strengthened and as the nature of the *umma* became increasingly one of religious fellowship, the ideological glue that bound the *umma* together can be said to be increasingly religious. As this process advanced, the same fervent pre-Islamic cultural attachment to kinship, with its attendant sense of commitment, responsibility, solidarity, and spirit, came to be transferred to the religious community, and it was this transference in conjunction with the growth in solidarity engendered by a severe outside threat that allowed the possibility of war based on religious rather than kinship solidarity.

The old kinship commitment was not yet ended, however, even with the evolution into the religious Umma. There continued to be tensions and occasional outright conflict between the *muhājirūn* and the *anṣār*, and of course between them and the Meccan Quraysh after the capitulation of Mecca in 630; and even among the *anṣār* there remained continued tension between the Aws and the Khazraj clans.[2] One still identified oneself as a member of a family, clan, and tribe, but the supertribal affiliation of Islam tended to claim the allegiance of the individual in ways that the large kinship group of the tribe no longer could. How this transfer of the fiery personal allegiance so inherent in Arabian culture came about may be inferred by examining the record of the history of inter- and intratribal relationships among Muḥammad's followers, the *muhājirūn* and the *anṣār*.

One key element is the particular history of kinship relations between the *muhājirūn* and the larger Quraysh tribe around the time of the Hijra. As a result of the physical and emotional abuse they received at the hands of their Meccan kin, Muḥammad's small group of Meccan followers were already feeling a sense of solidarity amid adversity, despite the fact that they derived from various clans among the Quraysh. The poor treatment they received enhanced a natural feeling of brotherhood among the devotees of the new Prophet, and a parallel program of "brothering" was implemented among Muḥammad's followers between the Meccan *muhājirūn* and the unrelated Medinan *anṣār*. This "religious brotherhood" (*ikhwān fil-dīn*) began to inform the nature of the *Umma* in its formation.[3]

When the *muhājirūn* moved to Medina, they were confronted with the additional problem of sustenance, for they had no reliable source of income in their new home. Medina was an oasis community based on date agriculture, and all the viable land had already been claimed and cultivated. Despite the attempt at "brothering," the *muhājirūn* had no traditional kinship ties with the attendant economic interdependence that such ties provided with the local Medinan populace. To improve the difficult economic situation, the *muhājirūn* or a faction among them naturally fell back on the old and honorable custom of the pre-Islamic tribal raid, the purpose of which was clearly material gain. The decision to engage in raiding was an obvious inclination toward traditional Arabian practice, and the kind of warring that did result clearly fit the pattern of materially driven war. This warring was not "holy war," aside perhaps from the fact that the people engaging in the violence saw themselves as living according to God's design. How, then, did such mundane raiding evolve into holy war?

The immediate problem the *muhājirūn* faced was, whom should they raid? The natural prey, it turned out, was their own Meccan tribe of Quraysh, despite the stern Arabian proscription against raiding one's own kin. The reason for breaking the old rule against attacking one's own kinship group is clear enough. The Meccans, first of all, regularly sent out transport caravans that were a potentially lucrative goal for a raiding party. Second, and more important, the *muhājirūn* had been treated so abusively by their own Meccan kith and kin that any sense of commitment or benefit from the traditional tribal relationship had vanished. The extent of their mistreatment was considered so excessive that it even altered the old tradition of revenge. The *muhājirūn* could have decided to raid unrelated tribes, or other schemes could have been attempted. The decision to raid their own kinsmen's Meccan interests certainly had a vengeful element within it.

The decision to raid their own kinsmen was something that had been unthinkable in pre-Islamic times, but now became an innovative idea. Such a daring adventure was only possible after the institution of the Medinan *umma*, for the *umma* served as protection against the inevitable reprisals that these raiders and their community would have to absorb. Lacking such protection, an errant band without allies attacking its own kin simply would have been destroyed by the combined forces of the mother tribe. The fact that such a daring act as raiding one's own tribe was difficult to initiate is clear from the great length of time it took for the first raid to be sent out. According to the Sīra, "[Muḥammad] then went out to raid in [the month of] Ṣafar, the beginning of the twelfth month from his arrival in Medina."[4] A number of initial forays were sent out, but it took another few months for the first raid to achieve results—that led by ʿAbdullah b. Jaḥsh. During the waiting period, according to the traditional Muslim chronologies and exegetical works, God provided divine authority for engaging in such raids.[5] Why was justification needed? Perhaps because it was felt that some higher authority was required to justify violation of the prohibition against attacking one's own kin or, perhaps, because transcendent sanction was felt needed to engage in organized violent acts of any kind. In any event, the array of scriptural texts that speak on the subject suggest that the community as a whole was not of one mind on the matter, and these texts are cited as support for the positions that are expressed in the early sources.

Ironically, the first successful raid initially caused strife within the new community of believers rather than enhance solidarity, because of the problem of the Sacred Months. The raiders' infringement of the old rule prohibiting violence during these months was seen by most believers as a grave transgression, and the shock of such an act threatened both the morale and solidarity of the community as a whole. Noting the gravity of the violation, the Meccans pressed their advantage in the name of old Arabian decency and fair play. It was only the new divine dispensation abrogating the absolute prohibition of fighting during this period that saved the community, and the fact that Muḥammad's recitation of God's word was successful demonstrates both the power of his leadership and the strength of his new religion among the believers in relation to the ancient Arabian norms. The revelation of *Sūra* 2:217 saved the community by providing divine sanction for warring during the Sacred Months, thereby unifying a community that was divided over the matter. By communicating about fighting and providing God's permission for doing so (even if only in a limited way), Scripture established the divinely sanctioned necessity or even desirability for engaging in combat against the enemies of Islam.

It must be admitted that the reading of this particular episode takes the traditional chronology largely at face value, but there is reasonable justification for doing so.[6] The point is that what began as traditional Arabian raiding forays (albeit against one's own kin) came to be considered divinely sanctioned because of historical circumstances. This typifies the transition process from mundane to holy war. The process continued with the eventual generalization of the enemy as anyone who opposed Muḥammad and his divinely guided following, but that took a little longer to come about.

At one level, the Hijra of the Meccan followers of Muḥammad relieved the pressure against them leveled by the Quraysh, because in Medina they were free from any immediate threat. For the Meccans, in turn, absence of the believers eliminated the pressure they had been applying against the traditional pagan religious practice and social system adhering in Mecca. On the other hand, when the *muhājirūn* began to attack Meccan interests (as some Meccans were afraid they would do), the Quraysh were obliged by their own economic and political interests—as well as traditional Arabian expectations of manliness and pride—to inflict punishment against them through reprisals. There was no avoiding a counterattack after the raid at Badr, but the damage that the Quraysh inflicted on Muḥammad and his followers at Uḥud did not achieve the goal of disgrace and the subsequent cessation of hostilities. On the contrary, it seemed to reinforce the solidarity of the Medinans (now both the *muhājirūn and* the *anṣār*) at the same time that it further weakened the kinship solidarity between the *muhājirūn* and their Meccan kinsmen and the old divisions between the Medinan Aws and Khazraj in the face of a larger communal threat.

The reprisal at Uḥud also stimulated the revelation of a number of qur'ānic verses, according to tradition.[7] Among them are those claiming that God granted the Muslims victory at Badr (3:123) and would help them in the future with a heavenly host (3:125). To the Muslims who were licking their wounds after Uḥud, these verses provided inspiration and hope. They also further sacralized the future violent encounters that ensued between those of the Umma and their opponents.

To the *muhājirūn*, it was their own kin who were trying to kill them, and in fact the Meccans pursued the *muhājirūn* and, after Uḥud, also the *anṣār*, simply because of who they were and what they represented—not for material gain as would have been the case in the pre-Islamic system.[8] This perception further reinforced the Umma members' own commitment to their new identity group. Such conflict reinforced the only real difference between the *muhājirūn* and their Meccan enemies. All belonging to the same extended kinship group, the only difference dividing them was religious ideology. Ideology (or if you wish, religion), therefore, evolved into a more important determinant of identity and solidarity than kinship. Ideological differences under these specific historical circumstances cut kinship ties, and the Muslim *muhājirūn* and their *anṣār* cohort "brethren" therefore saw the conflict increasingly in terms of ideological or religious differences. The Muslim believers were fighting the pagan Meccans, whatever their kinship relation, because the latter represented an enemy bent on destroying the Muslims, God's prophet, and God's religion itself. The Muslims naturally began to see their conflicts increasingly in ideological, religious terms.

This process also affected the native Medinans, who were in the process of transcending their old kinship ties through association with the *umma*. Muḥammad not only succeeded through the Medina Agreement in mediating the major feud between the clans of the Aws and the Khazraj: Creating the Muslim Umma eventually eliminated the blood feud altogether. The Qur'ān both prescribes and describes the sense of relationship that would attain in this new body (3:103):

> Find refuge and cling together with the bond of God. Do not divide into separate groups, but remember God's favor unto you when you were enemies at the edge of the fiery abyss, when He saved you from it and when He joined your hearts together and you became brothers through His grace. Thus does God make His signs clear to you so that you will be rightly guided.

Not only did the *anṣār* transcend the historic conflicts dividing them, but they also found a sense of solidarity with the *muhājirūn*, particularly after Uḥud, when they jointly took up arms to defend their community, their families, and their *umma* and prophet. This transition from divided and fractious groups to a unified religious community did not occur immediately or smoothly, nor was the transition ever complete. Centrifugal and centripetal forces constantly affect the unity and solidarity of any community, which was certainly the case among the early Muslims. The point is not to prove the existence of a unified religious community engaging in holy war under the undisputed leadership of Muḥammad but, rather, to suggest that religious ideological criteria became the dominant means of self-identification under the Medinan *umma* at the same time that the conflict with the Meccan Quraysh was being seen increasingly as a holy war that must be fought until victory.

Frictions always remained within the *umma*, and these frictions had many sources—ideological, political, and kinship-based. It is hoped that previous discussions in this study are convincing in their conviction that the followers of Muḥammad were not of one mind with regard to issues of warring, adherence to pre-Islamic norms of behavior, and certainly many other issues. The transition from pre-Islamic to Islamic Arabia occurred neither linearly nor smoothly. Various factions within the *umma* held different positions on many issues, as may be readily seen from the evidence cited in the Qur'ān, the Sīra and the Ḥadīth. The different factions expressed different positions, to which the Qur'ān and Muḥammad responded. These positions help us to understand the contradictory pronouncements and views expressed by these texts, which seem to have occurred at about the same time. Notwithstanding the various positions that naturally arose in the course of early Islamic history, the transition from mundane to holy war can be traced in the sources, from the early impossibility of Muḥammad's followers defining their own kinship group as the enemy, to the materialistic raids conducted even against their own kin, to the total declaration of war against all groups, whether kin or not, who did not accept the truth or the hegemony of Islam.

Notes

Abbreviations

BSOAS	*Bulletin of the School of Oriental and African Studies*
EI[1]	*The Encyclopaedia of Islam*, 1st ed., edited by M. T. Houtsma et al. (Leiden: E. J. Brill, 1913–1934, reprint edition, 1987)
EI[2]	*The Encyclopaedia of Islam*, 2nd ed., edited by H. A. R. Gibb et al. (Leiden: E. J. Brill, 1960–)
EJ	*Encyclopedia Judaica*
G	A. Guillaume, *The Life of Muhammad* (Oxford, 1955)
HTR	*Harvard Theological Review*
I.C.	*Islamic Culture*
I.I.	Ibn Isḥāq, *Al-Sīra al-Nabawiyya* (Beirut, n.d.)
IJMES	*International Journal of Middle East Studies*
I.S.	Ibn Saʿd, *Kitāb al-tabaqāt al-kabīr* (Leiden, 1917)
H	S. M. Haq, *Ibn Saʿd's Kitab al-Tabaqat al-Kabir* (New Delhi, n.d.)
JAOS	*Journal of the American Oriental Society*
JESHO	*Journal of the Economic and Social History of the Orient*
JNES	*Journal of Near Eastern Studies*
JRE	*Journal of Religious Ethics*
JSAI	*Jerusalem Studies in Arabic and Islam*
ZDMG	*Zeitschrift der Deutschen Morgenländischen Gesellschaft*

Introduction

1. On definitions of holy war and *jihād*, see chapter 1.

2. Friedrich Schwally, *Der Heilige Krieg im alten Israel*, vol. 1 of *Semitische Kriegsalterteumer* (Leipzig: Deiterich, 1901).

3. And a certain representation of tendentious intellectualism or uncautious moralizing. For a brief listing of recent scholarly approaches, see Susan Niditch's introduction to her *War in the Hebrew Bible* (New York: Oxford University Press, 1993). For a partial bibliography including popular and moralistic as well as scholarly studies, see Judith Sanderson, "War, Peace, and Justice in the Hebrew Bible: A Representative Bibliography," printed as an appendix to the English translation by Marva J. Dawn of Gerhard von Rad, *Der Heilige Krieg im alten Israel* (*Holy War in Ancient Israel*) (Grand Rapids, Mich.: Eerdmans, 1991), pp. 135–166.

4. See Roland Bainton, *Christian Attitudes toward War and Peace* (New York: Abingdon, 1960), pp. 101–121; H. E. J. Cowdrey, "The Genesis of the Crusades: The Springs of Western Ideas of Holy War," in Thomas Patrick Murphy, ed., *The Holy War* (Columbus: Ohio State University Press, 1976), pp. 9–32; James A. Brundage, "Holy War and the Medieval Lawyers," in Murphy, ed., *The Holy War*, pp. 99–140; James A. Brundage, *The Crusades, Holy War, and Canon Law* (Brookfield, Vt.: Variorum, 1991); LeRoy Walters, "The Just War and the Crusade: Antitheses or Analogies?" *Monist*, no. 57 (1973), pp. 584–594.

5. P. 356. Quite in this genre is Stephen van Rensselaer Trowbridge, "Mohammed's View of Religious War," *The Moslem World*, Vol. 3 (1913), pp. 290–305: "I imagine Mohammed on the battle field of Lule-Burgas, swinging the sword which he won from the plunder of Bedr, inspiring the ranks of Turks to dash into the fray, promising them the joys of paradise if they fall in the thick of the conflict! I imagine Christ standing with arms outstretched, like the silver figures of Christ in the old French court-rooms, His great, compassionate heart rent with pity, stooping now to give a draught of water to a dying Bulgar and now to stanch the wounds of a fallen Turk, pleading with the bloodstained antagonists to govern their passions and be reconciled to one another as children of God" (p. 305). This general approach is in keeping with an old Western tradition. A recent listing of an antiquarian book dealer, for example, included a work by Humphrey Prideaux, *The True Nature of Imposture Fully Display'd in the Life of Mahomet* (1708); cf. Edward W. Said, *Orientalism* (New York: Random House, 1979).

6. *Critical Exposition of Popular Jihād* (Calcutta, 1885) and as found in Edward Sell, *The Faith of Islam* (London, 1920; 4th ed. reprint, Wilmington, Del.: Scholarly Resources, 1976), pp. 448–456 ("Appendix B: The Law of *Jihād*").

7. *Tafsīr al-manār* in various volumes (see Rudolph Peters, "Djihad: War of Aggression or Defense," in *Akten des VII. Kongresses feur Arabistik und Islamwissenschaft* [Göttingen, 1976], p. 285 n. 6).

8. *Al-Tawḥīḍ* no. 1 (1404/1984), pp. 39–54.

9. With a foreword by Zia al-Haq (Lahore: Wajidalis, 1979).

10. Rudolph Peters, in his important early study mentioned above in note 7, describes the two contrasting trends among contemporary Muslims to the double challenge of Western colonialism/imperialism and polemic, naming the apologetic initial response "modernist" and the subsequent activist-revivalist response "fundamentalist" ("Djihad: War of Aggression or Defense"). For an interesting collection of papers on *jihād* delivered by Egyptian religious scholars responding to the 1967 Middle East war, see the English transcription, *The Fourth Conference of the Academy of Islamic Research*, al-Azhar University (Cairo: General Organization for Government Printing Offices, 1970).

11. The former, London: Grafton, 1988, and the latter, New Delhi: Voice of India, 1994.

12. Harfiya Abdel Haleem, Oliver Ramsbotham, Saba Risaluddin, and Brian Wicker, eds., *The Crescent and the Cross: Muslim and Christian Approaches to War and Peace* (New York: St. Martin's Press, 1998).

13. Baltimore: Johns Hopkins University Press, 1955. See also Khadduri, *The Islamic Law of Nations: Shaybani's Siyar* (Baltimore: Johns Hopkins University Press, 1966), and Muhammad Hamidullah, *Muslim Conduct of State* (Lahore: Muhammad Ashraf, 1953).

14. Universite de Lille, published by Service de Reproduction des Theses, 1975.

15. Rudolph Peters, *Jihad in Mediaeval and Modern Islam*, Nisaba Religious Texts Translation Series, vol. 5 (Leiden: Brill, 1977), reprinted and expanded in Rudolph Peters, *Jihad in Classical and Modern Islam* (Princeton: Marcus Weiner, 1996); and Rudolph Peters, *Islam and Colonialism: The Doctrine of Jihad in Modern History* (The Hague: Mouton, 1979).

16. Beirut: Dār al-Fikr, n.d.

17. Originally his doctoral dissertation, published in Beirut by Dār al-Bayāriq (1414/1993).

18. For the former, see W. Montgomery Watt, "Islamic Conceptions of the Holy War," in Murphy, ed., *The Holy War*, pp. 141–156; Watt, "The Significance of the Theory of *Jihād*," in *Akten des VII. Kongresses feur Arabistik und Islamwissenschaft*, pp. 390–394; Bernard Lewis, "War and Peace," in *The Political Language of Islam* (Chicago: University of Chicago Press, 1988), pp. 71–90; and Fred M. Donner, "The Sources of Islamic Conceptions of War," in John Kelsay and James Turner Johnson, eds., *Just War and Jihad: Historical and Theoretical Perspectives on War and Peace in Western and Islamic Traditions* (New York: Greenwood Press, 1991), pp. 31–69. On Shiʿite views, see Ann K. S. Lambton, "A Nineteenth Century View of Jihād," *Studia Islamica* 32 (1970), pp. 181–192, and Etan Kohlberg, "The Development of the Imāmī Shīʿī Doctrine of *Jihād*," *ZDMG* 126.1 (1976), pp. 64–86; and on Aḥmadī views, see Yohanan Friedmann, "*Jihād* in Aḥmadī Thought," in Moshe Sharon, ed., *Studies in Islamic History and Civilization in Honour of Professor David Ayalon* (Jerusalem and Leiden: Brill, 1986), pp. 221–235. Interest in modern "Islamist" (sometimes labeled as "fundamentalist," "revivalist," or other terms) movements is accelerating. Some good articles on Islamist views on war in this growing field include John Ralph Willis, "*Jihād fī Sabīl Allāh*—Its Doctrinal Basis in Islam and Some Aspects of Its Evolution in Nineteenth-Century West Africa," in *Journal of African History* 8.3 (1967), pp. 395–415; Richard Martin, "Religious Violence in Islam: Towards an Understanding of the Discourse on *Jihad* in Modern Egypt," in Paul Wilkinson and Alasdair Steward, eds., *Contemporary Research on Terrorism* (Aberdeen: Aberdeen University Press, 1989), pp. 55–71; and Tamara Sonn, "Irregular Warfare and Terrorism in Islam: Asking the Right Questions," in James Turner Johnson and John Kelsay, eds., *Cross, Crescent, and Sword: The Justification and Limitation of War in Western and Islamic Tradition* (New York: Greenwood Press, 1990), pp. 129–147. Less helpful are the articles by S. Abdullah Schleifer, "Understanding Jihad: Definition and Methodology," *Islamic Quarterly* 27.3 (1983), pp. 118–131, "Jihad and Traditional Islamic Consciousness," in *I.C.* 27.4 (1983), pp. 173–203; and "Jihad: Modernist Apologists, Modern Apologetics," *I.C.* 28 (1984), pp. 25–46. The pen-

dulum continues to swing among Muslims who are influenced by and respond to the challenges of the West. Of particular interest is the recent collection edited by Ralph Crow, Philip Grant, and Saad Ibrahim, *Arab Nonviolent Political Struggle in the Middle East* (Boulder, Col.: Lynne Rienner, 1990).

19. There are some exceptions, such as Fred Donner's work noted above.

20. One school of modern Islamic scholarship disputes this assertion, as well as any statement that is made about early Islam, by taking the position that everything we think we know about the earliest period developed at least a century later in the vicinity of today's Iraq and was "read back" retroactively into what we would erroneously consider to be early data extracted from the classic sources. This view, which was developed by John Wansbrough (*Quranic Studies* [Oxford: Oxford University Press, 1977] and *The Sectarian Milieu* [Oxford: Oxford University Press, 1978]) and his students, raises important issues regarding the use of source material, but its radical conclusion has not been accepted by Western scholarship.

21. That is, through an objective theory of historical development based on the observation of quantifiable social-structural criteria and not presuming an inexorable "progress" in the development and growth of human societies.

22. Or "a-modern" age among the majority of human civilizations that did not experience the same modern history of the West.

Part I

1. Said, *Orientalism*, p. 3.

2. Quincy Wright, *A Study of War*, 2nd ed. (Chicago: University of Chicago Press, 1965), pp. 636 ff.

3. His name was invariably pronounced by some in the Bush administration as "Sodom" Hussein and by the president himself in a way that rhymes with "Satan."

Chapter One

1. Frederick Denny, *An Introduction to Islam* (New York: Macmillan, 1985), p. 59.

2. Aziz al-Azmeh, *Islams and Modernities* (London: Verso, 1993), and al-Azmeh's essay therein on the many "Islams."

3. It was also during this period that the major heterodox views and concepts were formed. For a study of the concept of holy war in mainstream Shiʿite Islam, see Etan Kohlberg, "The Development of the Imāmī Shīʿī Doctrine of *jihād*," pp. 64–86. On the much later Aḥmadī view, see Friedmann, "*Jihād* in Aḥmadī Thought," pp. 221–235.

4. R. Brian Ferguson, "Studying War," in R. Brian Ferguson, ed., *Warfare, Culture, and Environment* (Orlando: Harcourt Brace Jovanovich, 1984), pp. 3–5; Martin Nettleship, "Definitions," in Martin Nettleship et al., eds., *War, Its Causes and Correlates* (The Hague: Mouton, 1975), pp. 73–90.

5. This definition is based on Ferguson, "Studying War," p. 5, and on Bruce Lincoln, *Death, War, and Sacrifice* (Chicago: University of Chicago Press, 1991), p. 138.

6. The tragedy of civil war or "war against brothers" is that the determination of who is within the group and who is the "enemy" may conflict with kinship or

other powerful bonds of relationship. This conflict, as noted below, becomes an issue of extreme importance in the context of early Islam.

7. Khadduri, *War and Peace in the Law of Islam*, pp. 62–65.

8. James Turner Johnson, *Ideology, Reason, and the Limitation of War* (Princeton: Princeton University Press, 1975), pp. 9–11.

9. The literature on just-war theory is quite large. For works treating just-war theory in the context of Islam, see Khadduri, *War and Peace in the Law of Islam*, and the works listed in note 20, this chapter.

10. Johnson, *Ideology, Reason, and the Limitation of War*, pp. 26–80. Johnson also includes "Hebraic culture" because of his occasional citations of Ambrose and Augustine ("Historical Roots and Sources of the Just War Tradition in Western Culture," in Kelsay and Johnson, eds., *Just War and Jihad*, 7–8), but the traditions of the Hebrew Bible lie mostly outside the conceptual development of the just-war tradition in the West. Their impact is greater on the holy war component.

11. Johnson, "Historical Roots," p. 4.

12. The question of motivation for warring is extremely complex and extremely controversial, whether one subscribes to psychoanalytic theories of aggression or materialist, social psychological, political, and/or a number of other motivations for warring, particularly in the fields of anthropology and sociology. Whatever historical, practical, psychological, or ideological motivations for engaging in war, material enhancement often plays a role in the motivational process at least within the leadership of decision making, if not among the masses. For a synopsis of the various disciplines and their views on the causes of war, see Ferguson, "Studying War," pp. 1–81, and cf. Berenice Carroll and Clinton Fink, "Theories of War Causation: A Matrix for Analysis," in Nettleship et al., eds., *War, Its Causes and Correlates*, pp. 55–70. Nettleship et al. provide a wide range of thinking in the social sciences on the etiology of war. For a synopsis of materialist thinking on the causes of war, see Ferguson, "Studying War," pp. 2, 22–37.

13. Not to mention the problem of guilt associated with the killing of others (see Rene Girard, *Violence and the Sacred*, Patrick Gregory, trans. [Baltimore: Johns Hopkins University Press, 1977]).

14. Edward Lane, *An Arabic-English Lexicon*, book 1 (London: Williams and Norgate, 1865) part 2, p. 473.

15. *Al-ʾamr bil-maʿrūf wal-nahy ʿan al-munkar*. This common phrase occurs repeatedly in the Qurʾān (*sūra* 3:110, 114, 9:71, etc.).

16. Muslim b. al-Ḥajjāj, *Ṣaḥīḥ Muslim* (Cairo: Dār al-Kitāb al-Miṣrī, n.d.), *K. al-Īmān*, 20.80 (1:69–70). All subsequent citations by Muslim refer to chapters in his collection, *Ṣaḥīḥ Muslim*.

17. Abū Dāwud, *Sunan Abī Dāwud* (Cairo, 1408/1988), *K. al-Malāḥim*, 4344 (4:122). All subsequent citations of Abū Dāwud refer to chapters of his collection, *Sunan Abī Dāwud*.

18. Much has been written about *jihād*, but little is unskewed by prejudice, apologetics, or political motives. Perhaps the best introductory article is that by E. Tyan, "Djihād," in *EI*², vol. 2, pp. 538–540. On the merits for engaging in war "in the path of God," see chapter 5, this volume.

19. Muḥammad ʿAlī, *Al-jihād fīl-sharʿiyya al-islāmiyya* (Cairo, 1393/1973), pp. 12–13; Watt, "Islamic Conceptions of the Holy War," p. 155. According to the oft-cited *ḥadīth*, Muḥammad, upon returning from battle, remarked: "We have re-

turned from the lesser *jihād* to the greater *jihād*." When asked what he meant by that, he is said to have replied, "The greater *jihād* is the struggle against the self." Its source is usually not given, and it is in fact nowhere to be found in the canonical collections.

20. Muḥammad Khayr Haykal, *Al-Jihād wal-qitāl fīl-siyāsa al-sharʿiyya*, 3 vols. (Beirut: Dār al-Bayāriq, 1414/1993), vol. 1, pp. 53–202; Khadduri, *War and Peace in the Law of Islam*, pp. 74–80; Joel L. Kramer, "Apostates, Rebels, Brigands," *Israel Oriental Studies* 10 (1980), pp. 34–73. These categories developed later than the earlier concept of warring in the path of God against non-Muslim enemies.

21. John Kelsay, "Religion, Morality, and the Governance of War: The Case of Classical Islam," *JRE* 18 (1990), pp. 123–139; John Kelsay, *Islam and War: A Study in Comparative Ethics* (Westminster: John Knox, 1993); Johnson and Kelsay, eds., *Cross, Crescent, and Sword*; Kelsay and Johnson, eds., *Just War and Jihad*; Robert Jeffrey Williams, "A Socio-Historical Analysis of Warfare (Jihād and Qitāl) in Primitive Islam" (Ph.D. diss., Florida State University, 1994).

22. To my knowledge, there has been no systematic study of the word as it appears in the Qurʾān. The root occurs there forty-one times in eighteen *sūras*. For new interpretations of *jihād* developed in the modern period, see Peters, *Islam and Colonialism*, pp. 105–35; Sonn, "Irregular Warfare and Terrorism," pp. 140–42.

23. But *qitāl* is far more specific in its narrower meaning of fighting. For *qitāl* in the path of God, see *sūras* 2:190, 244, 246; 3:13, 167; 4:74–76, 84; 9:111; 21:4; 73:20. *Ḥarb* is also common in the Qurʾān but is not found as part of the idiom, "in the path of God."

Chapter Two

1. For a survey of sources on biblical holy war, see note 3 in the Introduction.

2. Gwilym H. Jones, "The Concept of Holy War," in R. E. Clements, ed., *The World of Ancient Israel: Sociological, Anthropological, and Political Perspectives* (Cambridge: Cambridge University Press, 1989), pp. 299–302; Moshe Weinfeld, "Divine Intervention in War in Ancient Israel and in the Ancient Near East," in Moshe Weinfeld and Hayim Tadmor, eds., *History, Historiography, and Interpretation: Studies in Biblical and Cuneiform Literatures* (Jerusalem: Magnes, 1983).

3. On holy war in Christianity, see Roland Bainton, *Christian Attitudes toward War and Peace* (New York: Abington, 1960); Albert Marrin, *War and the Christian Conscience: From Augustine to Martin Luther King, Jr.* (Chicago: Henry Regnery, 1971). On Judaism, see Israel Historical Society, *Holy War and Martyrology in the History of Israel and the History of the Nations* (Hebrew), proceedings of the eleventh convention of the Israel Historical Society, March 1966 (Jerusalem: Israel Historical Society, 1968); Everette E. Gendler, "War and the Jewish Tradition," in *Contemporary Jewish Ethics*, Menachem Marc Kellner, ed., (New York: Sanhedrin Press, 1979), pp. 189–210.

4. No independent studies of the holy war phenomenon seem to exist for either tradition, but see E. W. Hopkins, *Ethics of India* (New Haven: Yale University Press, 1924), pp. 101–102, 243–244; S. C. Crawford, *The Evolution of Hindu Ethical Ideals* (Calcutta: Mukhopadhyay, 1974), pp. 87–89, 122–127, 153–154; Henry Thompson, *World Religions in War and Peace* (Jefferson, N.C.: McFarland, 1988), pp. 59–71; A. V. W. Jackson, *Zoroaster* (New York: Columbia University Press, 1919),

pp. 102–123, 210; William W. Malandra, *An Introduction to Ancient Iranian Religion* (Minneapolis: University of Minnesota Press, 1983), pp. 36, 59, 63–65, 71, 86, 102–103, 107–110.

5. Most of the classic scholarship in this field has focused on the remarkable parallels between the Bible and the Qur'ān. On the controversial issue of influence or independent development, see Jacques Waardenburg, "Toward a Periodization of Earliest Islam According to Its Relations with Other Religions," in *Proceedings of the Ninth Congress of the Union Europeene des Arabisants et Islamisants*, 1978 (Leiden: Brill, 1981), pp. 304–326; Reuven Firestone, *Journeys in Holy Lands: The Evolution of the Abraham-Ishmael Legends in Islamic Exegesis* (Albany: SUNY Press, 1990), pp. 3–19; Reuven Firestone, "Conceptions of Holy War in the Scriptures of Judaism and Islam," *Journal of Religious Ethics* 24 (Spring 1996), pp. 99–123.

6. The literature on the "influence" of Judaism and Christianity on Islam is vast and controversial. For an overview of the issues, see Firestone, *Journeys in Holy Lands*, pp. 3–21.

7. For a comparative examination of qur'ānic and biblical expressions of holy war, see Firestone, "Conceptions of Holy War in Biblical and Qur'ānic Tradition," *Journal of Religious Ethics* 24.1 (Spring 1996), pp. 99–123.

8. Reynold A. Nicholson, *A Literary History of the Arabs*, 2nd ed. (Cambridge: Cambridge University Press, 1930, and reprinted numerous times), pp. 30–31. The reliability of this poetry has been debated for much of the past century, with the scholarly trend recently being to accord a greater degree of authenticity to material in the collections.

9. The meaning of the term *jāhiliyya* and its implications regarding our topic will be examined later in this chapter.

10. Nabih Amin Faris, trans., *The Book of Idols, Being a Translation from the Arabic of the Kitāb al Asnām by Hishām Ibn Al Kalbi* (Princeton: Princeton University Press, 1952), p. vii; Jim G. Shaffer, "Origins of Islam: A Generative Model," *The Eastern Anthropologist* 31.4 (1978), p. 356. See the latter also for a synopsis of other modern approaches to the problem, pp. 355–363.

11. And excellent overview of the problem may be found in Fred Donner's introduction to A. A. Duri, *The Rise of Historical Writing among the Arabs*, Lawrence Conrad, trans. (Princeton: Princeton University Press, 1983), pp. vii–xvii. In addition to Duri, see D. M. Dunlop, *Arab Civilization to A.D. 1500* (Beirut: Librairie du Liban, 1971), pp. 70–149, and R. Stephen Humphreys, *Islammic History: A Framework for Inquiry* (Princeton: Princeton University Press, 1991).

12. See, for example, Fred M. Donner, *The Early Islamic Conquests* (Princeton: Princeton University Press, 1981), which is an excellent example of this type of study using modern ethnographies of Arab nomadic and sedentary groups as sources of data for reconstructing ancient Arabian sociopolitical systems.

13. This notwithstanding the respected view of Jibrail Jabbur: "With the experience of studying the ancient Arabic literature of pre-Islamic and Umayyad times, I saw that the way of life lived by those Arab bedouin authors was the same as that lived by their modern bedouin descendants, whose literature continues to give expression to desert ways just as that of their forefathers had done." (*The Bedouins and the Desert: Aspects of Nomadic Life in the Arab East* [Albany: SUNY Press, 1995], p. 12). As noted by Jabbur, twentieth-century ethnographic studies of the Bedouin indeed exhibit striking similarities with early descriptions. See (in addition to

Jabbur), for example, Alois Musil, *The Manners and Customs of the Rwala Bedouins* (New York: American Geographical Society, 1928); Charles M. Doughty, *Travels in Arabia Deserta*, 2 vols. (New York: Random House, 1937); Harold R. P. Dickson, *The Arab of the Desert: A Glimpse into Badawin Life in Kuwait and Sa'udi Arabia* (London: George Allen and Unwin, 1949); E. E. Evans-Pritchard, *The Sanusi of Cyrenaica* (Oxford: Clarendon, 1949). For a discussion and critique of some of these and other Western and modern Arabic works on the Bedouins, see Jabbur's introduction (pp. 9–28).

14. This observation is truer with regard to the tradition literature (the Ḥadīth) than to the Qur'ān, which because of its early provenance is more likely to reflect opinions and visions contemporary with the origins of Islam.

15. Dale Eickelman, "Musaylima: An Approach to the Social Anthropology of Seventh Century Arabia," *JESHO* 10 (1967), pp. 26–27, I. M. Lapidus, "The Arab Conquests and the Formation of Islamic Society," in G. H. A. Juynboll, ed., *Studies on the First Century of Islamic Society* (Carbondale, Ill.: Southern Illinois University Press, 1982), pp. 58–61.

16. Gorden D. Newby, *A History of the Jews of Arabia* (Columbia: University of South Carolina Press, 1988); J. Spencer Trimingham, *Christianity among the Arabs in Pre-Islamic Times* (London: Longman, 1979).

17. On the question of what forms of religious expression were represented by these groups and whether Islamic variations of practice, terminology, and ideas familiar to Judaism and Christianity represent "mainstream" or syncretistic practice of these traditions or unique Islamic forms, see David Halperin and Gordon Newby, "Two Castrated Bulls: A Study in the Haggadah of Kaʿb al-Aḥbār," *JAOS* 102.3 (1982), pp. 631–638, and Chaim Rabin, "Islam and the Qumran Sect," in Chaim Rabin, ed., *Qumran Studies* (London: Oxford University Press, 1957), pp. 112–130, in which the author also notes other scholarly attempts to associate Islamic artifacts with non-Rabbinic expressions (I am grateful to Professor Halperin for the latter reference).

18. Donner, *The Early Islamic Conquests*, pp. 12–14.

19. The invader was of Abyssinian origin but attempted to carve out a largely independent enclave. South Arabia had a major political and cultural impact on the central regions at various periods (Lapidus, "The Arab Conquests", p. 58).

20. Giorgio Levi Della Vida, "Pre-Islamic Arabia," in Nabih Amin Faris, ed., *The Arab Heritage* (New York: Russell and Russell, 1963), p. 32; A. F. L. Beeston, *Warfare in Ancient South Arabia*, Qahtan: Studies in Old South Arabian Epigraphy, Series fasc. 3 (London: Luzac, 1976), p. 23.

21. Beeston, *Warfare*, p. 1.

22. Uri Rubin, "The Kaʿba: Aspects of Its Ritual Functions and Position in Pre-Islamic and Early Islamic Times," *JSAI* 8 (1986), pp. 115–118.

23. Beeston, *Warfare*, p. 18.

24. Listed as 400 enemy children and women who were massacred along with 210 troops killed in battle and 130 taken captive, and 300 camels, 1,300 cattle, 270 asses, and 10,000 sheep and goats taken in spoil (ibid., p. 24).

25. A. K. Irvine, "Homicide in Pre-Islamic South Arabia," *BSOAS* 30.2 (1967), pp. 277–292.

26. Because the economies of organized polities could support larger populations in village and urban areas, when such systems collapsed causing their popula-

tions to revert to pastoralism, survivors were forced to spread out into larger geographical areas in order for the limited natural resources of the Arabian steppe to sustain them.

27. Della Vida, "Pre-Islamic Arabia," pp. 35–48; Werner Caskel, "The Bedouinization of Arabia," *The American Anthropologist* 56.2 (1954), pp. 36–46.

28. Eickelman, "Musaylima," pp. 24–25.

29. Julian Obermann, "Islamic Origins: A Study in Background and Foundation," in Faris, ed., *The Arab Heritage*, p. 61; Phillip Hitti, *History of the Arabs* (New York: St. Martin's, 1970), pp. 61–64. Dhū Nuwās's purported massacre of Najrani Christians will be examined later in this chapter.

30. *EJ*, vol. 12, pp. 739–744; *EI*², vol. 7, pp. 834–838.

31. Trimingham, *Christianity among the Arabs*, pp. 1–20; Michael Morony, *Iraq after the Muslim Conquest* (Princeton: Princeton University Press, 1984), pp. 214–223.

32. Hitti, *History of the Arabs*, pp. 78–84.

33. Patricia Crone, *Meccan Trade and the Rise of Islam* (Princeton: Princeton University Press, 1987), who counters the older view established by Henri Lammens, *La Mecque a la Veille de l'Hegire* (Beirut, 1924), and still held by a school of historians (Lapidus, "The Arab Conquests," p. 59). A digest and analysis of the two views may be found in F. E. Peters, *Muhammad and the Origins of Islam* (Albany: SUNY Press, 1993), pp. 70–75.

34. Caskel, "The Bedouinization of Arabia," pp. 36–46.

35. Sidney Smith, "Events in Arabia in the 6th Century A.D.," *BSOAS* 16.3 (1954), pp. 467–468; H. von Wissmann, "Badw," in *EI*², vol. 1, pp. 884–885.

36. Donner, *Conquests*, pp. 16–20.

37. Ibid., pp. 29–30.

38. The meaning of the words in Arabic is "gurgle" or "murmer." The origins of the settlement are shrouded in mystery, but the foundation stories are associated with the spring (Firestone, *Journeys in Holy Lands*, pp. 63–71).

39. Lapidus, "The Arab Conquests," pp. 59, 64.

40. Muḥammad Ibn Isḥāq, *Al-Sīra al-nabawiyya*, 2 vols. (Beirut: Dār al-Thiqāfa al-ʿArabiyya, n.d., a photo offset of the authoritative ed., Muṣṭafā al-Saqqā, Ibrāhīm al-Abyārī, and ʿAbdul-Ḥāfiẓ Shalabī, eds. [Cairo, 1937], and reprinted often), vol. 1, pp. 115–116. This Cairo edition was translated by Alfred Guillaume as *The Life of Muhammad: A Translation of Ibn Ishaq's Sirat Rasul Allah* (Oxford: Oxford University Press, 1955), but paginated according to the edition of Wustenfeld (Göttingen, 1856–1860), pp. 48–49. Henceforth, references will be given for the Arabic Cairo edition as I.I., followed by Guillaume's translation as G (I.I., vol. 1, pp. 115–116/G, pp. 48–49). See also Muḥammad b. Jarīr al-Ṭabarī, *Taʾrīkh al-rusul wal-mulūk*, ed. M. J. DeGoeje as *Annales* (Leiden: Brill, 1964), vol. 2, p. 1094 (henceforth cited as Ṭabarī, *Taʾrīkh*), English translation by W. Montgomery Watt and M. V. McDonald as *The History of al-Ṭabarī* (Albany: SUNY Press, 1988), vol. 6, pp. 20–21; cf. Ibn Saʿd, *Kitāb al-tabaqāt al-Kabīr*, ed. Sachau and entitled *Ibn Saad Biographien* (Leiden: Brill, 1917), vol. 1, pp. 36–138, English trans. by S. Moinul Haq as *Ibn Saʿd's Kitab al-Tabaqat al-Kabir* (New Delhi, Kitab Bhavan, n.d.), vol. 1, pp. 63–68 (henceforth I.S. [Arabic]/H [English translation]). This is challenged by some modern scholars (Shaffer, "Origins of Islam," p. 359).

41. Judges 6:5–6. The Midianites, according to the biblical genealogy, derive from Abraham and Qᵉturah (Genesis 25:2), whose name means frankincense and

is clearly associated with the Arabian spice trade. The children of the East derive from Ishmael's son, Qedmah (meaning, literally, "eastward," Genesis 25:15). Although the Bible tends to associate camels with non-Israelites (but see Genesis 12:16, 24:10–11, 30:43, 31:34), an interesting Bedouin legend assumes that the Jews introduced camels to the Bedouin (Musil, *Manners and Customs*, pp. 329–330).

42. Jabbur, *The Bedouins*, pp. 200–202.

43. For a classic but dated study of the patriarchal nature of Bedouin society and a theory of its early history as a matriarchal society, see W. Robertson Smith, *Kinship and Marriage in Early Arabia* (London: Adam and Charles Black, 1903).

44. Helmer Ringgren, *Studies in Arabian Fatalism* (Uppsala: A. B. Lundequistska, 1955), p. 14. Cf. Toshihiko Izutsu, *Ethico-Religious Concepts in the Qur'ān* (Montreal: McGill University Press, 1966), pp. 45–54.

45. Ringgren, *Arabian Fatalism*, pp. 6–9.

46. Ibid., pp. 9–14; L. Gardet, "Al-Ḳaḍā' wa'l-Ḳadar," in *EI*², vol. 4, pp. 365–367.

47. Ringgren, *Arabian Fatalism*, pp. 30–31. There are many such instances. Sometimes in place of *dahr* or *zamān* one finds *ayyām* ("days") or *layālī* ("nights") or together in poetic parallelism, such as in "Night and day together have destroyed us, Time is relentless and ever new" (Ringgren, *Arabian Fatalism*, p. 38).

48. The first poem is from Ḥātim al-Ṭā'ī, and the second from Sulmī b. Rabīʿa, as given in Ringgren, *Arabian Fatalism*, p. 50.

49. I.I., vol. 1, p. 543/G, pp. 254–255. Cf. Charles J. Lyall, *Translations of Ancient Arabian Poetry* (London: Williams and Norgate, 1930).

50. Ringgren, *Arabian Fatalism*, p. 57.

51. See ibid., pp. 58–60, for the views of Caskel, Gomez, and Watt, as well as his own predilections.

52. The influence of pre-Islamic Arabian religion on Arabian culture will be considered later in this chapter.

53. Ignaz Goldziher, "Muruwwa and Dīn," in his *Muslim Studies*, ed. S. M. Stern and trans. C. R. Barber and S. M. Stern (London: George Allen and Unwin, 1971), vol. 1, p. 13; W. Montgomery Watt, *Muhammad at Mecca* (Oxford: Clarendon, 1953), p. 24; Ringgren, *Arabian Fatalism*, p. 59.

54. Uri Rubin, "*Ḥanīfiyya* and Kaʿba: An Inquiry into the Arabian Pre-Islamic Background of *dīn ibrāhīm*, *JSAI* 13 (1990), pp. 85–112; Andrew Rippin, "RḤMNN and the Ḥanīfs," in Wael B. Hallaq and Donald P. Little, eds., *Islamic Studies Presented to Charles J. Adams* (Leiden: Brill, 1991), pp. 153–168; Hamilton Gibb, "Pre-Islamic Monotheism in Arabia," *HTR* 55 (1962), 269–280; Eickelman, "Musaylima," pp. 17–52; Watt, *Muhammad at Mecca*, pp. 162–164.

55. Yathrib was the name of the oasis settlement before Muḥammad made his famous Hijra there from Mecca in 622 C.E. After the Hijra, it was known as *madīnat al-nabī*, the "City of the Prophet," or simply *madīna*, usually spelled in English, Medina. It will be referred to here as Yathrib for references to the pre-Islamic period and Medina after the Hijra.

56. Goldziher, "Muruwwa and Dīn," in his *Muslim Studies*, vol. 1, pp. 12–27; Izutzu, *Ethico-Religious Concepts*, pp. 27, 75; W. Robertson Smith, *Kinship and Marriage*, pp. 41–72; Bichr Fares, "Murū'a," in *EI*², vol. 7, pp. 636–638.

57. Donner, *Conquests*, p. 287 n. 46.

58. Nicholson, *Literary History*, pp. 82–92; A. J. Arberry, *The Seven Odes* (London: George Allen and Unwin, 1957), p. 39.

59. Bichr Fares, "'Irḍ," in *EI*[2], vol. 4, p. 77.

60. W. Montgomery Watt, "Badw," in *EI*[2], vol. 1, p. 892. An excellent introduction to pre-Islamic poetry is still Nicholson, *Literary History*, pp. 71–83, and a good synopsis of themes can be found in A. J. Arberry, "Arabia Deserta," in his *Aspects of Islamic Civilization* (New York: A. S. Barnes, 1964), pp. 19–31. On the role of the poet in intertribal rivalry, see also Goldziher, *Muslim Studies*, vol. 1. pp. 48–54 (cf. I.I., vol. 1, pp. 411, 413–414/G, pp. 188, 190).

61. Goldziher, *Muslim Studies*, vol. 1, pp. 57–60; Bichr Fares, *L'Honneur chez Les Arabes Avant L'Islam* (Paris: Librairie d'Amerique et d'Orient Adrien-Maisonneuve, 1932), pp. 113–118.

62. Donner, *Conquests*, p. 17.

63. Ibid., pp. 39–40. I follow Donner here, who notes that although one could speak theoretically of culturally determined rules of behavior as law (as does Fares, *L'Honneur*, pp. 206 ff.): "Our understanding of law . . . demands not only a system of constraints and sanctions, but also that the imposed constraints reflect some general principle of justice *independent of the differences in actual social power exercised by specific groups*. That is, there is a difference between 'Thou shalt not kill' (a law) and 'Thou shalt not kill anyone whose tribal backing is more powerful than yours' (an imposed constraint accompanied by a sanction—the threat of retaliation)" (*Conquests*, p. 291 [italics in original]).

64. For the problems associated with the term "tribe" in the social sciences, see Donner, *Conquests*, pp. 283–284 n. 24.

65. Ibid., p. 22.

66. In general, "[t]he greater the competition for scarce resources, the greater the potential for and the probability of disputes; the great the number of disputes, the higher the likelihood of warfare in any particular region" (Ronald Cohen, "Warfare and State Formation: Wars Make States and States Make Wars," in Ferguson, ed., *Warfare*, p. 333.). This view, from the perspective of the cultural materialist theory of prestate warfare (see note 77, this chapter), would explain the highly warlike nature of pre-Islamic Arabian culture.

67. Abū Tammām Ḥabīb b. Aus, *Al-Ḥamāsa*, p. 378, as translated by Nicholson, *Literary History*, p. 83. So, too, in the following verse:

> Take for your brother whom you will in days of peace,
> But know that when fighting comes, your kinsman alone is near.
> Your true friend is your kinsman, who answers your call for aid
> With good will, when deeply drenched in bloodshed are sword and spear.
> Oh, never forsake your kinsman even when he does you wrong,
> For what he has marred he mends thereafter and makes sincere.
> (Nicholson's translation, with my few revisions).

68. Julius Wellhausen, "Muhammad's Constitution of Medina," in A. J. Wensinck, ed., *Muhammad and the Jews of Medina* (Berlin: Adiyok, 1982), p. 134.

69. W. Robertson Smith, *Kinship and Marriage*, pp. 41–44.

70. The Qur'ān refers to the practice and condemns it (16:57–59): "They consign daughters to God, may He be glorified, and [allow] to themselves what they desire. When one of them receives the news of a female [child], his face darkens in grief. He hides from the people because of the bad news [thinking], should he keep

it in disgrace [or contempt?], or bury it in the dust. These make an evil judgment." *Sūra* 17:31: "Do not kill your children in fear of poverty. We shall provide for them and for you. Killing them is a great sin!"

71. Fares, *L'Honneur*, pp. 143–146. It must be stressed here that the idea of blood purity within the tribe is a myth, for captured slaves intermingled within the tribe, as did certain levels of allies (*ḥulafā'*) who could be treated essentially as members. So, too, could a protected neighbor (*jār*) or client (*mawlā*) live among the tribe, and, as noted previously, tribal divisions resulted eventually in the existence of tribes that lost their awareness of kinship (W. Robertson Smith, *Kinship and Marriage*, pp. 41–72; Goldziher, *Muslim Studies*, vol. 1, pp. 65–68; Watt, "Badw," p. 891).

72. Watt, *Muhammad at Mecca*, p. 17.

73. The plural form is *ghazawāt*, but *maghāzī* is more common in the early material. The English word "razzia" is derived indirectly from colloquial Arabic (*ghazya*) through the French *razzier*.

74. For an economic analysis of raiding in the modern period, see Louise Sweet, "Camel Raiding of North Arabian Bedouin: A Mechanism of Ecological Adaption," *American Anthropologist*, no. 67 (1965), pp. 1132–1150.

75. The avoidance of bloodshed was not because of the inherent abhorrence of violence or killing but, rather, because of the resultant problem of blood feuds, which will be discussed later in this chapter.

76. Jawād ʿAlī, *Al-Mufaṣṣal fī taʿrīkh al-ʿArab qabl al-Islām* (Beirut: Dār al-ʿIlm, n.d.), vol. 5, pp. 333–341; Fares, *L'Honneur*, pp. 105–108; T. M. Johnstone, "Ghazw," in *EI*², vol. 2, pp. 1055–1056.

77. ʿAlī, Al-Mufaṣṣal, vol. 5, p. 403; Caskel, "Bedouinization of Arabia," p. 36 (cf. with the modern system described by Johnstone, "Ghazw," vol. 2, pp. 1055–1056). This description accords in general with the cultural materialist theory of prestate warfare, although most anthropological studies have not treated pastoral cultures. The theory, in general, holds that warfare in traditional cultures "enhanced the well-being and survivability of individuals and groups by regulating the balance between population size and crucial local and regional ecological variables" (Marvin Harris, "A Cultural Materialist Theory of Band and Village Warfare: The Yanomamo Test," in Ferguson, ed., Warfare, p. 111; cf. Andrew Vayda, "Primitive and Modern War," in Morton Fried, Marvin Harris, and Robert Murphy, eds., War: The Anthropology of Armed Conflict and Aggression [Garden City, N.Y.: Natural History Press, 1968], p. 86). In both the case of Amazonian cultures and Arab pastoralists, such cultures limit population growth at least as much through female infanticide as they do through war casualties, but the practice of the former is directly related to the necessity of favoring the rearing of male warriors.

78. These customs, according to observations, have continued into this century (Musil, *Rwala Bedouins*, p. 504). For a list of other traditional world cultures in which the nature of fighting obviously changes the more distantly related the enemy is, see Susan Niditch's synopsis in *War in the Hebrew Bible* (New York: Oxford University Press, 1993), pp. 17–18.

79. Donner, "Sources of Islamic Conceptions of War," p. 35.

80. Smith, *Kinship and Marriage*, p. 43. This principle was complicated as subgroups within the larger tribe grew and began to separate from one another. When a man killed a tribal relative from a different and separate clan, the kinship relationship might not be strong enough for that clan to offer up the killer or even to

pay the bloodwit. This situation could result in fratricidal wars that could drag on for decades if not generations. Examples of this phenomenon would be the famous blood feud between the Aws and the Khazraj in Yathrib, or the so-called Basūs War between the Bakr and Taghlib in Yamāma.

81. M. Ajmal Khan, "Jāhilīya: A Description of the State and Mode of Living," *Studies in Islam* 3.4 (1966), p. 179; Watt, "Badw," p. 892; Fares, *L'Honneur*, pp. 121–122. For parallels to such kinship-oriented fighting in other world cultures, see Alexander Lesser, "War and the State," in Fried, Harris, and Murphy, eds., *War: The Anthropology of Armed Conflict and Aggression*, pp. 94–95.

82. W. Robertson Smith, *Kinship and Marriage*, pp. 63–67.

83. As cited in Donner, *Conquests*, p. 291.

84. The famous War of Basūs (*ḥarb basūs*) between the Taghlib and the Bakr described repeatedly in the sources serves as a classic example of such a war (for a translation of the narrative found in al-Tibrīzī's commentary on *al-Ḥamāsa* of Abū Tammām, see Nicholson, *Literary History*, pp. 55–60). Whether or not the data regarding this intertribal conflict as extracted from the sources are historically accurate does not detract from the cultural issues and resultant expectations and motivations that they describe (cf. G. Levi Della Vida, "Kulayb b. Rabīʿa," *EI*^{2}, vol. 5, p. 362).

85. I.I., vol. 1, pp. 610–611/G, pp. 291–292.

86. Take, for example, the story of Qays b. Khaṭīm, who was assisted by a cousin of his grandfather's murderer to exact revenge against the perpetrator because of a favor that his dead father had bestowed on the cousin many years earlier (Abūl-Farāj al-Iṣfahānī, *Kitāb al-aghānī*, vol. 2, pp. 160 ff., and translated by Nicholson, *Literary History*, pp. 94–97).

87. Irvine, "Homicide," pp. 277–292. A similar system was instituted by the Qur'ān as centralized governance extended mutual relations between unrelated tribes under the new Islamic system (4:92–93; 6:151–152; 25:68).

88. Donner, *Conquests*, pp. 37–42.

89. Abū ʿUbayda Muʿammar b. al-Muthannā al-Taymī, *Kitāb ayyām al-ʿArab qablal-Islām*, ʿĀdil Jāsim al-Bayātī, ed. (Beirut, 1407/1987), part 1, pp. 59–65. Each conflict was named as a "day," such as Yawm Buʿāth ("Day of Buʿāth") and Yawm Dhī Qār (Taymī, *Kitāb ayyām al-ʿArab*, part 2, pp. 29–622; ʿAlī, *Al-Mufaṣṣal*, vol. 5, pp. 341–387).

90. Khan, *Jāhilīya*, pp. 179–180; E. Mittwoch, "Ayyām al-ʿArab" in *EI*^{2}, vol. 1, pp. 793–794.

91. ʿAlī, *Al-Mufaṣṣal*, vol. 5, pp. 343, 403.

92. Dickson, *Arab of the Desert*, p. 341.

93. Donner, *Conquests*, pp. 18–19.

94. For a brief survey of the issues, see Joseph Henninger, "La Religion bedouine preislamique," in F. Gabrieli, ed., *L'antica societa beduina* (Rome: Instituto di Studi Orientali, 1959), pp. 115–140, trans. Merlin Swartz as "Pre-Islamic Bedouin Religion," in Swartz, ed., *Studies on Islam* (New York: Oxford University Press, 1981), pp. 3–22.

95. F. E. Peters, *Muhammad*, pp. 121–127.

96. In addition to the sources listed above, see Michael Lecker, "Idol Worship in Pre-Islamic Medina (Yathrib)," *Le Museon* 106.3–4 (1993), pp. 331–346; Uri Rubin, "The Kaʿba," pp. 97–131; Rubin, "*Ḥanīfiyya* and Kaʿba, pp. 85–112.; Moshe

Gil, "The Origin of the Jews of Yathrib," *JSAI* 4 (1984), pp. 203–223; G. R. Hawting, "The Origins of the Muslim Sanctuary at Mecca," in G. H. A. Juynboll, ed., *Studies on the First Century of Islamic Society*, (Carbondale, Ill.: Southern Illinois University Press, 1982), pp. 23–47; M. J. Kister, "Labbayka, Allāhumma, Labbayka . . . ," *JSAI* 2 (1980), pp. 33–57; Kister, "Maqām Ibrāhīm: A Stone with an Inscription," *Le Museon* 84 (1971), pp. 477–491; Shaffer, "Origins of Islam," pp. 355–363; Toufic Fahd, *Le panthéon de l'Arabie centrale à la veille de l'hegire* (Paris: Paul Geuthner, 1968); Obermann, "Islamic Origins," pp. 58–80; Hamilton Gibb, "Pre-Islamic Monotheism in Arabia," pp. 268–280; René Dagorn, *La geste d'Ismael d'Après l'onomastique et la tradition arabes* (Paris: Champion, 1981); Rippin, "RḤMNN and the Ḥanīfs."

97. On the econonomy of prestige as a motivator for engaging in war, see Lincoln, *Death, War, and Sacrifice*, p. 138–140.

98. Faris, *The Book of Idols*, pp. 30, 41.

99. Or Yūsuf Ashʿar, or Yūsuf Shuraḥbīl, referred to usually as Dhū Nuwās in the Arabic sources but referred to often as Al-Masrūq in the Syriac sources.

100. This conflict seems to have begun as a campaign against foreign (Abyssinian) influence but may have expanded to include local Christians who would be expected to represent Abyssinian allies. The issue of the massacre and the general accuracy of the accounts have been questioned for years (see Abūl Ḥasan ʿAlī b. all-Ḥusayn al-Masʿūdī, *Murūj al-dhahab wa-maʿādin al-jawāhir* [Beirut: Universithy of Beirut Press, 1966], vol. 2, pp. 199–200; Ibn al-Athīr, *Al-Kāmil fīl-ta'rīkh*, ed. Carolus Tornberg as *Ibn-El-Athiri Chronicon [*Leiden: Brill, 1868], vol. 2, pp. 307–311; Axel Moberg, ed., *The Book of the Himyarites* [London: Humphrey Milford, 1924]; Jacques Ryckmans, *La persécution des Chrétiens himyarites au sixième siècle* [Istanbul: Nederlands Historisch-Archaelogisch Instituut, 1956]; Hayyim Hirschberg, "Yūsuf 'As'ar Yath'ar Dhū Nuwās," *EJ* 16 [1972], pp. 897–900; Sidney Smith, "Events in Arabia," pp. 456–463).

101. Josef Horovitz, *Koranische Untersuchungen* (Berlin: Walter de Gruyter, 1926), pp. 92–93.

102. The king or emperor of Abyssinia (*al-najāshī* in Arabic, *negūsh* in Amharic).

103. Or in some sources, the appeal was to the Byzantines, who subsequently appealed to the Ethiopians.

104. Ibn al-Athīr, *Al-Kāmil fīl-ta'rīkh*, vol. 2, pp. 307–311; Masʿūdī, *Murūj al-dḥahab*, vol. 2, pp. 199–200; F. Krenkow, "The Two Oldest Books on Arabic Folklore," *I.C.* 2 (1928), p. 228; Sidney Smith, "Events in Arabia," pp. 451–468; Ryckmans, *La persécution Des Chrétiens himyarites*; Moberg, *Book of the Himyarites*; Hayyim Hirschberg, *Yisrael baʿArav* (Jerusalem, 1946), pp. 76–111.

105. Sidney Smith, "Events in Arabia," pp. 449–450, 460–461.

106. F. E. Peters, *Muhammad*, p. 54.

107. Usually named as *Dhū al-Qaʿda*, *Dhū al-Ḥijja*, *Muḥarram*, and *Rajab* (Muḥammad b. Jarīr al-Ṭabarī [d. 925], *Jāmiʿ al-bayān ʿan ta'wīl āy al-Qur'ān*, 30 books in 15 vols. [Cairo: Muṣtafā al-Bābī al-Ḥalabī and Sons, 1373/1954; reprint, Beirut: Dār al-Fikr, 1405/1984], book 10, p. 124 [henceforth *Jamiʿ al-bayān* will be cited as Ṭabarī]; ʿImād al-Dīn Ismāʿīl Ibn Kathīr *Tafsīr al-Qur'ān al-ʿaẓīm*, 7 vols. [Beirut, 1405/1985], vol. 3, pp. 393–394; cf. Muḥammad b. Ismāīl al-Bukhārī, *Saḥīḥ al-Bukhārī*, 9 vols. [Lahore: Kazi, 1979], *K. Bad' al-Khalq*, 2.419 [vol. 4, p. 281], and *K. al-Tawḥīd*, 24.539 [vol. 9, pp. 405–406]; Abū Dāwud al-Sijistānī, *Sunan Abī Dāwud*

[Cairo: Dār al Miṣriyya al-Lubnāniyya, 1408/1988], *K. al-Manāsik*, 1947 [vol. 2, pp. 202–203]), although there is some disagreement over exactly how many months were sacred and which ones they were. This may have been a result of the problem of intercalating the calendar during this period, a practice which was later outlawed by Islam (F. E. Peters, *Muhammad*, pp. 251–253). Ibn Isḥāq mentions that some claim (*fī mā yazʿimūna*) there were eight sacred months among the ancient Arabs (*Al-Sīra al-Nabawiyya* [Beirut: Dār al-Thiqāfa al-ʿArabiyya, n.d.], vol.1, p. 102/G, p. 44).

108. Abūl-Walīd Muḥammad b. ʿAbdallah b. Aḥmad al-Azraqī, *Akhbār makka al-musharrifa*, ed. F. Wüstenfeld, as *Chroniken der Stadt Mecca* (Leipzig: F. A. Brockhaus, 1858), pp. 129–130. For a general synopsis of the pre-Islamic political and social background, see Lapidus, "The Arab Conquests," pp. 49–72.

109. A tradition recorded by Ṭabarī states that even if a man met the killer of his father or brother during one of the Sacred Months, he would not provoke him (Ṭabarī, book 2, p. 346). On the other hand, there was a period in Mecca, according to the tradition, during which the Sacred Months were broken. This was the period of the "War of Fijār" (I.I., vol.1, pp. 184–187/G, p. 82; I.S., vol. 1, part 1, pp. 80–82/H, vol.1, pp. 141–144).

110. Eickelman, "Musaylima," pp. 25, 42. There were sacred compounds in other parts of Arabia as well (I.I., vol. 1, p. 83/G, p. 38), and Bukhārī mentions one called *Kaʿbat al-Yamānīya* (*Kitāb al-Jihād* 154:262 and 192:310 [vol. 4, pp.163, 198]).

111. Cf. Exodus 21:14 and 1 Kings 1:50–53 and 2:28–30, in which, according to ancient biblical law, a person who had committed homicide could find protection by entering the sacred area and grasping hold of the handles of the altar. Both in 1 Kings and in Ibn Isḥāq (*Al-Sīra al-nabawiyya*, vol. 2, p. 172/G, p. 427]), a killer was forcibly removed from the protection of the sacred area and killed, a clear demonstration of how the rage of battle may cause infringement of the rule of protection afforded by such sacred sites. The same thing seems to have occurred also according to tradition, when Muḥammad victoriously entered Mecca and killed at least one person who had sought refuge by grasping onto the curtains of the Kaʿba (Bukhārī, *Kitāb al-jihād*, ch. 170 [vol. 4, p. 176]; Abu Dāwud, *K. al-jihād*, 2685 [vol. 3, pp. 59–60]).

112. R. B. Serjeant, "Haram and Hawtah, the Sacred Enclave in Arabia," in *Melanges Taha Husain* (Cairo: Dār al-Maʿārif, 1962), pp. 41–58.

113. For this distinction, see especially, Donner, "Sources of Islamic Conceptions of War," especially pp. 59–60, n. 5.

114. *Sūras* 3:154, 5:50, 33:33, and 48:26.

115. "What is Meant by 'al-Jāhiliyya,'" in Goldziher, *Muslim Studies*, vol. 1, pp. 201–208.

116. Ibid., p. 203. Cf. Khan, "Jāhilīya," pp. 175–176.

117. Goldziher, *Muslim Studies*, vol. 1, p. 205.

118. I.I., vol. 1, p. 336/G, p. 151.

119. Goldziher, *Muslim Studies*, vol. 1, p. 207.

Part II

1. I.S., vol. 1, part 1, pp. 151–152/H, vol. 1, pp. 260–261.
2. Alford T. Welch, "Ḳurān," in *EI*[2], vol. 5, pp. 404–406.

3. *Quranic Studies* (Oxford: Oxford University Press, 1977), especially pp. 44–46.

4. *The Collection of the Qur'ān* (Cambridge: Cambridge University Press, 1977), pp. 239–240.

5. Izutsu, *Ethico-Religious Concepts.*

6. Waardenburg, "Periodization of Earliest Islam," p. 307. For an excellent study of the transitional location of the Qur'ān (though overly judgmental with regard to its view of indigenous pre-Islamic culture), see Izutsu, *Ethico-Religious Concepts.*

7. H. A. R. Gibb, *Studies on the Civilization of Islam*, Standford Shaw and William Polk, eds. (Princeton: Princeton University Press, 1982), pp. 179–181, 187–196; Izutsu, *Ethico-Religious Concepts*, p. 16. See also M. M. Bravmann, *The Spiritual Background of Early Islam* (Leiden: Brill, 1972).

Chapter Three

1. An earlier version of this chapter was published in *JNES* 55 (1997) as "Disparity and Resolution in the Qur'ānic Teachings on War: A Re-evaluation of a Traditional Problem," pp. 1–19.

2. The relevant verses will be examined in some detail later in this chapter.

3. A number of other verses express a similar sentiment, such as 2:109, 5:13, 6:106, 15:94–95, 29:46, 42:15, 50:39, and 60:8.

4. See also 2:190 as understood by traditional Muslim exegetes, 16:110, and 22:39–40.

5. See also 2:190, 191(?), 217(?); 9:36(?).

6. The question of the "Sacred Months" will be treated in some detail later in this chapter.

7. See also 2:191, 193, 217; 8:39; 9:29, 123; 66:9.

8. See also 3:156, 167–168; 4:72–75, 77, 95; 9:38–39, 42, 86–87, 90; 33:16, 18; 47:20; 48:16–17; 61:2–4(?).

9. See also 2:154; 3:157–158, 169; 195; 4:74; 9:89, 111; 47:4b-6, 36.

10. See also 3:123–125, 166–167; 8:17; 9:14, 25–26; 48:23.

11. 4:94, 104; 8:15, 41; 47:4, 35.

12. 2:218; 3:139–140; 4:75; 8:65–66; 9:14, 20–22, 41, 111; 57:10; and see also some of the verses listed above (particularly in note 10) on the reward that accrues to those killed on the battlefield.

13. Proper names of contemporary historical personalities (as opposed to ancient characters such as Abraham, Moses, and Hud) almost never occur, nor do other proper nouns except on rare occasions. Even when a historical marker is given, such as the reference to the Byzantines' having been defeated in battle in 30:2–3 (*ghulibat al-rūm*), the particular battle is impossible to determine without additional evidence.

14. Rippin, "The Exegetical Genre *Asbāb al-nuzūl*," pp. 2–15. Western scholarship has likewise attempted an ordering of revelations, although much more modest. The so-called Nöldeke-Schwally system, named for Theodore Nöldeke (*Geschichte des Qorans* [Göttingen, 1860], and Friedrich Schwally, who revised Nöldeke's analysis in the second edition (3 vols. [Leipzig, 1909–1938], is flawed by its uncritical reliance on "the traditional Muslim substance, sequence, and dating of the events of the life of Muhammad" (F. E. Peters, *Muhammad and the Origins of Islam*, p. 259).

15. *Asbāb al-nuzūl* (Beirut: Dār al-Kutub al-ʿIlmiyya, n.d.) (henceforth, Wāḥidī).

16. On the problem of reliability of this genre, see Welch, "Ḳur'ān," pp. 415–416; Andrew Rippin, "Literary Analysis of *Qur'ān, Tafsīr,* and *Sīra*: The Methodologies of John Wansbrough," in Richard Martin, ed., *Approaches to Islam in Religious Studies* (Tucson: University of Arizona Press, 1985), p. 153. For a study of the problem with regard to warring in the Qur'ān, see Firestone, "Disparity and Resolution in the Qur'ānic Teachings on War, pp. 1–19.

17. David S. Powers, "The Exegetical Genre nāsikh al-Qur'ān wa mansūkhuhu," in Andrew Rippin, ed., *Approaches to the History of the Interpretation of the Qur'ān* (Oxford: Clarendon, 1988); Burton, *The Collection of the Qur'ān,* pp. 117–138; John Burton, *The Sources of Islamic Law: Islamic Theories of Abrogation* (Edinburgh: Edinburgh University Press, 1990).

18. 15:94–95, 16:125 (these verses and those in the following three notes will be translated and examined in detail in this and the following chapter); *Tafsīr Muqātil b. Sulaymān* (d. 767) (Cairo: al-Hay'a al-Miṣriyya al-ʿĀma lil-Kitāb, 1979), vol. 2, p. 437 (although this work is attributed to Muqātil, it is most likely somewhat later [M. Plessner and A. Rippin, "Muḳātil b. Sulaymān," in EI^2, vol. 7, pp. 508–509]; Ṭabarī, book 14, p. 69.

19. 2:190, 22:39–40; *Tafsīr al-imām Mujāhid b. Jabr* (d. 722) (Cairo: Dār al-Fikr al-Islāmī, 1410/1989), p. 482, which, although attributed to Mujāhid, is also later (A. Rippin, "Mudjāhid b. Djabr al-Makkī, in EI^2, vol. 7, p. 293); Ṭabarī, book 17, pp. 172–173; Aḥmad Muḥammad b. Ismāʿīl al-Naḥḥās (d. 949), *Al-Nāsikh wal-mansūkh fī kitāb Allah ʿazza wajalla* (Beirut: Mu'assasat al-Risāla, 1412/1991), vol. 2, pp. 233, 301 (henceforth, Naḥḥās).

20. 2:191, 217.

21. 2:216; 9:5, 29. *Sūra* 9:5 is of such importance that it is considered by early exegetes to have abrogated 114 or 124 verses treating war that were revealed before it (Ibn al-Jawzī [d. 1200], *Nawāsikh al-Qur'ān* [Beirut: Dār al-Kutub al-ʿIlmiyya, n.d.], p. 179 [henceforth, Ibn al-Jawzī]), and one modern scholar counts up to 140 verses (Muṣṭafā Zayd, *Al-Naskh fīl-Qur'ān al-Karīm* [Cairo?: Dār al-Fikr al-ʿArabī, 1383/1963], vol. 2, pp. 507–508. Naḥḥās considers 9:29 to have abrogated virtually all verses calling for patience or forgiveness toward Scriptuaries (e.g., vol. 1, p. 514; vol. 2, pp. 273, 355, 576, 614; vol. 3, p. 320).

22. In addition to the sources listed above, see the following exegetes on the verses listed: *Tanwīr al-miqbās min tafsīr Ibn ʿAbbās* (attributed to Ibn ʿAbbās [d. 686–688] but a later work) Beirut: Dār al-Jamīl, n.d.); Qatāda (b. Diʿāma al-Sadūsī, d. 735), *Kitāb al-nāsikh wal-mansūkh fī kitāb Allah taʿālā* (Beirut: Mu'assasat al-Risāla, 1406/1985). For a traditional Islamic viewpoint in a modern work collecting many of the traditional sources, see Haykal, *Al-Jihād,* vol. 1, pp. 371–465. Rudolf Peters provides a brief synopsis in *Islam and Colonialism,* pp. 13–14.

23. Exact dating is impossible, but it is quite certain that it could not have developed before the end of the Umayyad period in the mid-eighth century C.E.

24. Vol. 2, p. 437.

25. Ṭabarī, book 14, p. 68.

26. *Tafsīr Ibn ʿAbbās,* p. 220.

27. Richard Bell, *The Qur'ān Translated* (Edinburgh, 1937), vol. 1, p. 247; Muḥammad Asad, *The Message of the Qur'ān* (Gibraltar: Dār al-Andalus, 1980), p. 382.

28. See also *sūra* 29:46: "Do not argue with the People of the Book except in the best way, unless it be with those who do wrong but say, 'we believe in the revelation which has come down to us and in that which came down to you. Our God and your God is one, and it is to him we submit.'"

29. Wāḥidī, pp. 162–163.

30. I.I., vol. 1, pp. 95–96/G, p. 387. See also Naḥḥās, vol. 2, p. 484; Ṭabarī, book 14, pp. 195–196.

31. The versions of Al-Ṭaḥāwī (*Sharḥ Maʿānā al-ʾĀthār*, vol. 3, p. 183) and Wāḥidī, as quoted by the editor of Naḥḥās (vol. 2, p. 484 n. 4), has it that Muḥammad vowed to mutilate seventy men in revenge rather than simply kill them. The root *q.t.l.* may have been later substituted for *m.th.l.* to improve the image of the Prophet.

32. Or "punished." The verb here, *ʿāqaba*, means to alternate or to punish or to punish in return in the sense of retribution or revenge. The identical word is used in the verse three times and is translated variously as punishment, retribution, or affliction, depending on the translation.

33. Ṭabarī, book 14, p. 195.

34. Vol. 2, p. 494. This seems to be the view also of Ṭabarī (book 14, p. 195).

35. See *sūra* 9:29, discussed later in this chapter.

36. The Hijra occurred only in 622 C.E.

37. Mujāhid b. Jabr al-Makhzūmī (d. 104/722) was a prolific and well-respected transmitter of tradition and was a student of Ibn ʿAbbās (Abū ʿAbdallah Shams al-Dīn al-Dhahabī, *Tadhkirat al-Ḥuffāẓ* [Hyderabad, 1377/1958], vol. 1, pp. 92–93; *EI*[1], vol. 7, p. 293).

38. Ibn al-Jawzī, p. 188; *Tafsīr Mujāhid*, p. 427; Ṭabarī, book 14, p. 194 (repeated there). The aforementioned *ḥadīth* regarding Muḥammad's reaction upon seeing his mutilated uncle is found repeated also in the literature, but it is a *ḥadīth* and not an exegetical comment made in response to the text of the Qurʾān.

39. See also Ibn Kathīr, *Tafsīr*, vol. 4, p. 235, who calls for gentle persuasion in arguing against the idolaters.

40. This reference is to *sūra* 9:5, which will soon be examined in this chapter (Ibn al-Jawzī, p. 188). Naḥḥās cites the same opinion without providing sources (vol. 2, p. 487).

41. In his discussion of the following verse (16:126), however, Ibn al-Jawzī provides traditions in support of its abrogation on the authority of Ibn ʿAbbās and al-Ḍaḥḥāk (Ibn al-Jawzī, p. 189). According to this view, 16:126 in effect called for defensive fighting only but was ultimately abrogated by 9:5. Ṭabarī provides the same argument (vol. 14, p. 196). Both Ibn al-Jawzī and Ṭabarī, however, also cite the opinion that 16:126 is not abrogated, and they themselves take this view. That view holds that the verse does not treat war specifically but treats any case in which a believer is wronged by an unbeliever. In that case, the believer is allowed only to exact retribution to the level of the wrong perpetrated against him and not more, whether the wrong committed be in the realm of property or an injury to one's own person (Ibn al-Jawzī, p. 189; Ṭabarī, book 14, p. 197).

42. Ibn al-Jawzī, p. 188.

43. Naḥḥās, vol. 2, p. 487.

44. Bell considers 16:126 to have been a later addition, inserted in its present place perhaps because of the parallel theme of patient endurance (*The Qurʾān*, vol. 1, p. 261).

45. Or "those who have been fought against." The difference between the active and passive form of the verb depends on a very minor change in the pointing of the text (see Ṭabarī, book 17, pp. 171–172, for variant readings), but, as Ṭabarī says, the difference in meaning between the two readings is minor.

46. P. 177. Similar words put into the mouth of Abū Bakr are also found in a number of the sources listed in note 47, following.

47. Many authoritative statements to this effect (i.e., statements attributed to specific early authorities) are collected in Ṭabarī, book 17, pp. 172–173; Naḥḥās, vol. 2, pp. 233, 301, 525; *Tafsīr Ibn ʿAbbās*, p. 280; *Tafsīr Muqātil*, vol. 3, p. 129; *Tafsīr Mujāhid*, p. 482.

48. Ṭabarī, book 17, p. 172.

49. Naḥḥās, vol. 2, p. 525.

50. This interpretation is articulated as an unauthoritative minority opinion (Naḥḥās, vol. 2, p. 525).

51. Vol. 3, p. 129.

52. Ṭabarī, book 17, p. 172; Wāḥidī, p. 177.

53. Ṭabarī, book 17, p. 173. An interesting issue is taken up when Ṭabarī (book 17, pp. 171–173) treats the question of who was granted permission to fight by this verse. The options he provides are (1) only Muḥammad and his companions, (2) only those who were fought against, (3) only those who were wronged, (4) only the Emigrants (as opposed to the *anṣār*, or residents of Medina at the time of the Hijra), (5) everyone.

54. Wāḥidī, p. 29. Cf. *Tafsīr Muqātil*, vol. 1, p. 167.

55. W. Montgomery Watt, "Al-Hudaybiya," in *EI*², vol. 3, p. 539.

56. I.I., vol. 2, pp. 316–318/G, pp. 504–505.

57. The meaning and significance of this word will be examined in chapter 4.

58. *Sūra* 2:191 is treated separately in this chapter.

59. This change is reflected in virtually all the sources with the revelation of 2:217 in response to the raid of ʿAbdullāh b. Jaḥsh in 624 C.E. The raid is examined in the following section of this chapter.

60. See also Bell, *The Qur'ān*, p. 26.

61. Some Muslim traditionists claim 2:190 to have been the first verse about fighting revealed in Medina (cited on the authority of al Rabīʿ [Ṭabarī, book 2, p. 189] and of Abū al-ʿĀliya [Ibn Kathīr, *Tafsīr*, vol. 1, p. 400]. See also Abū Barakāt ʿAbdullāh b. Aḥmad b. Maḥmūd al-Nasafī, *Tafsīr al-Qur'ān al-jalīl*, also known as *Madārik al-tanzīl waḥaqā'iq al-ta'wīl* [Beirut, n.d.], vol. 2, p. 190 [henceforth, Nasafī]). This opinion clearly conflicts with the majority opinion that 22:39, revealed in relation to the Hijra some six years earlier, was the first verse revealed allowing the Muslims to engage in fighting—that is, defensive fighting. But those holding this view place its revelation much earlier than the pact at al-Ḥudaybiyya.

62. See *Tafsīr Ibn ʿAbbās*, p. 26.

63. Ibn al-Jawzī, p. 71. See also Naḥḥās, vol. 2, pp. 516–517; Ibn Kathīr, *Tafsīr*, vol. 1, p. 401; Nasafī, vol. 1, p. 123; Ṭabarī, book 2, p. 189–190, where the limits are extended to include old men, those who proffer peace, fighters who restrain their hands, and all protected peoples (*ahl al-jizya*) (Naḥḥās), and even the burning of trees and the killing of animals, which do not benefit the enemy (Ibn Kathīr).

64. Naḥḥās, vol. 1, p. 517; Ibn Kathīr, *Tafsīr*, vol. 1, p. 401.

65. The editor of Naḥḥās provides sources of this *ḥadīth* in virtually every collection of canonical Ḥadīth (vol. 1, p. 517 n. 2).

66. Ibn Kathīr, *Tafsīr*, vol. 1, p. 401.

67. Ibn al-Jawzī, pp. 70–72.

68. The abrogating verses cited are 9:36: "Fight the idolaters altogether as they fight you altogether"; 2:191: "and slay them wherever you find them"; 9:29: "Fight those who believe not in God nor in the Last Day"; 9:5: "kill the idolaters wherever you may find them."

69. Naḥḥās, vol. 1, pp. 516–518. See also Ṭabarī, book 2, p. 190.

70. Cf. Peters, *Islam and Colonialism*, p. 14.

71. Wāḥidī, pp. 36, 37. For this well-known story, see, for example, Ṭabarī, book 2, pp. 347–354, Abū Ḥasan ʿAlī al-Qummī, *Tafsīr al-Qummī*, vol. 1 (Najaf, 1385/1966), pp. 79–80; I.I., vol. 1, pp. 601–606/G, pp. 286–289; Ṭabarī, *Taʾrīkh*, pp. 1273–1280 (English trans., M. V. McDonald, *The History of al-Ṭabarī* [Albany: SUNY, 1987], vol. 7, pp. 18–23); *Tafsīr Ibn ʿAbbās*, p. 29; *Tafsīr Muqātil*, vol. 1, p. 184; *Tafsīr Mujāhid*, pp. 231–232; Ibn al-Jawzī, p. 80; Nasafī, vol. 1, p. 138; and Ibn Kathīr, *Tafsīr*, vol. 1, pp. 447 ff.

72. Naḥḥās, vol. 1, p. 538.

73. Wāḥidī, p. 36.

74. For a survey of the traditional dating of the Nakhla raid, see J. M. B. Jones, "The Chronology of the *Maghāzī*—A Textual Survey," *BSOAS* 19 (1957), p. 247.

75. See, for example, *sūra* 10:5; W. Hartner, "Zamān," in *EI*[1], vol. 8, pp. 1207–1212.

76. Wāḥidī, p. 37. See also Ṭabarī, book 2, p. 348; *I.I.*, vol. 1, p. 603/G, p. 287.

77. Wāḥidī, p. 38. See also *Tafsīr Muqātil*, p. 186. Some sources consider the day to have been both the last day of Jumāda al-Ākhira *and* the first day of Rajab (*Tafsīr Mujāhid*, p. 231 [2 traditions]; Ṭabarī, book 2, pp. 349–352 [four traditions given on the authorities of Mujāhid, al-Suddī, and Ibn ʿAbbās]). A very few traditions name the day as the *last* rather than the first day of Rajab (Wāḥidī, p. 36). See also Ibn al-Jawzī, p. 80; *Tafsīr Ibn ʿAbbās*, p. 30; Ibn Kathīr, *Tafsīr*, vol. 1, p. 447; *Tafsīr Muqātil*, vol. 1, p. 185; Nasafī, vol. 1, p. 138.

78. Ṭabarī, book 2, p. 351.

79. Qatāda, *Kitāb al-Nāsikh wal-Mansūkh*, p. 33; Ibn al-Jawzī, pp. 81–82; Naḥḥās, vol. 1, pp. 536–537; Nasafī, vol. 1, p. 138; Ṭabarī, book 2, p. 353.

80. See comments on *sūra* 9:5 later in this chapter.

81. Ibn al-Jawzī, p. 81; Ṭabarī, book 2, p. 353; Naḥḥās , vol. 1, p. 535.

82. Mahmoud Ayoub, *The Qur'an and Its Interpreters* (Albany: SUNY, 1984), p. 223.

83. Connected to this stubborn refusal to completely disregard the old pre-Islamic custom of peaceful months are the occasional references to pre-Islamic custom regarding the Sacred Months. One tradition cites an ancient ritual of acknowledging the arrival of the Sacred Month along with the vow not to seek revenge during that period (Ibn al-Jawzī, p. 81). Another acknowledges the effectiveness of the Sacred Month, during which a proud Arab might meet the killer of his own father or brother and still not make any move to enact revenge, while still another tradition mentions that a tribe referred to the Sacred Month as "the deaf" because of the tranquillity resulting from the lack of clatter from weapons during it (Ṭabarī, book 2, p. 346).

84. Ṭabarī, book 2, p. 354.

85. An earlier parallel to this phenomenon might be found in the Jewish Hasmonean decision to fight even during the Sabbath but only when necessary.

86. This word, for which the basic meaning is "temptation" is explained as the temptation of idolatry or sedition.

87. Naḥḥās, vol. 1, p. 521. *Sūra* 9 is also known as Al-Tawba.

88. *Sūra* 2 (Al-Baqara) tends to be dated from soon after the Hijra to the year 2 or 3 (624–625). This dating, of course, does not preclude the association of specific verses with later periods, however.

89. Nasafī, vol. 1, p. 123. See also Bell, *The Qur'ān*, vol. 1, p. 26.

90. *Tafsīr Ibn ʿAbbās*, p. 26; Ibn Kathīr, *Tafsīr*, vol. 1, p. 402; Nasafī, vol. 1, p. 123; Ṭabarī, book 2, p. 191.

91. Naḥḥās, vol. 1, p. 222.

92. *Tafsīr Muqātil*, vol. 1, p. 168.

93. Naḥḥās, vol. 1, p. 520; Ṭabarī, book 2, pp. 192–193.

94. Naḥḥās, vol. 1, p. 519.

95. Ibid., pp. 519–520; Ṭabarī, book 2, p. 192.

96. P. 29.

97. Attributed to ʿAṭā' (Naḥḥās, vol. 1, pp. 531–532; Ibn al-Jawzī, pp. 79–80; Ṭabarī, book 2, p. 344.

98. Attributed to Ibn ʿUmar, Ibn Shabrama, and Sufyān al-Thawrī (Naḥḥās, vol. 1, pp. 531–533).

99. *Tafsīr Ibn ʿAbbās*, p. 29; *Tafsīr Muqātil*, vol. 1, p. 184.

100. Ibn al-Jawzī, p. 79; Naḥḥās, vol. 1, pp. 532–534; Ibn Kathīr, *Tafsīr*, vol. 1, p. 446; Ṭabarī, book 2, pp. 344–345.

101. Ibn al-Jawzī, p. 79.

102. *Sūra* 4:77: "Have you not seen those unto whom it was said: withhold your hands, establish worship and pay the alms tax, but when fighting was prescribed for them, some of them fear mankind even as their fear of God or with greater fear, and say: 'our Lord! why have you ordained fighting for us? If only you would give us respite for a while!'"

103. *Sūra* 9:41: "Go forth lightly [armed] or heavily [armed] and strive (*jāhidū*) with your wealth and your lives in the way of God. That is best for you, if you only knew."

104. He does not cite 15:94–95 or 16:125 in support of this early stage.

105. Naḥḥās, vol. 1, pp. 530–532.

106. Ibn Kathīr, *Tafsīr*, vol. 1, p. 446. Or "good" is defined as God making the result "victory, spoils, and martyrdom" (*Tafsīr Muqātil*, vol. 1, p. 184); or "victory and spoils or martyrdom and the Garden" (Nasafī, vol. 1, p. 137); or "booty, splendor, martyrdom, but in refraining so that you do not conquer the idolaters, you will not be martyred and will not gain anything" (Ṭabarī, book 2, p. 345).

107. See I.I., vol. 2, pp. 543 ff./G, 617 ff. For an examination of the concept of "Dissociation," as it occurs in the Qur'ān, see Uri Rubin, "*Barā'a*: A Study of Some Quranic Passages," *JSAI* 5 (1984), pp. 13–32; and, in later usage, Etan Kohlberg, "Barā'a in Shiʿī Doctrine," *JSAI* 7 (1976), 139–175.

108. Ṭabarī, book 10, pp. 77, 79; Ibn Kathīr, *Tafsīr*, vol. 3, p. 364.

109. See discussion earlier in this chapter.

110. For a discussion on this issue, see Ṭabarī, book 10, pp. 77–79.

111. *Tafsīr Ibn ʿAbbās*, p. 153; *Tafsīr Muqātil*, vol. 2, p. 157. Both are referring to this period of nonbelligerency between the believers and those with whom they had previous agreements or pacts. It seems that later on, this period of fifty days of nonbelligerency was understood to have referred to those with whom there were no pacts. With regard to those with whom the Muslims had pacts, their period of nonbelligerency was a full four months (Ṭabarī, book 10, pp. 59–60).

112. Ṭabarī, book 10, p. 79. For a much fuller discussion, see Ṭabarī, book 10, pp. 58–63.

113. Ibid., p. 78; Ibn Kathīr, *Tafsīr*, vol. 3, pp. 364–365.

114. Ṭabarī, book 2, p. 195; Ibn Kathīr, *Tafsīr*, vol. 3, pp. 364–365.

115. Ibn Kathīr, *Tafsīr*, vol. 3, pp. 364–365.

116. The status of Scriptuaries or "Peoples of the Book" will be discussed later in this chapter.

117. Ibn Kathīr, *Tafsīr*, vol. 3, p. 364.

118. "If two parties among the believers fight one another, make peace between them; but if one of them treats the other unjustly, then fight against the one that transgresses until it complies with the command of God. But if it complies, then make peace between them with justice, and be fair, for God loves the just."

119. Ibn al-Jawzī, p. 173.

120. *Tafsīr Mujāhid*, p. 367; Ṭabarī, book 10, pp. 109–110; Ibn Kathīr, *Tafsīr*, vol. 3, pp. 382–383.

121. Some of the verses that *sūra* 9:29 is assumed to have abrogated follow. *Sūra* 2:109: "Many of the People of Scripture long to make you unbelievers after your belief, through envy on their own account, after the truth has become manifest to them. Forgive and be indulgent [toward them] until God gives the command. God is able to do all things" (Naḥḥās, vol. 1, p. 514); *sūra* 5:13: "And because of their breaking their covenant, We have cursed them and made hard their hearts. They change words from their context and forget a part of that whereof they were admonished. You will not cease to discover treachery from all save a few of them. But bear with them and pardon them. God loves the kindly" (Naḥḥās, vol. 2, p. 273); *sūra* 6:106: "Follow that which is inspired in you from your Lord; there is no God but Him; and turn away from the idolaters" (Naḥḥās, vol. 2, p. 355); *sūra* 29:46: "Do not argue with the People of Scripture unless it be in a way which is better" (Naḥḥās, vol. 2, p. 576); *sūra* 42:15: "Unto us our works and unto you your works" (Naḥḥās, vol. 2, p. 614); *sūra* 50:39: "So bear with what they say" (Naḥḥās, vol. 3, p. 320).

122. Naḥḥās, vol. 2, p. 432.

123. Ibid., vol. 1, p. 515.

124. *Palestinian Parties and Politics that Shaped the Old Testament* (New York: Columbia University Press, 1971; reprint, London: SCM, 1987).

Chapter Four

1. A far more complex, nuanced, and realistic accounting of ancient Medina is only now emerging, thanks primarily to the work of Uri Rubin, Michael Lecker, and other students of M. J. Kister. See especially Lecker, *Muslims, Jews, and Pagans: Studies on Early Islamic Medina* (Leiden: Brill, 1995).

2. See also 2:216, examined in chapter 3, and 9:38–39: "O Believers! What is with you, that when it is said to you: 'go forth in the path of God,' you are bowed

down to the ground with heaviness. Do you prefer the life of this world over the Hereafter? The comfort of the life of the world is but little in the Hereafter. If you do not go forth He will punish you with a painful doom, and will choose a different people in place of you."

3. *Sūras* 3:167; 4:75, 77; 9:38

4. Ṭabarī, book 2, p. 345.

5. ʿAbd al-Qāhir al-Baghdādī refers to a group as late as the ninth century known as the Mazyāriyya or Babākiyya that did not require the fighting of polytheists or fasting on Ramaḍān (*Mukhtaṣar kitāb al-farq bayn al-firaq*, Philip Hitti, ed. [Cairo, 1924], p. 163).

6. ʿAṭāʾ, who is referred to as being adamantly opposed to fighting during the Sacred Months, represents such an approach. His opinion that the prohibition or at least discouragement of fighting during those times was never abrogated is regularly cited in the discussions (Ibn al-Jawzī, pp. 80–81; Ṭabarī, book 2, p. 353; Naḥḥās, vol. 1, p. 535. Mujāhid also inclines in this direction and tends to take a less-militant stand than others on a number of issues.

7. This situation certainly would have been the norm for the century before the rise of Islam and subsequent to the demise of the Kinda in the early sixth century C.E. (A. Grohmann, "al-ʿArab," in *EI*², vol. 1, pp. 526–527).

8. For the significance of the Hijra for the development of Islamic holy war ideas, see chapter 6.

9. See Bell, *The Qurʾān*, vol. 1, pp. 125–126.

10. *Sūra* 9:5, which will be examined in detail later in this chapter, is cited as the verse that abrogates the conduct established in 6:106 (Ṭabarī, book 7, p. 308; Ibn al-Jawzī, p. 156).

11. This is also the nearly universal reading of the traditional commentators (*Tafsīr Muqātil* vol. 2, p. 437; Ṭabarī, book 14, pp. 67–69), who have suggested that this verse marks the first command to Muḥammad to preach Islam to the people of Mecca (cf. I.I., vol. 1, p. 409/G, p. 187).

12. That is, the *sajʿ* verse ending of *īn* (or *ūn*) is so simple and common in the Qurʾān that it cannot be relied on to suggest a necessary link between the verses.

13. Islamic tradition assigns the *sūra* to Mecca.

14. On the controversy over Muḥammad's treatment of the Jews of Medina, see Reuven Firestone, "The Failure of a Jewish Program of Public Satire in the Squares of Medina," *Judaism* 46 (1997), pp. 439–452.

15. As a rule, the term *Banū Isrāʾīl* is a reference to the biblical Israelites, while the term *Yāhūd* or *alladhīna hādū* refers to Jewish contemporaries of Muḥammad. Bell dates this to the second year of the Islamic calendar (*The Qurʾān*, vol. 1, p. 95).

16. Or *faʾfu ʿanhum waṣfaḥ*. The command is actually in the form of an idiom incorporating the trait of repetition common in Semitic languages.

17. Reuven Firestone, "Abraham," vol. 1, in *The Encyclopaedia of the Qurʾān* (Leiden: Brill, forthcoming); A. J. Wensinck, *Muhammad and the Jews of Medina*, W. H. Behn, trans. and ed., 2nd ed. (Berlin: Adiyok, 1982), p. 43; F. E. Peters, *Muhammad*, 203–204.

18. And others such as 5:13.

19. The Jews of Medina were allied with kinship groups of the *anṣār* who were Muslims, but they appear in the references as unrelated by kinship or by religious expression.

20. The significance of this transition is discussed in chapter 5.

21. *Tanwīr al-Miqbās*, p. 26; *Tafsīr Muqātil*, vol. 1, p. 167.

22. Ṭabarī, book 2, p. 189–190; Nasafī, vol. 1, p. 123. This restriction has become law among the Ḥanafī, Mālikī, and Ḥanbalī schools, although the Shāfiʿī school allows killing noncombatants based on the abrogative authority of more militant verses such as 9:5.

23. We do not know enough details about ancient rules of engagement to know whether this view was the norm in the pre-Islamic period as well. Noncombatants were certainly not to be harmed in intertribal raids, although this stricture may have been obeyed in the breech during extreme cases of all-out intertribal warfare. It should be noted here that the following verse, 2:191 (which will be considered in more detail in the following section), appears to call for unlimited warfare but nevertheless repeats the stricture against initiating aggression in the vicinity of the Sacred Mosque (*al-masjid al-ḥarām*).

24. See also 9:24 and 64:14–15.

25. *Tanwīr al-Miqbās*, p. 27; *Tafsīr Mujāhid*, p. 224; *Tafsīr Muqātil*, vol. 1, pp. 168–169; Ṭabarī book 2, pp. 196–197.

26. Asad, *The Message of the Qur'ān*, p. 41 and n. 171.

27. Ṭabarī, book 2, p. 198. In 22:30, the only other verse in which *ḥurumāt* may be found, the term refers in a general way to the ancient religious institutions of the pilgrimage. It appears that in our verse, it is a general reference to sacred institutions and may indeed refer, as Ṭabarī suggests, to sacred space and sacred status in addition to the Sacred Months.

28. *Kāffat^{an}*. Or "fight the idolaters during all [these months] just as they fight you during all [of them]." Another reading has "engage in fighting the idolaters as a unified army, just as they engage in fighting you as a unified army." The difficulty is in determining what *kāffat^{an}* refers to.

29. *Tanwīr al-Miqbās*, p. 157; *Tafsīr Muqātil*, vol. 2, pp. 169–170; Ṭabarī, book 10, pp. 124–128; al-Faḍl b. al-Ḥasan al-Ṭabarsī, *Jawāmiʿ al-jāmiʿ fī tafsīr al-Qur'ān al-karīm* (Beirut: Dār al-Aḍwā', 1405/1985), vol. 1, p. 602; Ibn Kathīr, *Tafsīr*, vol. 3, pp. 393–397.

30. See previous chapter, n.45.

31. Naḥḥās, vol. 2, pp. 233, 301, 525; *Tafsīr Ibn ʿAbbās*, p. 280; *Tafsīr Muqātil*, vol. 3, p. 129; *Tafsīr Mujāhid*, p. 482; Ṭabarī, book 17, pp. 172–173; Haykal, *Al-Jihād*, vol. 1, pp. 460–463; I.I., vol. 1, p. 467/G, pp. 212–213.

32. Ṭabarī, book 17, pp. 172–173.

33. The commentators are again unclear about exactly what type of institutions the words *ṣawāmiʿ*, *biyaʿ*, and *ṣalawāt* were referring to, but all the suggestions revolve around Christian and Jewish religious institutions (e.g., *Tafsīr Muqātil*, vol. 3, p. 129; Ṭabarī, book 17, pp. 175–178).

34. Compare with Morton Smith's study of the variety of positions that underlie the particular structure and content of the Hebrew Bible: *Palestinian Parties and Politics That Shaped the Old Testament.*

35. Ṭabarī, book 2, pp. 344–345.

36. Haykal, *Al-Jihād*, vol. 2, pp. 855–891; Naḥḥās, vol. 1, pp. 531–534; Ibn al-Jawzī, pp. 79–80; Ṭabarī, book 2, pp. 344–345; Ibn Kathīr, *al-ʿAzim*, vol. 1, p. 446.

37. *Sūra* 3:157–158. See also 2:154, 169; 3:158, 169, 195; 4:74; 9:89, 111; 47:4b–6, 36.

38. *Yawm iltaqā al-jamʿān* (3:166). A large number of verses in this part of *sūra* 3 (Āl-ʿImrān) treat various aspects of warring.

39. I.I., vol. 2, p. 106/G, pp. 391–392; Ṭabarī, book 1, p. 167; Ṭabarsī, *Jawāmiʿ al-Jāmiʿ*, vol. 1, p. 257; Ibn Kathīr, *Tafsīr*, vol. 2, p. 150–151.

40. *Alladhīna nāfaqū* or, more commonly, *al-munāfiqūn.*

41. *Tafsīr Muqātil*, vol. 1, p. 312; Ṭabarī, book 4, pp. 167–169; I.I., vol. 2, pp. 63–64/G, pp. 371–372.

42. A. Brockett, "Munāfiḳūn," in *EI*[2], vol. 7, pp. 561–562. The range of criticism against dissenters in Muḥammad b. Isḥāq's Sīra is wider. Some were considered more loyal to Judaism than the new Islam (I.I., vol. 1, pp. 513, 519, 527/G, pp. 239, 242, 246). One, Quzmān, who fought valiantly at Uḥud and was mortally wounded admitted that he fought only to protect his own kin and not for the Muslim cause (I.I., vol. 1, p. 525/G, p. 245). Others were called dissenters because they wanted to refer a dispute to the traditional *kāhins* rather than to Muḥammad (I.I., vol. 1, p. 526/G, p. 245), and some were referred to as such because they preferred to stay at home than fight (I.I., vol. 1, p. 525/G, p. 245). Hypocrites are likened to those Israelites who opposed Moses (I.I., vol. 1, pp. 534 ff./G, pp. 250 ff.).

43. Ṭabarī, book 26, p. 54 (on *sūra* 47:20).

44. *Sūra* 33:5.

45. See 2:154; 3:157–158, 169; 3:158, 169, 195; 9:89, 111; 47:4b–6, 36, and so on.

46. P. 74. Tanwīr al-Miqbās is referring to after the conquest of Mecca when Muḥammad placed ʿAttāb b. Usayd (Asīd?) b. Abīl-ʿĪs in charge of the town when Muḥammad went out to engage the Hawāzin in battle (cf. I.I., vol. 2, p. 440/G, p. 568).

47. Literally, "since you will not be wronged the [amount of] the skin in the cleft of a date pit." (*Tanwīr al-Miqbās*, p. 75; John Penrice, *Dictionary and Glossary of the Kur-ān* (London: Curzon, new ed. 1971), p. 107.

48. *Tanwīr al-Miqbās*, pp. 74–75; *Tafsīr Muqātil*, vol. 1, pp. 389–390; Qummī, *Tafsīr*, vol. 1, p. 151; Ṭabarī, vol. 5, pp. 170–171.

49. This phrase is cited as a proof text along with 48:17 indicating that those who are physically incapable of engaging in battle are not deprived of the status and merit of being religious warriors (*mujāhidūn*) because of their defect (see chapter 5).

50. Wāḥidī, p. 141; *Tanwīr al-Miqbās*, p. 157; *Tafsīr Mujāhid*, p. 368; *Tafsīr Muqātil*, vol. 2, p. 170; Ṭabarī, book 10, p. 133; Ṭabarsī, *Jawāmiʿ al-Jāmiʿ*, vol. 1, p. 604.

51. On the other hand, many Muslim scholars considered this requirement for the entire community to go on the march together (cf. 9:120–121) to have been abrogated by 9:122: "The believers should not all go out to fight" (Naḥḥās, vol. 2, p. 436; Ibn al-Jawzī, pp. 175–176).

52. Cf. Ṭabarī, book 10, pp. 141–142.

53. Cf. Ibn Kathīr, *Tafsīr*. vol. 6, p. 319.

54. Cf. 40:3; Ṭabarī, book 10, p. 207.

55. The conservative nature of the Bedouin as portrayed in these texts has been a difficult problem for the religious leadership of Islam throughout its history, but see also 9:99.

56. Jabbur, *The Bedouins*, pp. 375–376.

57. Ṭabarī, book 21, pp. 126 ff.; Ṭabarsī, *Jawāmiʿ al-Jāmiʿ*, vol. 2, pp. 313–314; Ibn Kathīr, *Tafsīr*, vol. 5, pp. 429 ff.

58. I.I., vol. 1, pp. 501–504/G, pp. 231–233. On this document, see chapter 5.

59. *Al-fitna ashaddu min al-qatl.* The meaning and significance of this word is treated in the following pages.

60. Ṭabarī, book 2, pp. 192–193; Nasafī, vol. 1, p. 123.

61. The traditional exegetes were the first to articulate the problem of contradiction in these verses and struggled with them a great deal.

62. See chapter 3 on defensive fighting and this chapter on restrictions on fighting.

63. Ṭabarī, book 2, pp. 192–193; Naḥḥās, vol. 1, p. 520. Others, however, are of the opinion that the restriction against initiating war in the Sacred Precinct was never abrogated (Naḥḥās, vol. 1, p. 519).

64. Wāḥidī, pp. 29–30.

65. *Fitna* has the basic definition of "testing," such as testing gold by putting it into fire to separate the pure from the impure (ʿAbdallah b. Muslim Ibn Qutayba, *Taʾwīl mashākil al-Qurʾān* [Cairo: Aḥmad Saqr, 1973], p. 362; Muḥammad Ibn Manẓūr, *Lisān al-ʿArab* [Beirut: Dār Ṣādir, 1375/1956], vol. 13, p. 317), but its meanings are quite diverse (Jamāl al-Dīn ʿAbd al-Raḥmān Ibn al-Jawzī, *Nuzhat al-aʿyun al-nawāẓir fī ʿilm al-wujūh wal-naẓāʾir* [n.p., n.d.], pp. 477–480). It may be related to the Hebrew root *p.t.w.* (*pātāh*), and the meaning for this verse suggested by the exegetes tends to be either (the temptation of) idolatry or sedition.

66. *Tanwīr al-Miqbās*, pp. 27, 30, 148; *Tafsīr Mujāhid*, pp. 223, 232; *Tafsīr Muqātil*, vol. 1, pp. 168, 187, 2:215; Maʿmar b. al-Muthanna Abū ʿUbayda, *Majāz al-Qurʾān* (Cairo, 1374/1954), vol. 1, p. 68; Qummī, *Tafsīr*, vol. 1, p. 180; Ṭabarī, book 2, pp. 191–192, 194, 347, book 9, pp. 248–249; Nasafī, vol. 1, pp. 124, 138; Ibn Kathīr, *Tafsīr*, vol. 1, p. 318.

67. Ibn Kathīr, *Tafsīr*, vol. 1, pp. 402–403, vol. 3, p. 317.

68. "The direct purpose of jihad is the strengthening of Islam, the protection of believers and voiding the earth of unbelief. The ultimate aim is the complete supremacy of Islam, as one can learn from K 2:193. . . ." (Rudolph Peters, *Islam and Colonialism*, p. 10).

69. Ṭabarī, book 2, p. 194.

70. Ibid., p. 195 (cf. Muslim, *K. al-īmān*, 35 (vol. 1, pp. 52–53); *Sunan Ibn Māja* (Beirut: al-Maktaba al-ʿIlmiyya, n.d.), *K. al-fitan*, 1 (vol. 2, p. 1295); Abū Dāwud, *K. al-jihād*, 2640 (vol. 3, pp. 44–45); and compare with Muslim, *K. al-īmān*, 34, 36 (vol. 1, pp. 52–53); Bukhārī, *K. al-īmān*, 17 (vol. 1, p. 25); Abu Dāwud, *K. al-jihād*, 2641 (vol. 3, p. 45), where the second part requiring witnessing belief in Muḥammad as God's apostle is included in the *ḥadīth*.

71. Other *ḥadīth*s, however, include both parts, as noted previously.

72. Ṭabarī, book 2, p. 195; Nasafī, vol. 1, p. 124; Ibn Kathīr, *Tafsīr*, vol. 1, p. 402; Haykal, *Al-Jihād*, vol. 1, pp. 758–759.

73. Ṭabarī, book 2, p. 195; Ibn Kathīr, *Tafsīr*, vol. 1, p. 402; Haykal, *Al-Jihād*, vol. 1, pp. 758–759.

74. "[E]ven if the idolaters ceased fighting, it is still a requirement (*farḍ*) for the Muslims to fight them until they become Muslims" (Ṭabarī, book 9, p. 250). The moderating interpretation can also be found in the literature, but it is not prominent (*Tanwīr al-Miqbās*, p. 27; Ṭabarī, book 2, pp. 195–196).

75. There is a somewhat different discussion on the meaning of *fitna* in Ṭabarī

and Ibn Kathīr, however, and this may be a response to the slight variation in this verse's rendering of "and religion becomes God's in its entirety (*wayakūn al-dīn kulluhu lillāh*)." Both commentators try to understand *fitna* in terms of the temptation within the Muslim community to stray away from the unity of God and the community of believers. Ṭabarī defines *fitna* as the temptation of outsiders to seduce the Muslims away from their belief (book 9, pp. 249–250), whereas Ibn Kathīr defines it as the temptation of the community to split apart and wage war on each other (*Tafsīr*, vol. 3, pp. 317–318).

76. See 9:1–5. Most but not all of the early exegetes were of this opinion (cf. Ibn Kathīr, vol. 3, p. 364, and see above, in this chapter and chapter 3).

77. For example, 2:43, 83, 177, 277; 4:77, 162; 5:12, 55; 9:11, 18, 71; 19:31, 55; 21:73; 22:41, 78.

78. *Tanwīr al-Miqbās*, p. 153; *Tafsīr Muqātil*, vol. 2, p. 157; Ṭabarī, book 10, p. 78; Haykal, *Al-Jihād*, vol. 1, p. 504.

79. Marc Cohen, *Under Crescent and Cross* (Princeton: Princeton University Press, 1994), pp. 56, 224 n. 26. See also M. J. Kister, "ʿAn Yadin (Qurʾān IX/29): An Attempt at Interpretation," *Arabica* 11 (1964), pp. 272–278; Meir Bravermann, "A propos de Qurʾān IX, 29. *ḥaṭṭa yuʿtū l-ğizyata wahum ṣāgirūna*," *Arabica* 10 (1963), pp. 94–95; idem., "The Ancient Arab Background of the Qurʾānic Concept *al-ğizyatu ʿan yadin*," *Arabica* 11 (1964), pp. 307–314; idem., "The Ancient Arab Background of the Qurʾānic Concept *al-ğizyatu ʿan yadin* (Suite)," *Arabica* 14 (1967), pp. 90–91; idem., "The Qurʾānic concept *al-ğizyatu ʿan yadin* (Addendum)," *Arabica* 14 (1967), pp. 326–327; C. Cahen, "Coran IX-29: *Haṭṭa yuʿtu l-ğizyata ʿan yadin wa-hum ṣāgirūna*," *Arabica* 9 (1962), pp. 76–79.

80. Cf. Bell, vol. 1, p. 177 n. 1.

81. Ibn Kathīr, *Tafsīr*, vol. 3, p. 383, cites Abū Ḥanīfa and al-Imām Mālik, who understand the verse to mean that the *jizya* may be collected from idolatrous people (*wathanī*) as well.

82. These verses are identical.

83. This verse is taken as the source for the rule that it is the duty of all Muslims to fight the enemies that are nearest to them (Ṭabarī, book 11, p. 71).

84. This verse is the source of the opinion of some that prisoners of war should not be killed (Rudolph Peters, *Islam and Colonialism*, pp. 27–28).

85. In fact, although ideological motivation was best, Islam itself acknowledged that the motivation of spoils may have been of greater importance for the success of the great conquests.

Part III

1. It remained an "oral literature" for a time precisely for the reason that the Jewish "Oral Law" was officially forbidden to having been written down—that it might be confused with Scripture (Muḥammad Abdul Rauf, "Ḥadīth Literature: The Development of the Science of Ḥadīth," in A. F. L. Beeston et al., eds., *Arabic Literature to the End of the Umayyad Period* [Cambridge: Cambridge University Press, 1983]), p. 271.

2. Ibid.

3. A. J. Wensinck, "Sunna," in *EI*[1], vol. 1, pp. 555–557.

4. The plural form in Arabic is *aḥādīth.*

5. Alfred Guillaume, *The Traditions of Islam: An Introduction to the Study of the Hadith Literature* (Lahore: Universal, 1977), p. 10.

6. J. Robson, "Ḥadīth," in EI², vol. 3, p. 23.

7. This *ṭalab al-ʿilm*—"traveling in search of traditions"—probably did not begin before the mid-eighth century, since the Ḥadīth remained largely local and confined to a few centers before that time. G. H. A. Juynboll, *Muslim Tradition: Studies in Chronology, Provenance, and Authorship of Early Ḥadīth* (Cambridge: Cambridge University Press, 1983), pp. 66–70.

8. This practice of associating positions with Muḥammad directly was not always felt to be necessary, because companions of the Prophet or other wise individuals were also considered authoritative sources for determining proper behavior and policies during much of the first century following his death. But as controversies between different Muslim approaches grew along with the community's growing interest in uniformity, the need to ground positions in the person of the Prophet became paramount.

9. W. Madelung, "ʿIṣma," in *EI²*, vol. 4, pp. 182–184; Moshe Zucker, "The Problem of ʿiṣma—Prophetic Immunity to Sin and Error in Islamic and Jewish Literatures" (Hebrew), *Tarbiz* 35 (1966), pp. 149–173.

10. The schema given here is simplified and omits much information contained in the sources and critical studies, such as the importance of the pre-Islamic custom of tribal *sunna*, the *sunna* of early Muslims aside from the Prophet, the evolution of the *isnād* along with the science of its criticism, and so on. A fuller picture is available from Juynboll, *Muslim Tradition*; Abdul Rauf, "Ḥadith Literature"; and Robson, "Ḥadith," as well as Goldziher, *Muslim Studies.*

11. See Abdul Rauf, "Ḥadith Literature," pp. 271–288; Nabia Abbott, "Ḥadīth Literature: Collection and Transmission of Ḥadīth," in Beeston et al., eds., *Arabic Literature*, pp. 289–298; and Robson, "Ḥadīth," pp. 23–28.

12. The Arabic term for the chain of authorities is *sanad* or *isnād.*

13. Which indeed it has become today among many Western scholars.

14. Juynboll, *Muslim Tradition*, p. 75; G. H. A. Juynboll, "On the Origins of Arabic Prose: Reflections on Authenticity, in G. H. A. Juynboll, ed., *Studies on the First Century of Islamic Society* (Carbondale, Ill.: Southern Illinois University Press, 1982), especially pp. 170–174.

15. This Western approach began in the mid-nineteenth century with A. Sprenger (*Das Leben und die Lehre des Mohammad* [Berlin, 1861–1865], especially vol. 3) but reached its apogee with Ignaz Goldziher (*Muhammedanische Studien*, vol. 2, trans. C. R. Barber and S. M. Stern as *Muslim Studies* [London: George Allen and Unwin, 1971]), and Jacob Schacht (*The Origins of Islamic Jurisprudence* [Oxford: Oxford University Press, 1950]). For a brief synopsis of the Western and traditional responses to the problem, see N. J. Coulson, "European Criticism of *Ḥadīth* Literature," in Beeston et al., eds., *Arabic Literature*, pp. 317–321; and for a critique of the Western approach as represented by Schacht, see M. M. Azami, *Studies in Early Hadith Literature* (Indianapolis: American Trust Publications, 1978).

16. F. E. Peters, *Muhammad*, p. 264.

17. See chapter 2.

18. In fact, it has been aptly suggested that the term *maghāzī* was simply an earlier reference for traditions treating the biography of the Prophet and that it was

not until the ninth century when they were considered separate fields. Martin Hinds, "'Maghāzī' and 'Sīra' in Early Islamic Scholarship," in *Vie du Prophete Mahomet: Colloque de Strasburg, 1980*, vols. 23–24 (Paris, 1983); and cf. J. M. B. Jones, "The *Maghāzī* Literature," in Beeston et al., eds., *Arabic Literature*, pp. 344–51.

19. Martin Hinds, "*Al-Maghāzī*," in *EI*[2], vol. 5, p. 1163. Modern scholars tend now to refer to the literature in general as *sīra-maghāzī* literature (J. M. B. Jones, "The Chronology of the Maghāzī—A Textual Survey," *BSOAS* 19 (1957), p. 259; J. M. B. Jones, "Ibn Ishāq and al-Wāqidī, The Dream of ʿĀtika and the Raid to Nakhla in Relation to the Charge of Plagiarism," *BSOAS* 22 [1959], p. 51; John Wansbrough, *The Sectarian Milieu* [Oxford: Oxford University Press, 1978]; Rizwi S. Faizer, "Muhammad and the Medinan Jews: A Comparison of the Texts of Ibn Ishaq's *Kitab Sirat Rasūl Allāh* without Wāqidi's Kitab al-Maqhāzī," *IJMES* 28 (1996), pp. 464–465.

20. In fact, the extant early works of *maghāzī* attributed to al-Wāqidī and Mūsā b. ʿUqba correspond closely in structure and content to Ibn Isḥāq's *Sīra* (Jones, "The Maghāzī Literature," pp. 346 ff.).

21. That is, we are seeking the evolution of an idea among the mainstream, leaving out for the purposes of this study the still important views of many groups among the Shīʿa and Khawārij.

Chapter Five

1. Bukhārī, *K. al-jihād*, 1.41 (vol. 4, p. 35).

2. Ibid., 1.44 (vol. 4, p. 36). See also Bukhārī, *K. al-jihād*, 2.45 (vol. 4, p. 37); Abū Dāwud, *K. al-jihād*, 2485 (vol. 3, p. 5); Tirmidhī, *Al-Jāmiʿ al-Ṣaḥīḥ* (Beirut: Dār al-Kutub al-ʿIlmiyya, 1408/1987), *K. faḍā'il al-jihād*, 17.1650 (vol. 4, pp. 155–156); and cf. Bukhārī, *K. al-ḥajj*, 4.594, 595 (vol. 2, p. 347); Ibn Māja, *Sunan Ibn Māja* (Beirut: Al-Maktab al-ʿIlmiyya, n.d.), *K. al-jihād*, 1.2754 (vol. 2, p. 920).

3. Tirmidhī, *K. faḍā'il al-jihād*, 17.1648–1649, 1651 (vol. 4, pp. 154–156); Ibn Māja, *K. al-jihād*, 2.2755–2757 (vol. 2, p. 921).

4. See A. J. Wensinck, *A Handbook of Early Muhammadan Tradition* (Leiden: Brill, 1971 reprint), p. 246, for the many references throughout the primary collections.

5. Bukhārī, *K. al-jihād*, 2.46 (vol. 4, p. 38), 10.59 (vol. 4, p. 46), *K. al-maghāzī*, 16.377–378 (vol. 5, pp. 260–261), *K. al-tawḥīd*, 28.549 (vol. 9, p. 413); Abū Dāwud, 2497 (vol. 3, p. 8); Tirmidhī, *K. Faḍā'il al-Jihād*, 13.1640–1641 (vol. 4, pp. 150–151). The very meaning of Tirmidhī's chapter is "The Book of the Merits of *Jihād*."

6. Bukhārī, *K. al-jihād*, 16:66 (vol. 4, p. 51); Tirmidhī, *K. faḍā'il al-jihād*, 7.1632 (vol. 4, p. 146).

7. Abū Dāwud, *K. al-jihād*, 2499–2501 (vol. 3, pp. 8–10); Nasā'ī, *Sunan al-Nasā'ī* (Cairo: Dār al-Ḥadīth, 1407/1987) *K. al-jihād*, *bāb mā takaffala Allah liman yujāhid fī sabīl Allah* (6:16–17), *thawāb man qātala fī sabīl Allah* (6:25–26). On the other hand, other traditions state that good Muslims will enter Paradise whether or not they actually engage in *jihād* in the path of God: ". . . Abū Hurayra: The Prophet said: Whoever believes in God and in His Apostle, establishes prayer and fasts on Ramaḍān, it is absolute to God that He cause him to enter the Garden whether he makes *jihād* in the path of God or sits on the land upon which he was born (*jalasa fī 'arḍihi allatī wulida fīhā*)" (Bukhārī, *K. al-jihād*, 4.48 [vol. 4, pp. 39–40]).

8. Abū Dāwud, *K. al-jihād*, 2522 (vol. 3, p. 15).

9. Bukhārī, *K. al-jihād*, 6.53 (vol. 4, p. 42); Tirmidhī, *K. faḍā'il al-jihād*, 13.1640 (vol. 4, p. 151), 25.1661 (vol. 4, p. 160).

10. Bukhārī, *K. al-jihād*, 7.54 (vol. 4, p. 42), 119.216 (vol. 4, p. 137).

11. Ibid., 22.73 (vol. 4, p. 55), 112.210 (vol. 4, p. 132–133), 156.266a (vol. 4, pp. 165–166); Muslim, *K. al-jihād wal-siyar*, 6.20/1742 (vol. 3, pp. 1362–1363); Abū Dāwud, *K. al-jihād*, 2631 (vol. 3, p. 42); Tirmidhī, *K. faḍā'il al-jihād*, 23.1659 (vol. 4, p. 159).

12. Bukhārī, *K. al-jihād*, 20–22.71–73 (vol. 4, pp. 54–55), 28.80 (vol. 4, p. 60); Nasā'ī, *K. al-jihād, Darajat al-mujāhid fi sabīl Allah* (6:19–20).

13. *Man māta walā yaghzu walam yuḥaddithu nafsahu bil-ghazw māta ʿalā shuʿbatin min nifāq* (Abū Dāwud, *K. al-jihād*, 2502 (vol. 3, p. 10).

14. Ibid., 2503. There are also traditions associated with *sūra* 4:95; "Not equal are those believers who sit [at home] . . . ," such as Bukhārī, *K. al-jihād*, 31 (vol. 4, pp. 62–63).

15. See chapter 4 for a discussion of this verse.

16. Wāḥidī, pp. 100–101; *Tafsīr Muqātil*, vol. 1, pp. 400–401; Ṭabarī, book 5, pp. 228–230; Ibn Kathīr. vol. 2, pp. 366–367; Bukhārī, *K. al-jihād*, 31.84, 85 (vol. 4, pp. 62–63); Abū Dāwud, *K. al-jihād*, 2507 (vol. 3, p. 11); Tirmidhī, *K. al-jihād*, 1.1670 (vol. 4, p. 164).

17. See Ṭabarī, book 18, pp. 175–176.

18. *K. al-jihād*, 113.211 (vol. 4, pp. 133–135).

19. *K. al-jihād wal-siyar*, 11.32 (vol. 3, pp. 1366). Cf. Deuteronomy 20:5–7. The Ḥadīth continues with a number of other parallels in the biblical book of Joshua.

20. *Fafīhimā fajāhid* (Muslim, *K. al-birr wal-ṣila wal-ādāb*, 1.5–6/2549 (vol. 4, p. 1975); Tirmidhī, *K. al-jihād*, 2.1671 (vol.4, p. 164–165).

21. Abū Dāwud, *K. al-jihād*, 2515 (vol. 3, p. 13), 2517 (vol. 3, p. 14).

22. Ibid., 2516 (vol. 3, pp. 13–14).

23. Muslim, *K. al-jihād wal-siyar*, 33.1748–1754 (vol. 3, pp. 1367–1375); Abū Dāwud, 2710–2716 (vol. 3, pp. 68–70).

24. Bukhārī, *K. al-tawḥīd*, 28.550 (vol. 9, pp. 413–414).

25. This definition certainly evolved. Like so many other terms found in the Qur'ān and employed from the earliest period, the meaning of fighting "in the path of God" certainly evolved and changed. Serjeant, for example, suggests that fighting "in the path of God" in the earliest layer of the Medina Agreement (see chapter 6) refers to fighting that was initiated by Muḥammad outside Medina, as opposed to defensive fighting to protect Medina and its community (R. B. Serjeant, "The 'Constitution' of Medina," *Islamic Quarterly* 8 (1964), p. 12).

Chapter Six

1. Faizer, "Muhammad and the Medinan Jews," pp. 463–489. Cf. M. J. Kister, "The *Sīra* Literature," in Beeston et al., eds., *Arabic Literature*, p. 352. The process of assembling the traditions into their biographical format was somewhat more complicated than in the canonical Ḥadīth in that the pool of data may have been broader from the outset and the process of filling in lacunae in the material with the creation of new traditions more lax (see W. Montgomery Watt, "The Materials

Used by Ibn Isḥāq," in Bernard Lewis, ed., *Historians of the Middle East* (London: Oxford University Press, 1962), pp. 23–34.

2. On the problem of historical accuracy and the pro-ʿAbbasid leanings of Ibn Isḥāq's *sīra*, see Jacob Lassner, *Islamic Revolution and Historical Memory*, American Oriental Series, vol. 66 (New Haven: American Oriental Society, 1986), especially pp. 3–36.

3. Kister, "The *Sīra* Literature," p. 357.

4. Ibid., p. 353.

5. J. M. B. Jones, "The *Maqhāzī* Literature," pp. 344–346. On the relationship of *maghāzī* with *sīra*, see the introduction to part III.

6. C. Brockelmann, "Ibn Isḥāḳ," in *EI*[1], vol. 3, pp. 389–390; Faizer, "Muhammad and the Medinan Jews," p. 463; D. M. Dunlop, "History and Historians," in *Arab Civilization to A.D. 1500*, pp. 72–73; Alfred Guillaume, *The Life of Muhammad* (Oxford: Oxford University Press, 1955), p. xvii.

7. Also entitled *Al-Sira al-Nabawiyya.* As noted previously, this edition is a photo offset of the authoritative edition edited by Muṣṭafā al-Saqqā, Ibrāhīm al-Abyārī, and ʿAbdul-Ḥafīẓ Shalabī, Cairo, 1937, and reprinted often. The Cairo edition was translated by Alfred Guillaume as *The Life of Muhammad: A Translation of Ibn Ishaq's Sirat Rasul Allah* but paginated according to the edition of Wustenfeld (Göttingen, 1856–1860.

8. Marsden Jones, ed., *Kitāb al-Maghāzī lil-Wāqidī*, 3 vols. (London: Oxford University Press, 1966), henceforth referred to as Wāqidī.

9. Eduard Sachau, ed., *Kitāb al-Tabaqāt al-Kabīr* (Leiden: Brill, 1904–1921).

10. I.S., vol. 1, part 1, p. 133/H, vol. 1, pp. 230–231.

11. I.I., vol. 1, p. 263/G, p. 118.

12. I.I., vol. 1, p. 591/G, p. 281.

13. "No archer who shoots an arrow at the enemy will be counted before me, O apostle of God" (G, p. 283). Saʿd later led a raid himself (I.I., vol. 1, p. 600/G, p. 286) and was one of the intrepid protectors of Muḥammad when the Prophet was threatened during the battle of Uḥud (I.I., vol. 2, p. 82/G, p. 381).

14. I.I., vol. 1, p. 290: *Fawallahi mā kunta jahūl*[an]. Guillaume translates *jahūl* as "violent" (p. 131). Perhaps "ferocious" would fit better in this particular context. This accusation of Muḥammad not being *jahūl* is an insult, given the importance among pre-Islamic Arabs of knowing when it is fitting to be so (see the discussion of *jāhiliyya* in chap. 2).

15. According to Jacob Lassner, this silence might be explained as a propagandistic ploy of the ʿAbbasid caliphal house in which their lack of active resistance against the ungodly house of Umayya is likened to the passivity of Muḥammad himself in the face of early injustice directed against him. The argument is cogent and the hypothesis sound, but its logic does not detract from independent evidence that supports Muḥammad's and most of his followers' lack of enthusiasm for physical engagement even in defense. According to Lassner, even blatant apologetics did not necessarily *alter* the historical record so much as they *manipulate* it (*Islamic Revolution and Historical Memory*, pp. 15–22, 31).

16. I.I., vol. 1, pp. 312–313/G, pp. 141–142.

17. The mother of ʿAmmār b. Yāsir (I.I., vol. 1, p. 320/G, p. 145).

18. I.I., vol. 1, p. 321/G, p. 145).

19. I.I., vol. 1, p. 331/G, p. 149).

20. I.I., vol. 1, p. 336/G, p. 151).

21. *Walammā aslama qātala quraysh ḥattā ṣallā ʿindal-kaʿba waṣallayna maʿahu.* This tradition is provided by Ibn Isḥāq twice, each with a separate *isnād* (I.I., vol. 1, p. 342/G, p. 155]).

22. I.I., vol. 1, p. 346/G, p. 157. Ḥamza b. ʿAbd al-Muṭṭalib's own conversion is lauded by the tradition because he was considered the first powerful individual with martial skills to become a follower of Muḥammad (I.I., vol. 1, pp. 291–292/G, pp. 131–132).

23. I.I., vol. 1, p. 349/G, p. 159.

24. In or about 619.

25. *Wadhālika qabla an tuftariḍu ʿalayhim al-ḥarb* (I.I., vol. 1, pp. 431, 433/G, pp. 198, 199). Because the pledge did not include taking responsibility to defend Muḥammad, it was called the "Pledge of Women" (*bayʿat al-nisāʾ*).

26. *ʿAlā ḥarb al-aḥmar wal-aswad min al-nās* (I.I., vol. 1, p. 446/G, p. 204). This second pledge is popularly known as the "Pledge of War" (*bayʿat al-ḥarb*). Montgomery Watt notes that the root of the word *anṣār* is *naṣara,* which has the connotation of helping a person wronged against his enemy ("Al-Anṣār," in *EI*^{2}, vol. 1, p. 514).

27. I.I., vol. 1, pp. 448, 454/G, pp. 205, 208.

28. I.I., vol. 1, pp. 467–468/G, pp. 212–213.

29. I.I., vol. 1, p. 480/G, p. 221.

30. I.I., vol. 1, p. 482/G, p. 222.

31. I.I., vol. 1, p. 590/G, p. 280. The text is very explicit that those whom he was commanded to fight were the nearby idolatrous Arabs: *waqitāl man amarahu Allah bih mimman yalīhi min al-mushriqīn mushriqay al-ʿarab.* Note the similarity to the command in Deuteronomy 20:15–18.

32. I.I., vol. 1, p. 590/G, p. 281. Ibn Saʿd places the first raid eight months after his arrival (I.S., vol. 2, part 1, p. 2/H, vol. 2, p. 3), and Wāqidī places it on the seventh month (vol. 1, p. 9).

33. "The Messenger of God sent . . . sixty or eighty riders from among the Emigrants, and not even one of the *Anṣār* was among them (*walaysa fīhum min al-anṣār aḥad*^{un}) (I.I., 591/G, 281). This phrase recurs consistently in the narrative, and Wāqidī notes the same thing (*fayuqāl: lam yabʿath rasūl Allah aḥad*^{an} *min al-anṣār mabʿath*^{an} *ḥattā ghazā bihim bibadr*) (vol. 1, p. 11).

34. I.I., vol. 1, pp. 601–606/G, pp. 286–289; I.S., vol. 2, part 1, p. 5/H, vol. 2, pp. 7–9; Wāqidī, vol. 1, pp. 13–19. This raid is discussed also in chapters 3 and 4 in relation to *sūra* 2:217. According to Ibn Isḥāq and Wāqidī, Muḥammad sent out the raiding party with sealed instructions that they were to open and read only after having gone out on the march. Muḥammad had apparently intended them to meet up with the caravan that they were to raid only after the end of the Sacred Month of Rajab, but the timing was slightly off and they caught up with them on the last day of the Sacred Month.

35. All three sources mention that there was some confusion over whether it was the last day of the Sacred Month or not but that they decided to attack anyway.

36. *Waʾajmaʿū ʿalā qatl man qadarū ʿalayhi minhum.*

37. And, in fact, the hotheaded Saʿd b. Abī Waqqāṣ mentioned was among the raiders.

38. *Wafarraja Allah ʿan al-misilmīn mā kābū fīhi min al-shafaq*. That the problem of the Sacred Months continues to disturb some Muslims may be adduced from Muḥammad Haykal's recent (1414/1993) *Al-jihād wal-qitāl fil-siyāsa al-sharʿiyya*, vol. 3, pp. 1505–1520.

39. *Wadhālika annahum lam yudhinnu an rasūl Allah yalqā ḥarb* (I.I., vol. 1, p. 607/G, p. 289.

40. I.I., vol. 1, p. 610/G, p. 294 (cf. Muslim, *K. al-jihād wal-siyar*, 30.83/1779 [vol. 3, pp. 1403–1404]).

41. *Mā lanā bikum min ḥāja* (I.I., vol.1, p. 625/G, p. 299; cf. Abū Dāwud, *K. al-jihād*, 2665 [vol. 3, p. 53]). It was customary for individuals to initiate independent combat before engagement of the full armies. This practice seems to have been a means of establishing a psychological advantage before the full engagement (cf. 1 Samuel 17:1–11).

42. The numerous distinctions and cleavages between the *muhājirūn* and the *anṣār* remained of great issue far beyond this point (e.g., they rarely intermarried until long after Muḥammad's death), but they were both equally welcome and encouraged to engage in war with the battle of Badr.

43. Watt, "Al-Anṣār," *EI²*, vol. 1, p. 514.

44. See previous section.

45. The Sīra notes that dust was thrown on his head and that someone even threw a sheep's uterus on him while he was praying (I.I., vol. 1, p. 416/G, p. 191), although Ibn Isḥāq himself finds the latter nearly incredible by adding, *fīmā dhukira lī* ("as was mentioned to me").

46. See chapter 3.

47. Cf. *sūra* 4:33. There is evidence that such "brothering" began as early as in Mecca, and Watt is of the opinion that it happened soon after Muḥammad's arrival in Medina, where *muhājirūn* and *anṣār* were "brothered" across broad kinship lines (W. Montgomery Watt, "Mu'ākhāt," in *EI²*, vol. 7, p. 253). According to Ibn Saʿd, this was a temporary measure that was superseded by allegience to the religious community as exemplified by *sūra* 8:75: "Those who have kinship relation are even closer to one another through the Book [or ordinance] of God" (I.S., vol. 1, part 2, p. 1/H, pp. 279–280).

48. I.I., vol. 1, pp. 627–628/G, p. 300.

49. That is, to the religious community of Muslims (W. Montgomery Watt, *Muhammad at Medina* [Oxford: Clarendon, 1956], p. 242).

50. *Al-Sha'm* or *al-shām*, the common Arabic term for the area comprising today's modern Israel, as well as Syria, Lebanon, and Jordan, even extending into today's Saudi Arabia (Jews, e.g., were allowed to remain in the towns of *wādī al-qura* despite ʿUmar's decree of expulsion because this area was considered to be a part of greater Syria).

51. Firestone, *Journeys in Holy Lands*, p. 25. Similarly, early radical Muslim groups considered their own followers *muḥajirūn* making their *hijra* to authentic Islam. One Kharijite sect called its camp the *dār al-hijra*, or the "abode of *hijra*" (Watt, "Hidjra," in *EI²*, vol. 3, p. 367). *Hijra*, like many symbolic terms, eventually took on a wider semantic range of meaning. Just as the meaning of *jihād* broadened to *jihād* of the heart, the hand, and so on, so, too, did the meaning of *hijra* expand to *hijra* of the heart when one turned one's mind away (i.e., "emigrated") from

temporal things, *hijra* of the hand when physical support for actions forbidden by Islamic law was withdrawn, and so on (Willis, "*Jihād fī Sabīl Allah*," p. 399).

52. Muḥammad arrived in the fall, according to the tradition. The beginning of that year is reckoned to coincide with July 16, 622 (G. S. P. Freeman-Grenville, *The Muslim and Christian Calendars* [London: Rex Collings, 1977], p. 14).

53. Watt, *Muhammad at Mecca*, pp. 142–143.

54. I.I., vol. 1, p. 429/G, p. 198. The ʿĀd and Iram were two Arabian tribes known from the legendary lore that had disappeared and become extinct.

55. Ibid.

56. I.I., vol. 1, p. 468/G, p. 213. Working back from the date of the Hijra, the pledge of the Second ʿAqaba occurred that same year according to Ibn Isḥāq, so Muḥammad's first meeting with the Medinans would have occurred two years previously in 620, shortly after the deaths of Abū Ṭālib and Khadīja.

57. I.I., vol. 1, pp. 454–467/G, pp. 208–212. Ibn Saʿd notes the confusion over the number who came to the Second ʿAqaba (I.S., vol. 1, part 1, p. 149/H, vol. 1, p. 256).

58. I.S., vol. 1, part 1, p. 149/H, vol. 1, p. 257.

59. I.I., vol. 1, p. 197/G, p. 86.

60. Serjeant, "Haram and Hawtah," pp. 41–58; Eickelman, "Musaylima," pp. 17–52.

61. On Muḥammad's making Medina a *ḥaram* similar to Mecca, see Bukhārī, *K. al-jihād*, 71.139 (vol. 4, pp. 89–90), and *K. al-maghāzī*, 26.410 (vol. 5, p. 282).

62. I follow F. E. Peters's use of the term "Medina Agreement" (*Muhammad and the Origins of Islam*, p. 198). "Constitution" is misleading because of its sense of institutional formality. It was much more of an agreement arrived at after protracted bargaining between Muḥammad and the individual parties.

63. Ibn Sayyid al-Nās (*ʿUyūn al-athar*, fol. 62ᵛ) derives the Medina Agreement from Ibn Isḥāq according to Wensinck, and parts of it may be found in the Ḥadīth collections of al-Bukhārī, Muslim, Abū Dāwud, and Nasāʾī (Wensinck, *Muhammad and the Jews of Medina*, pp. 61, 66–67). Wāqidī does not refer to it as such, although he notes that Muḥammad makes formal agreements with various Medinan parties. Serjeant claims that the Qurʾān itself refers to the Medina Agreement in 3:101–104, but is not convincing ("The 'Constitution' of Medina," pp. 5–16).

64. The issue of greatest surprise is the significant rights given to Medinan Jews in the Agreement. For an outline of the various positions, see Frederick Denny, "*Ummah* in the Constitution of Medina," *JNES* 36 (1977), p. 39 n. 3; and Watt, *Muhammad at Mecca*, pp. 225–226.

65. Watt, *Muhammad at Mecca*, p. 226, and cf. Moshe Gil, "The Constitution of Medina: A Reconsideration," *Israel Oriental Studies* 4 (1974), pp. 47–48.

66. The agreement's archaisms presented a problem even for its earliest copyists, and Ibn Isḥāq himself may not have understood it completely. The inclusion of non-Muslims in the *umma*, the anti-Qurayshite nature of much of the document (i.e., Qurayshite in the sense of the Meccan enemies of Muḥammad and not in the early sense of *muhājirūn* as depicted in the preamble and article 2 of the document), its apparent welcome of the Jews and the modest authority of Muḥammad all seem to contradict the natural inclination of later forgers (see Gil, "Constitution of Medina," p. 45, for a synopsis of the arguments put forth by Wellhausen, Caetani, Serjeant, and Watt).

67. Cf. Gil, "Constitution of Medina."

68. I.I., vol. 1, p. 503 (article 23), and cf. Serjeant, "Haram and Hawtah," p. 44. Henceforth, the agreement will be referred to according to Wensinck's division into 47 articles (*Mohammed en de Joden te Medina* [Leiden, 1908] and translated by Wolfgang Behn as *Muhammad and the Jews of Medina* [Berlin: Adiyok, 1982], pp. 51–60). The same division is used by Watt (*Muhammad at Medina*) and hence also by Denny ("*Ummah*").

69. Articles 14–15.

70. Peters, *Muhammad and the Origins of Islam*, p. 199.

71. Denny, "*Ummah*," pp. 42–44. In fact, the document places "the Believers and Muslims of the Quraysh and Yathrib and those who follow them, are attached to them, and strive (*jāhada*) along with them" within the *umma* in the preamble, but articles 25–31 specifically include Jewish clans (article 25: "The Jews of the Banī ʿAwf are an *umma* with the Believers; the Jews have their religion [*dīn*] and the Muslims have their religion.").

72. Article 39: *waʿin yathrib ḥarām jawfuhā liʾahli hādhihil-ṣaḥīfa.*

73. Article 36: *waʾinnahu lā yukhrij minhum aḥad illā biʾidhn muḥammad.*

74. There do seem to be some major lacunae, such as the three main Jewish kinship groups, the Qurayẓa, the Naḍīr, and the Qaynuqāʿ, who are not specifically mentioned.

75. Watt, *Muḥammad at Medina*, p. 229. He suggests that articles that did include the Jewish groups, such as the Qurayẓa and Naḍīr, were dropped from the document because of their irrelevance after their elimination (pp. 227–228). On Muḥammad's relations with the Jewish tribes of Medina, see Wensinck, *Muḥammad and the Jews of Medina*; Firestone, "Failure of a Jewish Program of Public Satire in the Squares of Medina"; or any of the many biographies of Muḥammad.

76. Another name for Muḥammad. This name is not in any way insulting.

77. I.I., vol. 2, p. 234/G, p. 461.

78. Lane, *Lexicon*, part 2, p. 477 col. 3.

79. Jews could be members of such an agreement in South Arabia even in this century (Serjeant, "Haram and Hawtah," pp. 50–51).

80. As noted previouisly, articles 25–31 specifically include Jewish groups as well. This has been understood as evidence to support the document's composite nature, but these Jews seem to have been allied or "attached to" the larger Medinan kinship groups listed in articles 3–10.

81. If the document is as early as believed, then the deficient early orthographic system for Arabic would not have included the long consonantal ā (*alif*). The form of the verb *j.h.d.* in the original document was most likely the first form (*jahada* and not *jāhada*). The long ā may have been added later under the influence of the Conquest, when the sense of "warring in the path of God" seemed more appropriate than "striving for the religious cause" as was most likely the original intent.

82. Following Gil ("Constitution of Medina," p. 50 n. 44) and contrary to Watt (*Muhammad at Mecca*, p. 221), who translates the phrase [*waman*] *jāhada maʿahum* as "[and those] who crusade along with them."

83. *Sūras* 2:195, 261–262; 8:60; 47:38; 57:10. Unbelievers, on the other hand, are noted in the Qurʾān for spending their resources in order to deter people from the path of God (8:36).

84. *Waʾin baynahum al-naṣr ʿalā man ḥāraba ahla hādhihi al-ṣaḥīfa.*

85. Wensinck, *Muḥammad and the Jews of Medina*, p. 58 n. 4.

86. *Wa'in baynahum al-naṣr ʿalā man dahima yathrib.*

87. It should be noted that those who consider the Medina Agreement to be post-Badr and after the destruction of Muḥammad's Jewish opposition regard the Jews mentioned in the document to be only the remnants of the once large Jewish community, which were rendered nonthreatening by the elimination of their powerful brethren.

88. Mostly in Mecca. Note the unification of disparate tribes into the Muslim Umma, in relation to the unification of the tribes of Israel into an Israelite nation. Such solidarity not only contributes to unification of the polity but also serves as an effective means of exacting revenge and engaging in combat (cf. Niditch, *War in the Hebrew Bible*, p. 19).

89. Abū Dāwud, *K. al-adab*, 4918 (vol. 4, p. 281).

90. Bukhārī, *K. al-maẓālim*, 4.622 (vol. 3, p. 373); Abū Dāwud, *K. al-mu'ākhāt*, 4893 (vol. 4, p. 275); Tirmidhī, *K. al-ḥudūd*, 3.1425 (vol. 4, p. 26).

91. I.I., vol. 2, p. 604/G, p. 651.

92. Ibn Māja, *K. al-ḥudūd*, 1.2533 (vol. 2, p. 847). The following tradition has, "Forbidden is the blood of a Muslim who witnesses that there is no god but God and that the Messenger of God [is Muḥammad] except one of three people: one who takes a life [willfully], the adulterer, and one who leaves his religion and separates from the collectivity (*wal-tārik lidīnihi al-mufāriq lil-jamāʿa*).

93. *Anṣur akhāka ẓālim*[an] *aw maẓlūm*[an] (Bukhārī, *K. al-maẓālim*, 5.623 [vol. 3, p. 373]). Compare this sentiment to that of the pre-Islamic poet cited in chapter 2 who boasted, "I am [of the tribe of] Ghaziyya: if she be in error, then I will err; And if Ghaziyya be guided right, I go right with her!" The moral implications of this tradition, however, was troubling enough to have engendered a related tradition in which the Prophet answers the question how one could possibly help an oppressor: "Keep him from his ways" (*ta'khudhu fawqa yadayhi*) (Bukhārī, *K. al-maẓālim*, vol. 3, pp. 373–374).

Chapter Seven

1. Such as the general urbanization of Bedouin culture among the Meccan Quraysh before the rise of Islam and the specific treatment of the Quraysh toward their kin who followed Muḥammad in pre-Hijra Mecca.

2. I.I., vol. 1, pp. 555–556/G, 261–262); F. E. Peters, *Muhammad*, p. 211. And that tension, of course, does not include the continuing tensions resulting from the lack of total allegiance among the dissident *munāfiqūn*.

3. As noted in the previous chapter, the formal "brothering" of *muhājirūn* with *anṣār* clearly enhanced such a feeling. There is evidence of previous "brothering" among the Quraysh before the Hijra, but it seems to have been a practice to influence who would become the beneficiary of one's inheritance (Watt, "Muʿākhāt," in EI^2, vol. 7, p. 254). In the Medinan case, however, the issue was not inheritance but solidarity.

4. I.I., vol. I, pp. 590–591/G, 281. This sentence is immediately followed by this heading: "The Raid on Waddān, which is [Muḥammad's] first raid" (*ghazwat waddān wahiyya awwal ghazawātihi ʿalayhi al-salām*).

5. *Sūra* 22:39–40 and, eventually, 2:217.

6. There is virtually no dissenting opinion that does not associate 2:217 with the raid of ʿAbdullah b. Jaḥsh. The yearlong wait before sending out probing forays makes great historical sense given, for example, the initial economic support that was accorded the *muhājirūn*, the need to become established in the new community, and the beginning of the formation of the early *umma*.

7. I.I., vol. 2, p. 106/G, 392.

8. Although their long-term material gain and prestige would certainly be enhanced by the destruction of the Muslims.

Glossary

Anṣār. "Helpers," or those followers of Muḥammad who derive from Medina. The *anṣar* are often distinguished from the *muhājirūn.*

Dhimmī. "Protected people," referring to the status of Peoples of the Book.

Farḍ. Religious duty or command.

Farḍ kifāya. Command or duty obligating the community in general but not every individual.

Farḍ wājib. Or *farḍ wujub,* or *farḍ ʿayn.* Command or duty obligating every individual Muslim.

Fitna. Temptation, idolatry, sedition.

Ḥadīth. "Report, news, tradition." A collection of literature that communicates the *sunna* (the behavior and words) of the prophet Muḥammad.

Ḥajj. The greater pilgrimage; a visit to Mecca and engagement in formal ritual requirements within the official pilgrimage season.

Ḥaram. "Sacred precinct." A certain area around a holy place; usually but not always refers to the area in and around Mecca, wherein certain behavioral restrictions apply.

Ḥijāz. "Barrier." The west-central region of Arabia in which Mecca and Medina are situated; named as such because of the range of mountains running north-south through it.

Hijra. "Emigration" of Muḥammad from Mecca to Medina in 622.

Jizya. An obscure term found in *sūra* 9:29 and eventually understood by Muslim scholars to be a special poll-tax obligation for Jews, Christians, and other Peoples of the Book.

Kaʿba. "Cube." The main Islamic sanctuary in Mecca.

Jāhiliyya. A term describing the pre-Islamic period of Arabia and connoting ignorance and barbarity.

Lex talionis or *talion.* The law of like-for-like, or punishment in kind, such as "a life for a life."

Muhājirūn. "Emigrants," or those followers of Muḥammad deriving from Mecca who joined him in his Hijra (emigration) to Medina in 622.

Munāfiqūn. Dissenters (sometimes translated as "hypocrites"). A qur'ānic term for nominal Muslims who did not assent entirely to the will of God and Muḥammad.

Murū'a. Or *muruwwa.* Ideal manly traits in Arabian culture.

Nabataea. A great civilization of Arab traiders centered in today's southern Jordan and Israel, existing roughly from 200 B.C.E. to 200 C.E.

Naskh. "Abrogation," referring to a solution for seeming internal contradictions in the Qur'ān. *Nāsikh* is an abrogating text, while *mansūkh* is an abrogated text.

People(s) of the Book (or "of Scripture"). Also referred to as "Scriptuaries." Jews and Christians (and later extended to included other religious communities) that are distinguished by the Qur'ān and Islamic tradition as having received divine revelation.

Quraysh. The major tribe in Mecca at the time of Muḥammad, who was a member of the Qurayshite clan of Banū Hāshim.

Sabab. A reason, in this context, for the revelation of a qur'ānic text. *Asbāb al-nuzūl* (occasions of revelation) refers to a *genre* of Islamic literature attempting to posit the historical contexts in result of which were revealed certain revelations of the Qur'ān.

Sacred Mosque. The central mosque in Mecca.

Saj'. Rhymed prose used in many—and especially the earlier—parts of the Qur'ān.

Scriptuaries. *See* People of the Book.

Sunna. See ḥadīth.

Sūra. The Arabic term for a chapter in the Qur'ān.

Umma. The community of Muslims. In this book, *umma* (in lowercase italic type) relates to a generic community, including the inclusive political community of Medina (that included Jews and idolaters) under Muḥammad's leadership immediately after the Hijra, while Umma (in uppercase roman type) refers only to the later sense of a purely Muslim community, including the later, more religiously defined Medinan community exclusive of Jewish tribes and idolaters.

'Umra. The lesser pilgrimage; a visit to Mecca and engagement in formal ritual requirements outside the official pilgrimage season.

Zakāt. Legally enjoined donation of personal wealth to the community of Muslims.

Bibliography

Abbott, Nabia, "Ḥadīth Literature: Collection and Transmission of Ḥadīth," in A. F. L. Beeston et al., eds., *Arabic Literature to the End of the Umayyad Period* (Cambridge, Cambridge University Press, 1983), pp. 289–298.

Abdel Haleem, Harfiya, Oliver Ramsbotham, Saba Risaluddin, and Brian Wicker, eds., *The Crescent and the Cross: Muslim and Christian Approaches to War and Peace* (New York: St. Martin's Press, 1998).

Abdul Rauf, Muḥammad, "Ḥadīth literature: The Development of the Science of Ḥadīth," in A. F. L. Beeston et al., eds., *Arabic Literature to the End of the Umayyad Period* (Cambridge: Cambridge University Press, 1983), pp. 271–288.

Abū Dāwud al-Sijistānī, *Sunan Abī Dāwud* (Cairo: Dār al-Miṣriyya al-Lubnāniyya, 1408/1988).

Abū Ubayda Maʿmar b. al-Muthannā, *Majāz al-Qur'ān* (Cairo, 1374/1954).

Al-Azhar University, *The Fourth Conference of the Academy of Islamic Research* (1388/1968) (Cairo: General Organization for Government Printing Offices, 1970).

ʿAlī, Jawād, *Al-Mufaṣṣal fī taʿrīkh al-ʿArab qabl al-Islām* (Beirut, n.d.).

ʿAlī, Muḥammad, *Al-Jihād fīl-shurʿiyya al-islāmiyya* (Cairo, 1393/1973).

Arberry, A. J., *The Seven Odes* (London: George Allen and Unwin, 1957).

———, "Arabia Deserta," in A. J. Arberry, *Aspects of Islamic Civilization* (New York: A. S. Barnes, 1964), pp. 19–31.

Asad, Muḥammad, *The Message of the Qur'ān* (Gibraltar: Dār al-Andalus, 1980).

Ayoub, Mahmoud, *The Qur'an and Its Interpreters* (Albany: SUNY, 1984).

Azami, M. M., *Studies in Early Hadith Literature* (Indianapolis: American Trust Publications, 1978).

Azmeh, al-, Aziz, *Islams and Modernities* (London: Verso, 1993).

Azraqī, al-, Abūl-Walīd Muḥammad b. ʿAbdallah, *Akhbār makka al-musharrifa*, ed. F. Wüstenfeld, as *Chroniken der Stadt Mecca* (Leipzig: F. A. Brockhaus, 1858).

Baghdādī, al-, ʿAbd al-Qāhir, *Mukhtaṣar kitāb al-farq bayn al-firaq*, Philip Hitti, ed. (Cairo, 1924).

Bainton, Roland, *Christian Attitudes toward War and Peace* (New York: Abingdon, 1960).

Beeston, A. F. L., *Warfare in Ancient South Arabia*, Qahtan: Studies in Old South Arabian Epigraphy Series, fasc. 3 (London: Luzac, 1976), pp. 1–73.

Bell, Richard, *The Qur'ān Translated*, 2 vols. (Edinburgh: T. and T. Clark, 1937).

Bravermann, M. M., *The Spiritual Background of Early Islam* (Leiden: Brill, 1972).

Bravermann, Meir, "*A propos de Qur'ān IX, 29, ḥattā yu'tū l-ğizyata wahum ṣāgirūna*," *Arabica* 10 (1963), pp. 94–95.

———, "The Ancient Arab Background of the Qur'ānic Concept *al-ğizyatu 'an yadin*," *Arabica* 11 (1964), pp. 307–314.

———, "The Ancient Arab Background of the Qur'ānic Concept *al-ğizyatu 'an yadin* (Suite)," *Arabica* 14 (1967), pp. 90–91.

———, "The Qur'ānic Concept *al-ğizyatu 'an yadin* (Addendum)," *Arabica* 14 (1967), pp. 326–327.

Brockelmann, C., "Ibn Isḥāḳ," *EI*[1], vol. 3, pp. 389–390.

Brockett, A. "Munāfiḳūn," in *EI*[2], vol. 7, pp. 561–562.

Brundage, James A., "Holy War and the Medieval Lawyers," Thomas Patrick Murphy, ed., *The Holy War* (Columbus: Ohio State University Press, 1976) pp. 99–140.

———, *The Crusades, Holy War, and Canon Law* (Brookfield, Vt.: Variorum, 1991).

Bukhārī, al-, Muḥammad b. Ismā'īl, *Ṣaḥīḥ al-Bukhārī*, 9 vols. (Lahore: Kazi, 1979).

Burton, John, *The Collection of the Qur'ān* (Cambridge: Cambridge University Press, 1977).

———, *The Sources of Islamic Law: Islamic Theories of Abrogation* (Edinburgh: Edinburgh University Press, 1990).

Caetani, L., *Annali dell'Islām*, vol. 1 (Milan: Hoepli, 1905).

Cahen, C., "*Coran IX-29: Haṭṭa yu'tu l-ğizyata 'an yadin wa-hum ṣāgirūna*," *Arabica* 9 (1962), pp. 76–79.

Carroll, Berenice, and Clinton Fink, "Theories of War Causation: A Matrix for Analysis," in Martin Nettleship et al., eds., *War, Its Causes and Correlates* (The Hague: Mouton, 1975), pp. 55–70.

Caskel, Werner, "The Bedouinization of Arabia," *The American Anthropologist* 56.2 (1954), pp. 36–46.

Cohen, Marc, *Under Crescent and Cross* (Princeton: Princeton University Press, 1994).

Cohen, Ronald, "Warfare and State Formation: Wars Make States and States Make Wars," in R. Brian Ferguson, ed., *Warfare, Culture, and Environment* (Orlando: Harcourt Brace Jovanovich, 1984), pp. 329–358.

Coulson, N. J., "European Criticism of Ḥadīth Literature," in A. F. L. Beeston et al., eds., *Arabic Literature to the End of the Umayyad Period* (Cambridge: Cambridge University Press, 1983), pp. 317–321.

Cowdrey, H. E. J., "The Genesis of the Crusades: The Springs of Western Ideas of Holy War," in Thomas Patrick Murphy, ed., *The Holy War* (Columbus: Ohio State University Press, 1976), pp. 9–32.

Crawford, S. C., *The Evolution of Hindu Ethical Ideals* (Calcutta: Mukhopadhyay, 1974).

Crone, Patricia, *Meccan Trade and the Rise of Islam* (Princeton: Princeton University Press, 1987).

Crow, Ralph, Philip Grant, and Saad Ibrahim, eds., *Arab Nonviolent Political Struggle in the Middle East* (Boulder, Col.: Lynne Rienner, 1990).

Dagorn, René, *La geste d'Ismaël d'Après l'onomastique et la traditional arabes* (Paris: Champion, 1981).

Della Vida, Giorgio Levi, "Pre-Islamic Arabia," in Nabih Amin Faris, ed., *The Arab Heritage* (New York: Russell and Russell, 1963), pp. 25–57.

———, "Kulayb b. Rabīʿa," *EI*², vol. 5, p. 362.

Denny, Frederick, "*Ummah* in the Constitution of Medina," *JNES* 36 (1977), pp. 39–47.

———, *An Introduction to Islam* (New York: Macmillan, 1985).

Dhahabī, al-, Abū ʿAbdallah Shams al-Dīn, *Tadhkirat al-Ḥuffāẓ*, 4 parts in 2 vols. (Hyderabad: Osmania University, 1377/1958).

Dickson, Harold R. P., *The Arab of the Desert: A Glimpse into Badawin Life in Kuwait and Sa'udi Arabia* (London: George Allen and Unwin, 1949).

Donner, Fred M., *The Early Islamic Conquests* (Princeton: Princeton University Press, 1981).

———, "The Sources of Islamic Conceptions of War," in John Kelsay and James Turner Johnson, eds., *Just War and Jihad: Historical and Theoretical Perspectives on War and Peace in Western and Islamic Traditions* (New York: Greenwood Press, 1991), pp. 31–69.

Doughty, Charles M., *Travels in Arabian Deserta*, 2 vols. (New York: Random House, 1937).

Dunlop, D. M., *Arab Civilization to A.D. 1500* (Beirut: Librairie du Liban, 1971).

Duri, A. A., *The Rise of Historical Writing among the Arabs*, Lawrence Conrad, trans. (Princeton: Princeton University Press, 1983).

Eickelman, Dale, "Musaylima: An Approach to the Social Anthropology of Seventh Century Arabia," *JESHO* 10 (1967), pp. 17–52.

Evans-Pritchard, E. E., *The Sanusi of Cyrenaica* (Oxford: Clarendon, 1949).

Fahd, Toufic, *Le panthéon de l'Arabie centrale à la veille de l'hégire* (Paris: Paul Geuthner, 1968).

Faizer, Rizwi S., "Muhammad and the Medinan Jews: A Comparison of the Texts of Ibn Ishaq's *Kitāb Sirat Rasūl Allāh* with al-Wāqidi's *Kitāb al-Maghāzī*," *IJMES* 28 (1996), pp. 463–489.

Fares, Bichr, *L'Honneur Chez Les Arabes Avant L'Islam* (Paris: Librairie d'Amerique et d'Orient Adrien-Maisonneuve, 1932).

———, "Murū'a," in *EI*², vol. 7, pp. 636–638.

Faris, Nabih Amin, ed., *The Arab Heritage* (New York: Russell and Russell, 1963).

Faris, Nabih Amin, trans., *The Book of Idols, Being a Translation from the Arabic of the Kitāb al-Aṣnām by Hishām Ibn-Al-Kalbi* (Princeton: Princeton University Press, 1952).

Ferguson, R. Brian, "Studying War," in R. Brian Ferguson, ed., *Warfare, Culture, and Environment* (Orlando: Harcourt Brace Jovanovich, 1984), pp. 1–81.

Firestone, Reuven, *Journeys in Holy Lands: The Evolution of the Abraham-Ishmael Legends in Islamic Exegesis* (Albany: SUNY Press, 1990).

———, "Conceptions of Holy War in Biblical and Qur'ānic Tradition," *Journal of Religious Ethics* 24.1 (Spring 1996), pp. 99–123.

———, "Conceptions of Holy War in the Scriptures of Judaism and Islam," *Journal of Religious Ethics* 24 (Spring 1996), pp. 801–824.

———, "Disparity and Resolution in the Qur'ānic Teachings on War: A Re-evaluation of a Traditional Problem," *JNES* 55 (1977), pp. 1–19.

———, "The Failure of a Jewish Program of Public Satire in the Squares of Medina," *Judaism* 46 (Winter 1997), pp. 438–452.

———, "Abraham," vol. 1, in *The Encyclopaedia of the Qur'ān* (Leiden: Brill, forthcoming).

Freeman-Grenville, G. S. P., *The Muslim and Christian Calendars* (London: Rex Collings, 1977).

Friedmann, Yohanan, "*Jihād* in Aḥmadī Thought," in Moshe Sharon, ed., *Studies in Islamic History and Civilization in Honour of Professor David Ayalon* (Jerusalem and Leiden: Brill, 1986), pp. 221–235.

Gardner, W. R., "Jihad," *The Moslem World* 2.4 (1912), pp. 347–357.

Gardet, L., "Al-Ḳaḍā' wa'l-Ḳadar," in *EI²*, vol. 4, pp. 365–367.

Gendler, Everette E., "War and the Jewish Tradition," in Menachem Marc Kellner, ed., *Contemporary Jewish Ethics* (New York: Sanhedrin Press, 1979), pp. 189–210.

Gibb, H. A. R., *Studies on the Civilization of Islam*, Standford Shaw and William Polk, eds. (Princeton: Princeton University Press, 1982).

Gibb, Hamilton, "Pre-Islamic Monotheism in Arabia," *HTR* 55 (1962), pp. 269–280.

Gil, Moshe, "The Constitution of Medina: A Reconsideration," *Israel Oriental Studies* 4 (1974), pp. 44–66.

———, "The Origin of the Jews of Yathrib," *JSAI* 4 (1984), pp. 203–223.

Girard, Rene, *Violence and the Sacred*, Patrick Gregory, trans. (Baltimore: Johns Hopkins University Press, 1977).

Goldziher, Ignaz, *Muslim Studies*, 2 vols., ed. S. M. Stern and trans. C. R. Barber and S. M. Stern (London: George Allen and Unwin, 1971).

Grohmann, A., "al-ʿArab," in *EI²*, vol. 1, pp. 524–527.

Guillaume, Alfred, trans., *The Life of Muhammad: A Translation of Ibn Ishaq's Sirat Rasul Allah* (Oxford: Oxford University Press, 1955).

———, *The Traditions of Islam: An Introduction to the Study of the Hadith Literature* (Lahore: Universal, 1977).

Halperin, David, and Gordon Newby, "Two Castrated Bulls: A Study in the Haggadah of Kaʿb al-Aḥbār," *Journal of the American Oriental Society* 102.3 (1982), pp. 631–638.

Hamidullah, Muhammad, *Muslim Conduct of State* (Lahore, n.d.).

Haq, S. Moinul, trans., *Ibn Saʿd's Kitab al-Tabaqat al-Kabir* (New Delhi: Kitāb Bhavan, n.d.).

Harris, Marvin, "A Cultural Materialist Theory of Band and Village Warfare: The Yanomamo Test," in Brian Ferguson, ed., *Warfare, Culture, and Environment* (Orlando: Harcourt Brace Jovanovich, 1984), pp. 111–140.

Hartner, W., "Zamān," in *EI¹*, vol. 8, pp. 1207–1212.

Hawting, G. R., "The Origins of the Muslim Sanctuary at Mecca," in G. H. A. Juynboll, ed., *Studies on the First Century of Islamic Society* (Carbondale, Ill.: Southern Illinois University Press, 1982), pp. 23–47.

Haykal, Muḥammad Khayr, *Al-jihād wal-qitāl fīl-siyāsa al-sharʿiyya*, 3 vols. (Beirut: Dar al-Bayāriq, 1414/1993).

Henninger, Joseph, "Pre-Islamic Bedouin Religion," trans. Merlin Swartz from "La religion bedouine preislamique," in *L'antica societa beduina*, F. Gabrieli, ed.

(Rome: Instituto di Studi Orientali, 1959), pp. 115–140, in Swartz, ed., *Studies on Islam* (New York: Oxford University Press, 1981), pp. 3–22.
Hinds, Martin, "*Al-Maghāzī*," in *EI*², vol. 5, pp. 1161–1164.
———, "'Maghāzī' and 'Sīra' in Early Islamic Scholarship," in *Vie du Prophete Mahomet: Colloque de Strasburg, 1980*, vols. 23–24 (Paris, 1983), pp. 57–66.
Hirschberg, Hayyim, *Yisrael ba'Arav* (Jerusalem, 1946).
———, "Yūsuf 'As'ar Yath'ar Dhū Nuwās," *EJ* 16 (1972), pp. 897–900.
Hitti, Phillip, *History of the Arabs* (New York: St. Martin's, 1970).
Hopkins, E. W., *Ethics of India* (New Haven: Yale University Press, 1924).
Horovitz, Josef, *Koranische Untersuchungen* (Berlin: Walter de Gruyter, 1926).
Humphreys, R. Stephen, *Islamic History: A Framework for Inquiry* (Princeton: Princeton University Press, 1991).
Ibn al-Athīr, 'Izz al-Din Abūl-Hussayn 'Alī, *Al-Kāmil fīl-ta'rīkh*, ed. Carolus Tornberg, as *Ibn-El-Athiri Chronicon* (Leiden: Brill, 1868).
Ibn al-Jawzī, Jamāl al-Dīn 'Abd al-Raḥmān, *Nuzhat al-a'yun al-nawāẓir fī 'ilm al-wujūh wal-naẓā'ir* (n.p., n.d.).
———, *Nawāsikh al-Qur'ān* (Beirut: Dār al-Kutub al-'Ilmiyya, n.d.).
Ibn Isḥāq, Muḥammad, *Al-Sīra al-nabawiyya*, 2 vols. (Beirut: Dār al-Thiqāfa al-'Arabiyya, n.d.).
Ibn Kathīr, 'Imād al-Dīn Ismā'īl, *Tafsīr al-Qur'ān al-'aẓīm*, 7 vols. (Beirut, 1405/1985).
Ibn Manẓūr, Muḥammad, *Lisān al-'Arab*, 15 vols. (Beirut: Dār Ṣādir, 1375/1956).
Ibn Māja, *Sunan Ibn Māja* (Beirut: Al-Maktaba al-'Ilmiyya, n.d.).
Ibn Qutayba, 'Abdallah b. Muslim, *Ta'wīl mashākil al-Qur'ān* (Cairo: Aḥmad Saqr, 1973).
Ibn Sa'd, Muḥammad b. Manī' al-Baṣrī al-Hāshimī, *Kitāb al-tabaqāt al-kabīr*, ed. Edward Sachau as *Ibn Saad: Biographien*, 9 vols. (Leiden: Brill, 1904–1921).
Irvine, A. K., "Homicide in Pre-Islamic South Arabia," *BSOAS* 30.2 (1967), pp. 277–292.
Israel Historical Society, *Holy War and Martyrology in the History of Israel and the History of the Nations* (Hebrew), proceedings of the eleventh convention of the Israel Historical Society, March 1966 (Jerusalem: Israel Historical Society, 1968).
Izutsu, Toshihiko, *Ethico-Religious Concepts in the Qur'ān* (Montreal: McGill University Press, 1966.
Jabbur, Jibrail S., *The Bedouins and the Desert: Aspects of Nomadic Life in the Arab East*, Lawrence I. Conrad, trans. (Albany: SUNY Press, 1995).
Jackson, A. V. W., *Zoroaster* (New York: Columbia University Press, 1919).
Jannatī, Āyatullāh Aḥmad, "Defence and Jihād in the Qur'ān," *Al-Tawḥīd*, no. 1 (1404/1984), pp. 39–54.
Johnson, James Turner, *Ideology, Reason, and the Limitation of War* (Princeton: Princeton University Press, 1975).
———, "Historical Roots and Sources of the Just War Tradition in Western Culture," in John Kelsay and James Turner Johnson, eds., *Just War and Jihad: Historical and Theoretical Perspectives on War and Peace in Western and Islamic Traditions* (New York: Greenwood Press, 1991).

———, and John Kelsay, eds., *Cross, Crescent, and Sword: The Justification and Limitation of War in Western and Islamic Tradition* (New York: Greenwood Press, 1990).

Johnstone, T. M., "Ghazw," in *EI*[2], vol. 2, pp. 1055–1056.

Jones, Gwilym H., "The Concept of Holy War," in *The World of Ancient Israel: Sociological, Anthropological, and Political Perspectives*, edited by R. E. Clements (Cambridge: Cambridge University Press, 1989), pp. 299–321.

Jones, J. M. B., "The Chronology of the Maghāzī—A Textual Survey," *BSOAS* 19 (1957), pp. 245–280.

———, "Ibn Isḥāq and al-Wāqidī, The Dream of ʿĀtika and the Raid to Nakhla in Relation to the Charge of Plagiarism," *BSOAS* 22 (1959), pp. 41–51.

———, "The *Maghāzī* Literature," in A. F. L. Beeston et al., eds., *Arabic Literature to the End of the Umayyad Period* (Cambridge: Cambridge University Press, 1983), pp. 344–351.

Jones, Marsden, ed., *Kitāb al-Maghāzī lil-Wāqidī*, 3 vols. (London: Oxford University Press, 1966).

Juynboll, G. H. A., "On the Origins of Arabic Prose: Reflections on Authenticity, in G. H. A. Juynboll, ed., *Studies on the First Century of Islamic Society* (Carbondale, Ill.: Southern Illinois University Press, 1982), pp. 161–175.

———, *Muslim Tradition: Studies in Chronology, Provenance, and Authorship of Early Ḥadīth* (Cambridge: Cambridge University Press, 1983).

Kelsay, John, "Religion, Morality, and the Governance of War: The Case of Classical Islam," *JRE* 18 (1990), pp. 123–139.

———, *Islam and War: A Study in Comparative Ethics* (Westminster: John Knox, 1993).

———, and James Turner Johnson, eds., *Just War and Jihad: Historical and Theoretical Perspectives on War and Peace in Western and Islamic Traditions* (New York: Greenwood Press, 1991).

Khadduri, Majid, *War and Peace in the Law of Islam* (Baltimore: Johns Hopkins University Press, 1955).

———, *The Islamic Law of Nations: Shaybani's Siyar* (Baltimore: Johns Hopkins University Press, 1966).

Khan, M. Ajmal, "Jāhilīya: A Description of the State and Mode of Living," *Studies in Islam* 3.4 (1966), pp. 175–184.

Kister, M. J., "ʿAn Yadin (Qurʾān IX/29): An Attempt at Interpretation," *Arabica* 11 (1964), pp. 272–278.

———, "Maqām Ibrāhīm: A Stone with an Inscription," Le Museon 84 (1971), pp. 477–491.

———, "Labbayka, Allāhumma, Labbayka . . . ," *JSAI* 2 (1980), pp. 33–57.

———, "The *Sīra* Literature," in A. F. L. Beeston et al., eds., *Arabic Literature to the End of the Umayyad Period* (Cambridge: Cambridge University Press, 1983), pp. 352–367.

Kohlberg, Etan, "Barāʾa in Shiʿī Doctrine," *JSAI* 7 (1976), pp. 139–175.

———, "The Development of the Imāmī Shīʿī Doctrine of *Jihād*," *ZDMG* 126.1 (1976), pp. 64–86.

Kramer, Joel L., "Apostates, Rebels, and Brigands," *Israel Oriental Studies* 10 (1980), pp. 34–73.

Krenkow, F., "The Two Oldest Books on Arabic Folklore," *I.C.* 2 (1928), pp. 55–89, 204–286.
Lambton, Ann K. S., "A Nineteenth Century View of Jihād," *Studia Islamica* 32 (1970), pp. 181–192.
Lane, Edward, *An Arabic-English Lexicon* (London: Williams and Norgate, 1865).
Lapidus, I. M., "The Arab Conquests and the Formation of Islamic Society," in G. H. A. Juynboll, ed., *Studies on the First Century of Islamic Society* (Carbondale, Ill.: Southern Illinois University Press, 1982), pp. 49–72.
Lassner, Jacob, *Islamic Revolution and Historical Memory*, American Oriental Series, vol. 66 (New Haven: American Oriental Society, 1986).
Lecker, Michael, "Idol Worship in Pre-Islamic Medina (Yathrib)," *Le Museon* 106.3–4 (1993), pp. 331–346.
———, *Muslims, Jews and Pagans: Studies on Early Islamic Medina* (Leiden: Brill, 1995).
Lesser, Alexander, "War and the State," in Morton Fried, Marvin Harris, and Robert Murphy, eds., *War: The Anthropology of Armed Conflict and Aggression* (Garden City, N.Y.: Natural History Press, 1968), pp. 92–96.
Lewis, Bernard, *The Political Language of Islam* (Chicago: University of Chicago Press, 1988).
Lincoln, Bruce, *Death, War, and Sacrifice* (Chicago: University of Chicago Press, 1991).
Lyall, Charles J., *Translations of Ancient Arabian Poetry* (London: Williams and Norgate, 1930).
Madelung, W., "ʿIsma," in *EI²*, vol. 4, pp. 182–184.
Majumdar, Suhas, *Jihād: The Islamic Doctrine of Permanent War* (New Delhi: Voice of India, 1994).
Malandra, William W., *An Introduction to Ancient Iranian Religion* (Minneapolis: University of Minnesota Press, 1983).
Malik, S. K., *The Quranic Concept of War* (Lahore: Wajidalis, 1979)
Marrin, Albert, *War and the Christian Conscience: From Augustine to Martin Luther King, Jr.* (Chicago: Henry Regnery, 1971).
Martin, Richard, "Religious Violence in Islam: Towards an Understanding of the Discourse on *Jihad* in Modern Egypt," in Paul Wilkinson and Alasdair Steward, eds., *Contemporary Research on Terrorism* (Aberdeen: Aberdeen University Press, 1989), pp. 55–71.
Masʿudı, al-, Abul Ḥasan ʿAlī b. all-Ḥusayn, *Murūj al-dhahab wamaʿādin al-jawāhir* (Beirut: University of Beirut Press, 1966),
McDonald, M. V., trans., *The Foundation of the Community*, vol. 7 of *The History of al-Ṭabarī* (Albany: SUNY Press, 1988).
Mittwoch, E., "Ayyām al-ʿArab," in *EI²*, vol. 1, pp. 793–794.
Moberg, Axel, ed., *The Book of the Himyarites* (London: Humphrey Milford, 1924).
Morabia, Alfred, "La notion de gihad dans la'Islam medieval," Ph.D. diss., Universite de Lille, 1974, published by Service de Reproduction des Theses, 1975.
Morony, Michael, *Iraq after the Muslim Conquest* (Princeton: Princeton University Press, 1984).
Murphy, Thomas Patrick, ed., *The Holy War* (Columbus: Ohio State University Press, 1976).

Musil, Alois, *The Manners and Customs of the Rwala Bedouins*, American Geographical Society Oriental Explorations and Studies, no. 6 (New York: American Geographical Society, 1928).

Muslim b. al-Ḥajjāj, *Ṣaḥīḥ Muslim* (Cairo: Dār al-Kitāb al-Miṣrī, n.d.).

Nasafī, al-, ʿAbdullāh b. Aḥmad b. Maḥmūd, *Tafsīr al-Qurʾān al-jalīl*, also known as *madārik al-tanzīl waḥaqāʾiq al-taʾwīl* (Beirut, n.d.).

Nasāʾī, al-, Abū ʿAbd al-Raḥmān, *Sunan al-Nasāʾī* with the commentary of Jalāl al-Dīn al-Suyūṭī (Cairo: Dār al-Ḥadīth, 1407/1987).

Naḥḥās, al-, Aḥmad b. Muḥammad b. Ismāʿīl, *Al-Nāsikh wal-mansūkh fī kitāb Allah ʿazza wajalla*, 3 vols., Sulaymān b. Ibrāhīm b. ʿAbdullāh al-Rāḥim, ed. (Beirut: Muʾassasat al-Risāla, 1412/1991).

Nettleship, Martin, et al. eds., *War, Its Causes and Correlates* (The Hague: Mouton, 1975).

Newby, Gordon D., *A History of the Jews of Arabia* (Columbia: University of South Carolina Press, 1988).

Nicholson, Reynold A., *A Literary History of the Arabs*, 2nd ed. (Cambridge: Cambridge University Press, 1930, and reprinted numerous times).

Niditch, Susan, *War in the Hebrew Bible* (New York: Oxford University Press, 1993).

Nöldeke, Theodore, *Geschichte des Qorans* (Göttingen, 1860).

Obermann, Julian, "Islamic Origins: A Study in Background and Foundation," in Nabih Amin Faris, ed., *The Arab Heritage* (New York: Russell and Russell, 1963), pp. 58–79.

Penrice, John, *Dictionary and Glossary of the Kur-ān* (London: Curzon, new ed. 1971).

Peters, F. E., *Muhammad and the Origins of Islam* (Albany: SUNY Press, 1994).

Peters, Rudolph, "Djihad: War of Aggression of Defense," in *Akten des VII. Kongresses feur Arabistik und Islamwissenschaft* (Göttingen, 1976).

———, *Islam and Colonialism: The Doctrine of Jihad in Modern History* (The Hague: Mouton, 1979).

———, *Jihad in Mediaeval and Modern Islam*, Nisaba Religious Texts Translation Series, vol. 5 (Leiden: Brill, 1977), reprinted and expanded as *Jihad in Classical and Modern Islam* (Princeton: Marcus Weiner, 1996).

Plessner, M., and Rippen, A., "Muḳātil b. Sulaymān," in *EI²*, vol. 7, pp. 508–509.

Powers, David S., "The Exegetical Genre nāsikh al-Qurʾān wa mansūkhuhu," in Andrew Rippin, ed., *Approaches to the History of the Interpretation of the Qurʾān* (Oxford: Clarendon, 1988), pp. 117–138.

Qatāda b. Diʿāma al-Sadūsī, *Kitāb al-nāsikh wal-mansūkh fī kitāb Allah taʿālā* (Beirut: Muʾassasat al-Risāla, 1406/1985).

Qummī, al-, Abū Ḥasan ʿAlī b. Ibrāhīm b. Hāshi b. Mūsā al-Bābawayhī, *Tafsīr al-Qummī*, 2 vols. (Najaf, 1385/1966).

Rabin, Chaim, "Islam and the Qumran Sect," in Chaim Rabin, ed., *Qumran Studies* (London: Oxford University Press, 1957), pp. 112–130.

Ringgren, Helmer, *Studies in Arabian Fatalism* (Uppsala, 1955).

Rippen, Andrew, "Mudjāhid b. Djabr al-Makkī," in *EI²*, vol. 7, p. 293.

———, "The Exegetical Genre *Asbāb al-nuzūl*: A Bibliographical and Terminological Survey," *BSOAS* 48 (1985), pp. 2–15.

———, "Literary Analysis of *Qurʾān*, *Tafsīr*, and *Sīra*: The Methodologies of John

Wansbrough," in Richard Martin, ed., *Approaches to Islam in Religious Studies* (Tucson: University of Arizona Press, 1985), pp. 151–163.
———, "RḤMNN and the Ḥanīfs," in Wael B. Hallaq and Donald P. Little, eds., *Islamic Studies Presented to Charles J. Adams* (Leiden: Brill, 1991), pp. 153–168.
Robson, J., "Ḥadīth," in *EI*[2], vol. 3, pp. 23–28.
Rubin, Uri, "*Barāʾa*: A Study of Some Quranic Passages," *JSAI* 5 (1984), pp. 13–32.
———, "The Kaʿba: Aspects of Its Ritual Functions and Position in Pre-Islamic and Early Islamic Times," *JSAI* 8 (1986), pp. 97–131.
———, "*Ḥanīfiyya* and Kaʿba: An Inquiry into the Arabian Pre-Islamic Background of *dīn ibrāhīm*, *JSAI* 13 (1990), pp. 85–112.
Ryckmans, Jacques, *La persécution des Chrétiens himyarites au sixième siècle* (Istanbul: Nederlands Historisch-Archaeologisch Instituut, 1956).
Said, Edward W., *Orientalism* (New York: Random House, 1979).
Sanderson, Judith, "War, Peace, and Justice in the Hebrew Bible: A Representative Bibliography," in Gerhard von Rad, *Holy War in Ancient Israel*, Marva J. Dawn, trans. (Grand Rapids, Mich.: Eerdmans, 1991).
Schacht, Jacob, *The Origins of Islamic Jurisprudence* (Oxford: Oxford University Press, 1950).
Schleifer, S. Abdullah, "Jihad and Traditional Islamic Consciousness," *I.C.* 27.4 (1983), pp. 173–203.
———, "Understanding Jihad: Definition and Methodology," *Islamic Quarterly* 27.3 (1983), pp. 118–131.
———, "Jihad: Modernist Apologists, Modern Apologetics," *I.C.* 28 (1984), pp. 25–46.
Schwally, Friedrich, *Der Heilige Krieg im alten Israel*, vol. 1 of *Semitische Kriegsaltertumer* (Leipzig: Deiterich, 1901)
Sell, Edward, *The Faith of Islam* (London, 1920; 4th ed. reprint, Wilmington, Del.: Scholarly Resources, 1976).
Serjeant, R. B., "Haram and Hawtah, the Sacred Enclave in Arabia," in *Melanges Taha Husain* (Cairo: Dār al-Maʿārif, 1962), pp. 41–58.
———, "The 'Constitution' of Medina," *Islamic Quarterly* 8 (1964), pp. 3–16.
Shaffer, Jim G., "Origins of Islam: A Generative Model," *The Eastern Anthropologist* 31.4 (1978), pp. 355–363.
Smith, Morton, *Palestinian Parties and Politics that Shaped the Old Testament* (New York: Columbia University Press, 1971; reprint, London: SCM, 1987).
Smith, Sidney, "Events in Arabia in the 6th Century A.D.," *BSOAS* 16.3 (1954), pp. 424–468.
Smith, W. Robertson, *Kinship and Marriage in Early Arabia* (London: Adam and Charles Black, 1903).
Sonn, Tamara, "Irregular Warfare and Terrorism in Islam: Asking the Right Questions," in James Turner Johnson and John Kelsay, eds., *Cross, Crescent, and Sword: The Justification and Limitation of War in Western and Islamic Tradition* (New York: Greenwood Press, 1990), pp. 129–147.
Sprenger, A., *Das Leben und die Lehre des Mohammad* (Berlin, 1861–1865).
Sweet, Louise E., "Camel Raiding of North Arabian Bedouin: A Mechanism of Ecological Adaption," *American Anthropologist*, no. 67 (1965), pp. 1132–1150.

Ṭabarī, al-, Muḥammad b. Jarīr, *Jāmiʿ al-bayān ʿan taʾwīl āy al-Qurʾān*, 30 books in 15 vols. (Cairo: Muṣṭafā al-Bābī al-Ḥalabī and Sons, 1373/1954; reprint, Beirut: Dār al-Fikr, 1405/1984).

———, *Taʾrīkh al-rusul wal-mulūk*, ed. M. J. DeGoeje as *Annales* (Leiden: Brill, 1964).

Ṭabarsī, al-, Radī al-Dīn Abū ʿAlī al-Fadl b. al-Ḥasan, *Jawāmiʿ al-jāmiʿ fī tafsīr al-Qurʾān al-karīm* (Beirut: Dār al-Aḍwāʾ, 1405/1985).

Tafsīr al-Imām Mujāhid b. Jabr (Cairo: Dār al-Fikr al-Islāmī, 1410/1989).

Tafsīr Muqātil b. Sulaymān, 5 vols. (Cairo: Al-Hayʾa al-Miṣriyya al-ʿĀma lil-Kitāb, 1979).

Tanwīr al-miqbās min tafsīr Ibn ʿAbbās (Beirut: Dār al-Jamīl, n.d.).

Taymī, al-, Abū ʿUbayda Muʿammar b. al-Muthannā, *Kitāb ayyām al-ʿArab qablal-Islām*, ʿĀdil Jāsim al-Bayātī, ed. (Beirut, 1407/1987).

Thompson, Henry, *World Religions in War and Peace* (Jefferson, N.C.: McFarland, 1988).

Tirmidhī, al-, Muḥammad b. ʿĪsā b. Sawra, *Al-Jāmiʿ al-Ṣaḥīḥ*, 5 vols., Aḥmad Muḥammad Shākir, ed. (Beirut: Dār al-Kutub al-ʿIlmiyya, 1408/1987).

Trimingham, J. Spencer, *Christianity among the Arabs in Pre-Islamic Times* (London: Longman, 1979).

Trowbridge, Stephen van Rensselaer, "Mohammed's View of Religious War," *The Moslem World*, no. 3 (1913), pp. 290–305.

Tyan, E., "Djihād," in *EI²*, vol. 2, pp. 538–540.

Vayda, Andrew, "Primitive and Modern War," in Morton Fried, Marvin Harris, and Robert Murphy, eds., *War: The Anthropology of Armed Conflict and Aggression* (Garden City, N.Y.: Natural History Press, 1968), pp. 85–91.

Von Rad, Gerhard, *Holy War in Ancient Israel*, Marva J. Dawn, trans. (Grand Rapids, Mich.: Eerdmans, 1991).

Von Wissman, H., "Badw," in *EI²*, vol. 1, pp. 884–885.

Waardenberg, Jacques, "Toward a Periodization of Earliest Islam According to Its Relations with Other Religions," in *Proceedings of the Ninth Congress of the Union Europeene des Arabisants et Islamisants*, 1978 (Leiden: Brill, 1981), pp. 304–326.

Wāḥidī, Abūl-Ḥasan ʿAlī b. Aḥmad, *Asbāb al-nuzūl* (Beirut: Dār al-Kutub al-ʿIlmiyya, n.d.).

Walters, LeRoy, "The Just War and the Crusade: Antitheses or Analogies?" *Monist*, no. 57 (1973), pp. 584–594.

Wansbrough, John, *Quranic Studies* (Oxford: Oxford University Press, 1977).

———, *The Sectarian Milieu* (Oxford: Oxford University Press, 1978).

Watt, W. Montgomery, *Muhammad at Mecca* (Oxford: Clarendon, 1953).

———, *Muhammad at Medina* (Oxford: Clarendon, 1956).

———, "The Materials Used by Ibn Ishaq," in Bernard Lewis, ed., *Historians of the Middle East* (London: Oxford University Press, 1962), pp. 23–34.

———, "Islamic Conceptions of the Holy War," in Thomas P. Murphy, ed., *The Holy War* (Columbus: Ohio State University Press, 1976).

———, "The Significance of the Theory of *Jihād*," in *Akten des VII. Kongresses für Arabistik und Islamwissenschaft* (Göttingen, 1976), pp. 390–394.

———, "Al-Ansar," in *EI²*, vol. 1, pp. 514–515.

———, "Al-Hudaybiya," in *EI²*, vol. 3, p. 539.

———, "Badw," in *EI²*, vol. 1, pp. 889–892.

———, "Hidjra," in *EI²*, vol. 3, pp. 366–367.

———, "Mu'ākhāt," in *EI²*, vol. 7, pp. 253–254.

———, and M. V. McDonald, trans., *Muhammad at Mecca*, vol. 6 of *The History of al-Tabarī* (Albany: SUNY Press, 1988).

Weinfeld, Moshe, "Divine Intervention in War in Ancient Israel and in the Ancient Near East," in Moshe Weinfeld and Hayim Tadmor, eds., *History, Historiography, and Interpretation: Studies in Biblical and Cuneiform Literatures* (Jerusalem: Magnes, 1983).

Welch, Alford T., "Ḳurān," in *EI²* vol. 5, pp. 400–429.

Wellhausen, Julius, *Prolegomena to the History of Ancient Israel* (1885; Chicago: World, 1957 reprint)

———, "Muhammad's Constitution of Medina," in A. J. Wensinck, *Muhammad and the Jews of Medina* (Berlin: Adiyok, 1982), pp. 128–138.

Wensinck, A. J., *A Handbook of Early Muhammadan Tradition* (Leiden: Brill, 1971 reprint).

———, *Muhammad and the Jews of Medina*, trans. and ed. W. H. Behn, 2nd ed. (Berlin: Adiyok, 1982).

———, "Sunna," in *EI²*, vol. 1, pp. 555–557.

Williams, Robert Jeffrey, "A Socio-Historical Analysis of Warfare (Jihad and Qital) in Primitive Islam (Ph.D. diss., Florida State University, 1994).

Willis, John R., "*Jihād fī Sabīl Allāh*—Its Doctrinal Basis in Islam and Some Aspects of Its Evolution in Nineteenth-Century West Africa," *Journal of African History* 8.3 (1967), pp. 395–415.

Wright, Quincy, *A Study of War*, 2nd ed. (Chicago: University of Chicago Press, 1965).

Zayd, Muṣṭafā, *Al-Naskh fil Qur'ān al-karīm* (Cairo?: Dār al-Fikr al-ʿArabī, 1383/1963).

Zucker, Moshe, "The Problem of ʿiṣma—Prophetic Immunity to Sin and Error in Islamic and Jewish Literatures" (Hebrew), *Tarbiz* 35 (1966), pp. 149–173.

Zuḥaylī, al-Wahba, *Āthār al-ḥarb fīl-fiqh al-Islāmī* (Beirut: Dār al-Fikr, n.d.).

Index of Scriptural Citations

QUR'ĀN

Subject Index